HEARTS AND MINDS

THE COMMON JOURNEY OF SIMONE de BEAUVOIR AND JEAN-PAUL SARTRE

HEARTS

~/∗ AND ∗/~

MINDS

THE COMMON JOURNEY
OF SIMONE de BEAUVOIR
AND JEAN-PAUL SARTRE

by

Axel Madsen

WILLIAM MORROW AND COMPANY, INC.

NEW YORK   1977

1   2   3   4   5   6   7   8   9   10

Library of Congress Cataloging in Publication Data

Madsen, Axel.
    Hearts and minds.

    "Works by Sartre and Beauvoir": p.
    Bibliography: p.
    Includes index.
    1. Beauvoir, Simone de, 1908-   2. Sartre,
Jean Paul, 1905-   3. Authors, French—20th
century—Biography.   I. Title.
PQ2603.E362Z84   848'.9'1409   77-2896
ISBN 0-688-03206-0

BOOK DESIGN   CARL WEISS

CONTENTS

5

HEARTS AND MINDS

THE COMMON JOURNEY OF SIMONE de BEAUVOIR AND JEAN-PAUL SARTRE

CHAPTER

I

SUMMER OF 1929

No BOOKS, Jean-Paul Sartre had decreed, just long walks and longer talks, even if the boggy hollows of the Limousin uplands were too much chlorophyll, as he joked. Simone de Beauvoir joined him every morning as soon as she could get away from her family, running across still dewy meadows to reach their secret rendezvous. There was so much to talk about—the friends, books, life and, of course, their future. They took long walks, two figures in an August landscape; she tall and gangly; he short and square and with a crossed right eye behind the schoolmaster glasses. He laughed a lot. They were brand-new teachers, the two top graduates of their class. They had worked terribly hard, but still, she said, she was sure her first paycheck would be a practical joke.

All too soon it was time for her return to Meyrignac for lunch while he sat under a hedgerow eating the cheese or gingerbread smuggled out of the Beauvoir kitchen by Simone's cousin Madeleine who adored anything romantic. In the afternoon they were together again, picking up the discussions started in Paris before the holidays or in a chestnut grove before lunch. She had told her parents they were working on a book, a *critical* study of Marxism. Her idea had been to butter them up by pandering to their hatred of communism. All too soon the sun plunged into the hills beyond the Auvezère River, sending her back to Meyrignac and him to the Hôtel de la Boule d'Or and dinner among the traveling salesmen.

Teachers college graduate Sartre

Simone in Marseille

Like him, she was born in Paris—they might have played together in the Luxembourg Gardens, they discovered. Both had spent precocious childhoods in coddled surroundings and both thought a lot of themselves. The difference was the country. Every summer since she had been a little girl she had scratched at earth, played with lumps of clay, polished chestnuts and learned to recognize buttercups, ladybirds, and glowworms at her grandfather's five-hundred-acre estate. Meyrignac, which had been in the family since the 1830s, had a dammed-up stream with waterlilies and goldfish and a tiny island that could be reached via stepping stones. It had fields, cedars, willows, magnolias, shrubberies and thickets. At Meyrignac and at La Grillière, her uncle's estate twenty kilometers away, she had always been allowed to run free and to touch everything. Uncle Maurice's park was bigger and wilder but also monotonous and it surrounded a sinister turreted château that looked much older than it really was. Uncle Maurice, a member of the local gentry, had married Papa's sister, Hélène.

Jean-Paul had an eccentric grandfather. Charles Schweitzer was a handsome language teacher with a passion for the sublime, who in old age looked so much like God Almighty that repentent parishioners in a dimly lit church once took him for an apparition. Charles spent his life turning little events into great circumstances that his pudgy and cynical wife reduced to insignificance with a raising of her eyebrows. The Schweitzers were Alsatians and Protestants. Charles' brother had become a Lutheran minister who in turn had begotten a minister, Albert, who was now a doctor-missionary in darkest Africa. Charles had become a teacher and co-author of a *Deutsches Lesebuch,* used in German classes in all schools in France, and the father of two sons and a daughter. The elder son had settled into civil service and the younger had been a teacher of German until he died, still a bachelor, with a revolver under his pillow and twenty pairs of worn-out shoes in his trunks. Anne-Marie Schweitzer was gifted and pretty, but the family thought it distinguished to leave her gifts undeveloped. She had met Jean-Baptiste Sartre at Cherbourg, a young naval officer already wasting away with tropical fever. They had been married two years when he died and Anne-Marie had returned to her parents with her baby. Charles Schweitzer had found his son-in-law's untimely death insolent and blamed his daughter for not having foreseen or forestalled it. He had applied for retirement but without a word of reproach went back to teaching to support Anne-Marie and her infant son. Chilled with gratitude she had given herself unstintingly, keeping house for her parents and becoming an adolescent again, asking for permission to go out.

* * *

There was so much to talk about. The friends were René Maheu, who had introduced Simone to Sartre, and Paul Nizan, Sartre's best friend, who was already married and, with his wife, Henriette, believed in sexual freedom. It was Maheu who had nicknamed Simone *Le Castor* (Beaver) because, he said, beavers like company and have a constructive bent.[1] Maheu was also married. He never brought his wife to the Sorbonne and disappeared into a suburban train every evening. To Beaver, he liked to underline the difference between himself and Sartre and Nizan. He was a sensualist, he said, enjoying works of art, nature and women; *they* heaped scorn on exalted principles and had to find the reason behind everything. Weren't they the ones who had thrown water bombs at the mundane and vaguely Nietzschean elitist students with shouts of "Thus pissed Zarathustra!"? Nizan, who was always biting his nails and wore steel-rimmed glasses, was up on artistic fashion and introduced the others to James Joyce and the new American novel. He belonged to various literary circles, had joined the Communist Party and lived with his in-laws in a smart apartment where his and Henriette's studio was decorated with a portrait of Lenin, cubist posters and a reproduction of Botticelli's *Venus*. Most important, Nizan had had a book published.

Sartre had been writing since he was ten—stories, poems, essays, epigrams, puns, ballads and a novel—and he never stopped telling girls he met that they should also write. Only by creating works of the imagination could anyone escape from contingent life, he said. Art and literature were absolutes, which didn't mean he had any intention of becoming a professional man of letters. He detested literary movements and hierarchies and couldn't really reconcile himself to become a career person with faculty colleagues and college presidents.

There were many things Sartre didn't want to become. He would never be a family man, he would never marry, never settle down and never clutter up his life with possessions. He would travel instead and accumulate experiences that would benefit his writing. In theory, Simone admired dangerous living, lost souls and all excesses, but for her graduation had meant liberation, moving away from home. For her, life would begin in October.

She had never felt she was a "born" writer, but at fifteen, when writing in a girl friend's scrapbook about the future, she had scribbled that she wished to become a famous author. At eighteen she had written the first

[1] The nickname was to remain permanently hers. Sartre would dedicate several of his books "au Castor." This book drops the article and translates Le Castor as Beaver throughout.

pages of a novel—about an eighteen-year-old girl whose obsessive concern was to defend herself against other people's inquisitiveness. When
they had all crammed together in the Nizans' studio, Sartre had made fun
of her parochial-school vocabulary, although he, too, admitted he was
really seeking "salvation" in literature.

What Simone liked about Sartre was that he never stopped thinking,
never took anything for granted and that on the subject that interested
her above all others—herself—he tried to understand her in the light of
her own set of values and attitudes. He told her she should hold on to
her personal freedom, should remain curious and open and really do something about wanting to write. Only two and a half years older than she,
Sartre impressed her by his maturity. Her cousin Jacques had been her
first adolescent crush, Maheu had been the first man to make compliments
on her figure. Sartre was the first man who was like her, only much more
so, someone who wanted the same things as she, but who had more self-
assurance than she could muster.

There were differences of course. Simone thought it was a miracle that
she had managed to break free from her narrow upbringing and looked
toward the future with excitement; Sartre detested adult life. At twenty-
four, he didn't particularly look forward to military service and the
necessity of teaching for a living, but all this didn't prevent him from
saying that people should create their own lives and that freedom had to
be the essence of *his* future. As a tolerable solution to the question of
earning a living, he was applying for a French lectureship in Tokyo for
the fall of 1931 when he would be through with the army. If accepted,
he would have to spend two years in Japan, but the payoff would be that
he could get similar appointments in other exotic capitals.

And he liked women. He found them less comical than men and had
no intention of depriving himself of their company. The first time Simone
had seen him at the Sorbonne, he had been talking with a great gawk of
a student. Before that he had been engaged to and was still the admirer
of Simone-Camille Sans, a sensuous would-be actress everybody at the
teachers' college had talked about. Together with Pierre Guille and Maheu
he was also the platonic admirer of Madame Morel, a storied Argentinian
lady of the exotic age of forty, whose son Guille and Sartre had tutored for
his *baccalauréat*. While Simone realized that for a girl with her upbringing
marriage was perhaps unavoidable, Sartre positively hated matrimony.
What we have, he liked to tell her, was an essential love, which meant
they could both experiment with contingent love affairs. They were two
of a kind, he told her, their relationship would endure, something she had

also felt. But it could not make up entirely for the fleeting riches of encounters with others. The question was of course how to avoid such emotions as regret and jealousy.

Maheu had been jealous of her friendship with Sartre and Nizan and had demanded preferential treatment. When they had all crammed together, they had often piled into Nizan's little car and spent the afternoon at the Porte d'Orléans amusement park playing pinball machines and mini-football, and stopping for beer at a sidewalk café on the way back. When the question of their all going out together had come up one evening, Maheu had insisted on taking her to the movies alone. But Maheu had agreed that Sartre could spend the evening of the Fourteenth of July with them. After watching the fireworks on the lawn of the Cité Universitaire, Sartre had invited them all to a night of bar crawling on Montparnasse. Out in the streets at 2 A.M., Maheu had ostentatiously taken her arm. Maheu had said that if he flunked, he would take a grade-school teaching job in the provinces. Maheu did fail and left Paris without saying good-bye to anyone. In a short note to Sartre, he added, "Give Beaver my best wishes for her happiness."

There was so much to talk about. On the fourth day, however, as they sat on the edge of a meadow, Simone suddenly saw her parents trooping toward them. As they came closer, she could see her father wearing a resolute but somewhat embarrassed expression under his straw boater. Sartre sprang to his feet and Simone introduced her friend to her parents. Monsieur de Beauvoir was brief and to the point. Politely, he asked Sartre to leave the area. People were gossiping, he said; besides, it was hoped to get Simone's cousin married and the way Simone kept seeing a strange young man all day and every day could only harm Madeleine's reputation.

Sartre, who happened to be wearing an aggressive red shirt, replied that he would certainly not leave the area a minute sooner than he intended. Georges de Beauvoir was a small man who hated arguments and bad manners and the standoff at the edge of the meadow remained civilized. Mortified, Simone followed her parents back to Meyrignac, but her father didn't return to the attack and Sartre stayed another week at the Boule d'Or. He and Simone merely arranged more secret meeting places in a chestnut grove. After he left they wrote each other every day. In October they would begin their future.

Simone was born on January 8, 1908, on Boulevard Raspail in an apartment above the Rotonde café. Georges and Françoise de Beauvoir—he thirty, she twenty-one—were happy with their firstborn. They were a genteel couple, far from wealthy but trying to keep up the appearances of a noble, if obscure name. Blue-eyed Georges de Beauvoir was the grandson of a tax inspector who had amassed sufficient wealth to allow even his youngest son to live on a private income, although Georges' father took up a civil service career in Paris and eventually retired as the head of his department. Brought up in moderate opulence, Georges was the youngest of three children. He was his mother's favorite and his teachers' pet. He disliked sports and violence of any kind and won academic prizes year after year at the Collège Stanislas. His mother's death when he was thirteen touched him deeply and, Simone de Beauvoir was to write in *Memoirs of a Dutiful Daughter,* from then on "he stopped trying." [2]

The Beauvoirs were halfway between aristocracy and *haute bourgeoisie* and could not bring themselves to allow young Georges to take up the career he loved most passionately—acting. Instead, he studied law, for its dramatic possibilities. His name, family connections, certain childhood friends and those he associated with as a young man convinced him he belonged to the aristocracy. He appreciated social graces, style, wit and the free-and-easy self-assurance of the rich. He dressed to the teeth, took elocution lessons and, to imitate actors, sported neither beard nor mustache. He passed his exams but didn't bother to present himself to the bar. Instead he registered at the Court of Appeals and became the secretary to a well-established lawyer.

Suspended somewhere between aristocratic loftiness and bourgeois earnestness, Georges de Beauvoir attached little importance to the careers that were open to him. Clerking for the lawyer during the daytime, he became at night and during vacations an amateur actor, performing at charities in fashionable drawing rooms and resort hotels while slowly eating his way through his legacy and through a substantial cash payment that his brother Gaston gave him in return for renouncing all claims to Meyrignac. He devoted all his leisure to comedy and mime, took a special delight in makeup, kept up with stage gossip, idolized great actors, had actors as intimate friends, read prodigiously about the theater and on the very eve of his marriage acted in a play.

His wife came from a rich and devout provincial family. Born in Verdun, Françoise was the eldest of three children. Her father was a banker; her mother had been brought up by nuns and she herself attended a con-

---

[2] Simone de Beauvoir, *Mémoires d'une jeune fille rangée,* Paris: Gallimard, 1958; *Memoirs of a Dutiful Daughter,* Cleveland and New York: World Publishing, 1959.
    See page 297 for "Works by Sartre and Beauvoir" in French and English.

vent school. Her parents were reserved and she spent a pallid childhood and adolescence devoted to school and religious duties. At twenty, she was a brooding but beautiful girl, who without enthusiasm consented to meet Georges de Beauvoir. His vitality and charm overwhelmed her and in her eyes he would always enjoy the greatest prestige. The transition to married life was not without difficulties. Transported to a milieu where her convent morality was barely respected, she dreaded criticism and, to avoid it, took pains to be like everybody else. "In all matters, she accepted my father's ideas without ever appearing to find any difficulty in reconciling them with her religion," Simone would write.[3] "My father was constantly astonished by the paradoxes of the human heart, by the playful tricks of heredity, and by the strangeness of dreams; I never saw my mother astonished by anything."

When Simone was two and a half, the Beauvoirs had a second daughter, Hélène, who was instantly and for good nicknamed Poupette (little doll). The two sisters spent their early years between Louise, their nursemaid, and their young mother, who took up the responsibilities of motherhood with Christian devotion. She chose her daughters' private school, supervised their reading and learned English and Latin to follow their progress. She took them to mass, said prayers with them morning and evening; she read works of piety, regularly received holy communion, but lost her temper too easily, even if the warmth of her affection made up for her unpredictability. Corporal punishment was rare, but she could shatter her daughters' self-confidence with a phrase she often used: "It's ridiculous." One metaphysical difficulty in Simone's young life was the fact that her father never went to mass. Feeling herself deeply penetrated by the presence of God, but taught by her mother that Papa was always right, her father's agnosticism would have been a shock if it wasn't for the fact that her mother found his attitude quite natural. "The consequence was that I grew accustomed to the idea that my intellectual life—embodied by my father—and my spiritual life—expressed by my mother—were two radically different fields of experience which had absolutely nothing in common. Sanctity and intelligence belonged to two quite different spheres . . . My situation resembled that of my father in his childhood and youth: he had found himself suspended between the airy skepticism of my grandfather and the bourgeois earnestness of my grandmother. In my own case, too, my father's individualism and pagan ethical standards were in complete contrast to the rigidly moral conventionalism of my mother's teach-

[3] *Ibid.*

ing. This imbalance, which made my life a kind of endless debate, is the main reason why I became an intellectual." [4]

Her father's interest in her increased as she grew up. He took great pains with her handwriting and spelling and during holidays dictated tricky passages to her, usually from Victor Hugo. No one she knew was as funny, as interesting and as brilliant as he; no one else had read so many books, or knew so much poetry by heart, or could argue with such passion. Always the life and soul of parties and family gatherings, he treated her as a fully developed person while her mother was more indulgent and found it natural that she should be a silly little girl now and then. "I was flattered most by praise from my father," she would remember, "but if he complained because I had made a mess in his study, or if he cried, 'How stupid these children are!' I took such censure lightly because he obviously attached little importance to the way it was said. On the other hand any reproach made by my mother, or even her slightest frown was a threat to my security. Without her approval, I no longer felt I had any right to live." [5]

For Poupette, life was more complicated. Although great pains were taken to treat both girls with scrupulous fairness, Simone enjoyed certain advantages. Poupette, who looked like her father, was hurt and perplexed and often sat crying in her little chair. She was accused of being sulky and clung to Simone with absolute devotion, grateful for her bigger sister's approval. Poupette was to grow up prettier than Simone and to possess more of the social grace her father appreciated so much in young girls.

When Simone was five and a half, her mother enrolled her in a parochial girls' school with an alluring name, Le Cours Désir. Simone could already read and write and immediately enjoyed having her own books, homework and schedules. At six, she taught Poupette to read and write, something that gave her a sense of pride in her own efficiency. They were all at Meyrignac that summer when one day in August the general alarm was sounded and it was announced that war had been declared. Orders for the requisitioning of horses and vehicles were nailed to doors and their grandfather's horses were taken to the county seat of Uzerche. A month later at La Grillière, Simone was helping her mother knit woolen caps for soldiers and with Aunt Hélène went to the railway station to distribute apples to turbaned Indian troops on their way to the front. Georges de Beauvoir had been discharged from the Reserves because of heart trouble, but was called up for active service in the infantry. After

[4] *Ibid.*
[5] *Ibid.*

his basic training, Simone went with her mother to visit him in his camp near Paris and was impressed by the gravity of his face since he had let his mustache grow. Patriotically, she had trampled to pieces a celluloid doll, "Made in Germany," which actually belonged to Poupette, and went around sticking Allied flags in flower pots and scribbling *Vive la France!* everywhere with colored chalk. One part of her school became a temporary hospital and a refugee girl joined her class. In October, her father left for the front, and together with her mother and Poupette, Simone prayed for his safety. She was convinced that God would protect her father especially for her. A new heart attack felled him and he was evacuated to a military hospital, then transferred to a desk job at the War Ministry. He changed uniforms, shaved off his mustache and together with forty million other Frenchmen, the Beauvoirs settled into the war.

Simone learned her catechism from a pale young priest and, dressed in white tulle and with her head covered with a veil of Irish lace, received her first communion. Books helped broaden her horizon although they were carefully chosen for her by her parents. Curious about others, she never dreamed her fate could be different from what it was, and she felt no disappointment at being a girl. With the exception of her cousin Jacques, the boys she knew were in no way remarkable. Six months older than she, Jacques dazzled her with his brilliant compositions, his knowledge and assurance. He treated grownups as if he were their equal and although he usually despised girls made Simone an exception. "Simone is a precocious child," he declared, words that pleased her immensely.

If the coronary spared Georges de Beauvoir the horrors of the trenches, the war ruined him, swept away his dreams, and destroyed his myths and his hopes. Earning only a soldier's pay, he was obliged to move his family to a smaller cold-water flat at 71 Rue de Rennes. Thanks to the influence of a distant cousin, he supplemented his income by selling newspaper advertising space. The job bored him and brought in very little money and he began to go out in the evenings to play bridge with friends. The daughters wore their clothes until they were threadbare and after the maid, Louise, found a husband and left, Madame de Beauvoir decided she could do without domestic help.

For the 1917–18 school year a new girl joined Simone's class at the Cours Désir. She was Elizabeth Mabille—Zaza, to everybody—and she immediately captivated Simone. "The manner in which she spoke to the teachers astounded me; her natural inflections contrasted strongly with the stereotyped expressionless voices of the rest of the pupils. Her conquest of me was complete when, a few days later, she mimicked Mademoiselle Bodet to perfection; everything she had to say was either interesting or amusing." [6] Zaza could play the piano, her handwriting was elegant and puberty didn't make her lose her good looks. She dressed with affectation and behaved with all the ease of a young lady. She was selective in her interests and between twelve and fifteen ridiculed not only the majority of the people she and Simone knew, but established habits and conventional ideas. Zaza, people said, had personality. Simone was obliged to come to terms with her own timidity and her own subjectivity.

The happiest times for Simone were the summers at Meyrignac, where her family was still welcome. There, her mother was more relaxed than in Paris, her father devoted more time to her and she had her own little room overlooking the woodshed and the carriage house. Grandpapa came down at noon, his chin freshly shaven between his white sideburns, and after a solid lunch, he and his son Georges would sing, joke and retell the family anecdotes. In the afternoon, Simone and Poupette usually went for walks, discovering the world for miles around. On rainy days, they would ransack the drawing-room library for some Fenimore Cooper novel or Mama would prop the scores of grandfather's favorite airs on the slightly off-key piano and he would join in the choruses with the rest of the family. On starry nights, Simone would go for walks in the garden, smelling the magnolias and keeping an eye open for shooting stars.

Her awakening to the "facts of life" was slow but her loss of faith was abrupt and lasting. If Cousin Madeleine, who was allowed to read anything, was the person who told Simone and Poupette that men, like her pet dog, had two balls between their legs and explained how children were born, Simone reached puberty and her first period without her mother ever mentioning menstruation. The sisters had long felt that adults concealed something of importance behind deceptive fronts, but when they found out, the disillusionment only served to reduce the prestige of grownups. Simone did not ponder long over pregnancy and childbirth, but came to dread the idea that her mother would find out that she knew and would therefore want to have a talk with her. With puberty came pimples, acne and nervous tics and remarks by her father about her complexion and clumsiness, which only aggravated her misery and bad habits.

The loss of faith came one balmy evening in her little room at Meyrignac. Having said her prayers, she realized with no great surprise that she no longer believed in God. Her father's agnosticism had prepared her, but she was nevertheless taken aback by her discovery. The greatest writers and the finest thinkers were skeptics and she found it upsetting that it was

[6] *Ibid.*

women who went to church and therefore possessed divine truth when men were so clearly their superiors. She could not reveal her spiritual turmoil to her father since it would embarrass him. For a while she lived a double life, continuing to go to confession while realizing that God could no longer influence her behavior. When she finally told a father confessor that she had lost faith, he asked what mortal sins she had committed. When she protested she hadn't committed any, he didn't believe her. She resigned herself to the life of an outcast.

Together with her father, Simone rated writers higher than scholars, philosophers and professors because novels were read by everybody and touched peoples' imagination and because they brought their authors universal and intimate fame. Also, the most celebrated women had distinguished themselves in literature, and although Georges de Beauvoir considered women's intelligence should be no more than a social ornament, he admired Colette's literary style. Simone was also attracted to teaching. Rather than have her own children, she could easily see herself forming other minds and, to be able totally to plan her pupil's education, wouldn't mind becoming a governess in a family. Her parents threw up their hands in horror but she contended that educating the young could never be considered a menial job.

As Georges de Beauvoir's finances slipped and, with the Bolshevik Revolution, he lost shares he held in Russian railway companies, his daughters' future loomed painfully large on his horizon. To people of his pretensions. training a girl for a profession was a sign of defeat. The daughters of his brother, his sister and his friends would be ladies; Simone would not. Approaching fifty and financial uncertainty, he resolved that if nothing else Simone should become a civil servant, earn a government salary and, on retirement, receive a pension.

Librarianship was considered a possibility, but Simone preferred philosophy because she had seen an illustrated article about a woman who had taken her doctorate in philosophy and had adopted a young niece, thereby reconciling her intellectual life with the demands of feminine sensibility. The number of women who had such degrees could be counted on one hand and Simone wanted to be one of these pioneers. From a practical point of view, the only career open to her with a degree in philosophy was teaching. Simone did not object to that, nor did her father, provided she didn't give private tuition in pupils' homes but taught in a *lycée,* or college. This solution was to Simone's taste and her mother talked to her teachers about the decision. The ladies at the Cours Désir had given their lives to combating secular education and abhorred state colleges. They told

Mme. de Beauvoir that the study of philosophy would corrupt the soul and that after one year at the Sorbonne Simone would have lost her faith and good character. Her father backed off slightly. Instead of philosophy, Simone could major in literature, but no daughter of his should become a private tutor, whatever the saintly ladies at the Cours Désir said. In July 1924, Simone passed her exams and in September, shortly before her grandfather and her Uncle Gaston died, sat down in a lecture hall together with boys for the first time. With some trepidation the Mabille family allowed Zaza to follow French literature classes with Simone.

The literature professor was Robert Garric, an ardent Catholic who had assured Monsieur Mabille that a young girl could indeed take a degree without losing her soul. Garric was just over thirty, had thinning blond hair and was founder and director of Les Equipes Sociales, a noble postwar experiment in bringing culture to the underprivileged. In a few years, the Social Teams movement had spread all over France, with ten thousand members, including two hundred teachers. Simone's cousin Jacques was a member and an admirer of Garric who felt the cultural segregation of bourgeois and working-class youths as a personal mutilation.

Simone found Garric's lectures spellbinding and, through Jacques, joined the students-for-the-underprivileged action program. She heard Garric speak in chic Neuilly homes about everyone's right to culture and how social progress was possible only if class hatred was overcome. His ideas were not at variance with her own, yet seemed to strike her as absolutely new. In Garric, she had met someone who, instead of submitting to fate, had chosen a way of life that had meaning and was governed by its own overriding necessity. She was shocked when Zaza didn't share her hero worship.

Simone's relationship with her father became difficult. He attached extreme importance to her diplomas and encouraged her to accumulate them. This insistence convinced her he was proud of having a brainy daughter, but the contrary was true. After a casual look at her favorite and newly discovered authors—André Gide, Jean Cocteau, Henry de Montherlant and Paul Claudel—he pronounced them pretentious and decadent and was indignant with Jacques for having lent their books to her. She felt her father harbored a deep resentment against her as he took to making violent scenes about the sacrifices his daughters imposed upon him. He was annoyed when Simone attacked certain traditions or tried to skip the dinners which several times a year reunited the whole family. She couldn't accept his concept of marriage and he couldn't see what love and friendship had in common. "I couldn't accept that if one of the partners should be un-

faithful to the other, if they didn't get along together, they should sep-
arate," she was to remember late in life. "I was not a feminist to the
extent of caring about politics, but in my opinion men and women had
the right to be considered equal and I demanded that they should have
reciprocal benefits and privileges. My father's attitude toward 'the fair sex'
wounded me deeply. Taken as a whole, the frivolity of bourgeois love
affairs and adulteries made me sick." Her upbringing had persuaded her
that the interests of the bourgeoisie were closely linked with the interest
of humanity as a whole, but when she tried to enlist the support of her
family in the pursuit of truths that would be valid for everyone, her father
and mother turned against her. Her mother regarded her with suspicion;
her father accused her of renouncing the values of her class. When Simone
told her mother that for some time she had no longer believed in God,
her mother attempted to prove God's existence, then, with a helpless gesture and her eyes full of tears, suddenly stopped. Simone was sorry to
hurt her, but felt relieved to be able to live without false pretenses.

Simone passed her literature exams with distinction—and congratula-
tions from Garric—and spent the summer of her eighteenth year at Meyrignac feeling miserable and lonely. She had started a diary and the first
chapter of a novel and now wrote her first complete work, the story of a
futile escape. The heroine was eighteen and spending a holiday with her
family in a country house where she was awaiting the arrival of her fiancé.
Suddenly, she discovered the "something else" in life. A genius musician
made her see art, sincerity and disquiet. She felt she had been living a lie
and a strange, feverish longing overtook her. The musician went away,
and from her upstairs room she saw her fiancé arrive. She hesitated but her
courage failed her and she went downstairs to greet her future husband.

Jacques became her hope. He was now a good-looking youth, independent and already in charge of his family's stained-glass manufacturing
business. To Simone, he was both a somewhat remote elder brother and
someone she felt she could reasonably fall in love with. He treated her as
"good old Sim" and responded to her needs for affectionate understanding
with a mixture of cozy sarcasm and sincere concern. To a desperate letter
she sent him from Meyrignac that summer he responded that if she were
more human she would shock her parents less. His advice touched her
although she didn't feel she was deliberately trying to shock her family.
But Jacques failed too many exams, spent too much time with fashionable
friends in fashionable bars and on two occasions told her he loathed himself to prevent her disillusionment in him. The next year she saw little
of him, but his visit on her nineteenth birthday made her fantasize about

marriage. For Jacques, however, marriage was an end in itself. She could not imagine herself accepting an end to *anything*.

Zaza remained Simone's only friend, although Monsieur Mabille's sudden appointment to an executive position with the Citroën car company imposed such a heavy social schedule on Zaza that the two friends only saw each other on Sunday mornings. More vexing, Zaza's mother discouraged the friendship, for fear that her daughter would become too intellectual to find a husband. Simone's circle of friends broadened when, at nineteen and a half, she entered the Ecole Normale, the teachers' college of the Sorbonne, which trained for higher education professorates. While she found most of her fellow students uninteresting, she got to know Pierre Nodier, an older student with serious blue eyes who never spoke to anyone except a little thin-faced dark girl. Nodier belonged to a group who founded the magazine *L'Esprit,* and he was her first contact with left-wing intellectuals. He believed philosophy could never be separated from revolutionary aspirations although he felt economics played only a secondary role to spiritual progression. Simone asked him a lot of questions, but her political ideas remained hazy. Several of the students were socialists, but she suspected the communists were as dogmatic as Jesuits. At the end of the term, Nodier told her he had found a teaching post in Australia and, together with the skinny dark girl, disappeared forever.

Simone was introduced to pacifism—she had never imagined that her father's jingoist patriotism wasn't shared by all Frenchmen—signed a petition for the reprieve of Sacco and Vanzetti in America, and made a fleeting acquaintance with Simone Weil. The future Christian philosopher always strolled around the Sorbonne courtyard in a bizarre getup. She was very concerned about famine in China. When the two Simones got into a conversation, Weil said the only important thing was revolution, which would feed all starving people, and Beauvoir retorted that the problem was not so much making people happy as finding the reason for their existence. "It's easy to see you've never gone hungry," La Weil snapped. In the philosophy exams, Weil was No. 1, Beauvoir No. 2.

More important was her friendship with an uncomplicated student of independent means who was also trying to emancipate himself from a long Catholic upbringing. Jean Pradelle had a limpid, pretty face and a knack for listening to people with a handsome meditative air. When Simone told him about her qualms, he disapproved of her uncompromising attitudes—and she of his readiness to accept the bourgeois life laid out for him. They became fast friends and when he walked her home one day and they bumped into her mother in the Rue de Rennes, he was formally introduced. To Simone's surprise, her mother rather liked him. Like Jacques, however, Pradelle seemed to be a little afraid of her and for a while she wondered whether men ever married women like her.

Simone worked hard and in the spring of 1928 toyed with the idea of taking up philology. She found the study of ancient records too boring, however, and gave it up. Her father was disappointed. He would have liked her to have two degrees. It would have been the smart thing to do. To her astonishment, her father did not shunt Poupette into a safe career but let her choose to study art.

Simone wondered whether, instead of philology, she shouldn't start right away on her *agrégation*—that difficult, competitive postgraduate examination for university and lycée teaching positions. That would mean she could be finished with the Sorbonne and leave home in eighteen months. She talked to her philosophy dean, Léon Brunschvicg. He said Why not? and advised her to do her thesis on Gottfried Wilhelm von Leibniz (1646–1716). The philosophy of the Hanoverian thinker-mathematician-diplomat was not easy. For two centuries his fame had rested on his metaphysics while his logical works had remained unpublished and unappreciated until the beginning of the twentieth century. What Professor Brunschvicg wanted was that she write her thesis on Leibniz's logical doctrine.

She was unhappy again that summer. Meeting Pradelle after the Easter recess, he told her he had taken holy communion and had decided he was still a believer. She felt betrayed. Jacques was on the eve of induction for his military service and told Simone with such romantic fervor about an affair he had had that for the first time she felt favorably disposed toward the idea of illicit love. A night with him on Montparnasse, where he hoisted her onto a tall barstool and ordered her a dry martini, ended with a hysterical reminder that she was still very much under her parents' sway. Jacques deposited her safely at 71 Rue de Rennes at 2 A.M., but when she got upstairs she was greeted by tears and thunder. Her parents had just come back from Jacques' home, where they had roused his mother and wailed that they wanted their dishonored daughter back. Simone told them Jacques and she had simply gone for coffee at the Rotonde. Her parents refused to calm down and the scene ended with Simone in tears also. The next day when Simone met her cousin for a last good-bye and he saw her red eyes and heard about her mother's suspicion, he looked her deep in the eyes and said he respected her too much ever to want to treat her with disrespect. She was touched and went off to study her Leibniz.

Jacques would do his army stint in Algeria but would be back in eighteen months.

The life of bars and the glitter and fauna of Boulevard Montparnasse after midnight intrigued Simone and, with Poupette, she went bar crawling. She became a regular at the Jockey Club, learned to drink gin fizz, allowed men to accost her and went to drink with strangers. "Refuse nothing," was the motto of Gide and the surrealists. When the driver of a car following her one night, leaned out and asked her to go for a spin, she hopped in. When he tried to kiss her, she ran off, followed by a flood of curses. She realized she had got off lightly, but was pleased with herself for having dared a truly "gratuitous" act.

A new friend was Stefanie Avdicovitch, a Polish student of vast experience who had spent the summer as the governess of Zaza's younger sisters, attended lectures at the Sorbonne and received an allowance from her parents in Lvov. Stépha, as Simone and Zaza called her, was graceful and feminine, spoke with a warbling voice and told Zaza she was naïve to believe that young Catholic men were virgins when they married. Stépha had a bright room in a hotel in the Rue Saint Sulpice where she hung reproductions of Cézanne, Renoir, El Greco and drawings of a Spanish painter who lived in the same hotel. Prematurely bald and with a round face, Fernando Gerassi was a Sephardic Jew, born in Constantinople and educated in Berlin. Although penniless, he managed to continue to paint. Simone introduced Stépha and Fernando to Poupette, who was now taking commercial art and attending drawing classes in a studio on Montparnasse. One day Fernando pointed to a sketch of a naked woman on his wall and said Stépha had posed for it. Simone didn't know where to look and Stépha told him not to say such silly things. He hurriedly admitted it was only a joke. Stépha took great care not to shock Simone while at the same time making gentle attempts at opening her eyes. "But I'm telling you, physical love is very important, especially for men," Stépha would try. Simone didn't think she would languish in virginity forever, but she was sure her wedding night should be a white mass.

In January 1929, Simone began her teaching "internship" at the Lycée Janson de Sailly. Her fellow interns were Maurice Merleau-Ponty and Claude Lévi-Strauss. Merleau-Ponty was preparing for his *agrégation* in philosophy also. Lévi-Strauss wasn't afraid of being funny in class, expounding with deadpan irony on the folly of human passions. There were days when Simone found it silly to discourse upon the life of the emotions in front of forty teenage boys who obviously couldn't care less, but on other days she felt she could catch a glimmer of intelligence in certain eyes. She read *My Life* by Isadora Duncan and daydreamed about her own existence. It wouldn't be a stormy life, nor even a startling one. All she wanted was to be in love, to write good books, to have children and friends to whom she could dedicate her books. After the Easter recess, she met René Maheu who introduced her to Sartre.

Jean-Paul Charles Aymard Sartre was born June 21, 1905, at 2 Rue Mignard in the 16th *arrondissement* near the Bois de Boulogne. The year before, in May, Jean-Baptise Sartre had married Anne-Marie Schweitzer. The courtship had been brief. They had met in Cherbourg, where the thirty-year-old Jean-Baptiste was second lieutenant in the navy and suffering from bouts of intestinal fever contracted during a tour of duty in French Indochina.

The whole thing was pathetic. Jean-Paul was barely born before he and his father began to waste away. When the baby was a few months old, Jean-Baptiste's condition was such that he, his wife and infant son moved to a farm near Thiviers, south of Limoges, so that Jean-Baptiste's father could cure him. Inexperienced and without advice, the twenty-year-old Anne-Marie cared for her husband as best she could. Her milk dried up and it seemed the baby would die of an inflammation of the intestines. Dr. Aymard Sartre did his best for his son and his grandson. Little Jean-Paul was put out to nurse with a healthy farmer's wife but the enteritis persisted. Meanwhile, Jean-Baptiste's intestinal fever worsened.

Dr. Sartre was a taciturn country doctor who visited his patients in the Dordogne Valley in a buckboard. After medical school, he had married Marie-Marguerite Chavois, the daughter of a rich landowner from Périgord, and set up practice on the dreary main street of Thiviers opposite the pharmacist. The day after the wedding, he had discovered that his father-in-law was penniless. Outraged, he did not speak to Marie-Marguerite for forty years. At the table, he expressed himself by signs, but he shared her bed and, from time to time, made her pregnant. She had given him two sons and a daughter. Jean-Baptiste was the eldest of these children of silence. Late in life his sister had married a cavalry officer who went mad and his younger brother retired early from the military to his parents' home, developed a stammer and shot himself.

On September 17, 1906, Jean-Baptiste died in his bewildered young wife's arms. After the funeral, Anne-Marie said good-bye to the Sartres and, with her baby, returned to her parents—Charles (or Karl, according to moods) and Louise Schweitzer. Fifty years later, Jean-Paul would write

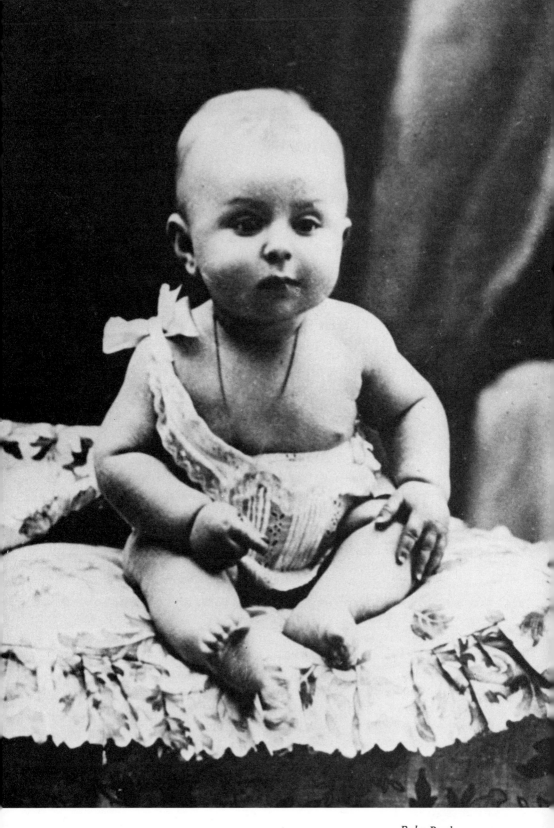

Baby Poulou

in *The Words,* his autobiography that didn't go beyond his childhood,[7]
how his grandmother kept repeating that Jean-Baptiste had shirked his
duties while his grandfather, proud of the Schweitzers' longevity, would
not hear of anyone dying at thirty-two and eventually forgot all about his
son-in-law. "Even now I am surprised at how little I know about him,"
Sartre would write. "Yet he loved, he wanted to live, he saw himself dying; that is enough to make a whole human being. But no one in my
family was able to make me curious about the man. For several years, I
was able to see over my bed the photograph of a little officer with frank
open eyes, a round baldish head and a thick mustache. The picture disappeared when my mother remarried."

Charles Schweitzer was sixty-two when his widowed daughter returned
with her infant son to his home in Meudon, on the western outskirts of
Paris. A teacher who had earned his Ph.D. with a thesis on the medieval
poet Hans Sachs and had become a pioneer in direct-language methods,
Schweitzer had applied for retirement. To support his daughter and bring
up his grandson, he remained a teacher until he was forced to retire at
sixty-seven, then moved to Paris and founded The Institute for Living
Languages. Until the age of twelve, Poulou—as his mother affectionately
called him—spent his life in a vast apartment at 1 Rue Le Goff, a tiny
Latin Quarter street near the Sorbonne, "between an old man and two
women."

Schweitzer, who tyrannized his wife and daughter and constantly pes-
tered his grown sons, took to grandfatherhood with a vengeance. "In the
struggle between generations, children and old people often join forces,"
Sartre would write about his early years in his grandfather's benevolent
shadow, admired and meditated upon, doted over, and taught to make
grownup remarks. "I was extremely worried about my grandmother. It
pained me to note that she didn't admire me sufficiently. In point of fact,
Louise had seen through me. She openly found fault with me for the
hamming with which she didn't dare reproach her husband. I was a buffoon, a clown, a humbug; she ordered me to stop 'smirking and smiling.'
I was all the more indignant in that I suspected her of belittling my grandfather too. I would answer back; she would demand an apology. Sure of
being backed up, I would refuse. My grandfather would seize the opportunity to show his weakness; he would side with me against his wife, who
would stand up, outraged, and go lock herself up in her room. My mother,
anxiously fearing my grandmother's rancor, would speak in a low voice

[7] Jean-Paul Sartre, *Les Mots,* Paris: Gallimard, 1964; *The Words,* New York: Braziller,
1964.

Charles Schweitzer

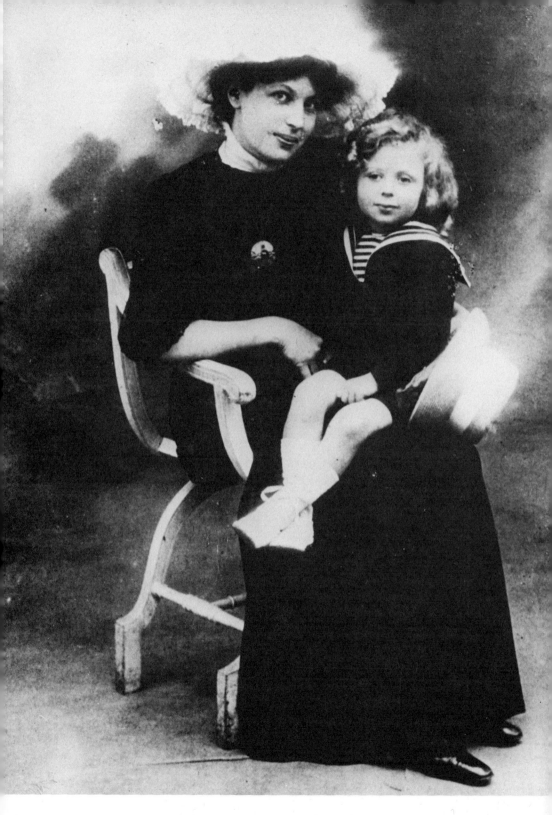

Anne-Marie with Poulou

and humbly lay the blame on my grandfather, who would shrug and with-
draw to his study. Finally, she would beg me to ask my grandmother to
forgive me. I enjoyed my power." [8]

Poulou could read at four. Adventures were in books, not in the Luxembourg Gardens across Boulevard St. Michel. He climbed perilously on
chairs to reach the upper shelves of his grandfather's library, picked volumes at random, art books which his grandfather's students had given him
as New Year's gifts, major French and German classics, and, especially,
the big Larousse Encyclopedia. "With difficulty I would put a volume on
my grandfather's blotter and open it," he would remember. "Men and
animals were there in person; the engravings were their bodies, the texts
were their souls, their individual particularities. Outside, one would encounter rough approximations of archetypes that never reached perfection.
The monkeys in the zoo were less monkey, people in the Luxembourg
Gardens were less people. In Platonic fashion, I went from knowledge to
its object. I found more reality in ideas than in things. It was in books that
I encountered the universe—assimilated, classified, labeled, thought out
yet still formidable; and I confused the disorder of my bookish experiences
with the random course of actual events, which explains why it took me
thirty years to shake off my idealism."

He read voraciously, Guy de Maupassant's short stories because they provided the best translation material for his grandfather's students, Corneille,
Voltaire, Hugo and—unforgettably before he was seven—*Madame Bovary*. He read the last pages twenty times without understanding why the
widowed Charles Bovary let his beard grow because he had found some
letters. To bring Poulou back to childhood, Anne-Marie bought him illustrated magazines and Jules Verne adventures. He loved, too, *The Last of
the Mohicans,* Phineas Fogg's sideburns, a world of murder and pillage,
Hindus and Hottentots, and closing-chapter heroics. When Charles found
out about the trashy reading, he lost his temper on the two women, who
lied and said it was Poulou himself who had wanted comic books. Summers were spent in Auvergne, roaming villages and admiring architecture.
Charles appreciated religious architecture and although he loathed papists,
never failed to enter a church if it was Gothic. Romanesque churches depended on his mood.

School was a jarring experience. Charles had decided his grandson
should go to the Lycée Montaigne and when he talked to the principal
said the only trouble with the child was that he was *too* advanced for his
age. The principal accepted Professor Schweitzer's recommendation, but

8 *Ibid.*

when Poulou flunked a composition test, his grandfather scolded him for the first time in his life. Charles engaged a private tutor to drum spelling into Poulou and next enrolled him in a public school. Here, he lasted until the following fall when Anne-Marie decided he should go to a private school. L'Institution Poupon practiced "advance" teaching methods, with the mothers attending classes, sitting against the wall while the teacher addressed the children spread out in a half circle in front of her. After one semester, Poulou was taken out of the Poupon Academy. For a while one of its teachers gave him private lessons at home, but Charles dismissed her after she complained to her pupil that she was terribly lonely and would give anything to have a man, regardless of who he was.

Between five and seven, Poulou went through intense death anxiety. He saw death, a very run-of-the-mill skeleton with a scythe, appear at his bed every night until he turned to lie on his right side. Once on the Quai Voltaire, an old madwoman dressed in black muttered, "I'll put that child in my pocket," but when his grandmother Sartre passed away and he and his mother were summoned to Thiviers, he didn't feel anything walking behind the hearse to the cemetery. Anne-Marie refused to cut his locks even in the face of her father's objections that she was making a girl out of her son. "She would, I think, have liked me to be a girl really and truly," Sartre was to write. "That would have revived her sad childhood and she would have been able to heap blessings on it. But since Heaven had not heard her prayers, she made her own arrangements. I would have the sex of the angels, indeterminate, but feminine around the edges. Being gentle, she taught me gentleness: my solitude did the rest and kept me away from violent games." One day when Poulou was seven Charles could take it no longer and, saying he was taking his grandson for a walk, took him to get a haircut. When they returned, Anne-Marie shrieked and locked herself in her room to cry. As long as Poulou's ringlets fluttered around his ears, they made it possible to deny the obvious fact that he was ugly. Strabismus was already beginning to blind his right eye; he had worn glasses since he was five and even if his features were regular, he had already caught friends of the family looking at him with a worried or puzzled expression. But he was twelve before he fully realized he was no Prince Charming but a toad.

That same year, he began to write. When the family spent the summer at Arcachon on the Atlantic coast and Louise, Anne-Marie and Poulou left Paris before Charles finished his semester, the grandfather would write three times a week—two pages for his wife, a postscript for his daughter and a whole letter in verse for the grandson. "In order to make me fully aware of my good fortune, my mother learned and taught me the rules of versification. Someone caught me scribbling a versified reply. I was urged to finish it. I was helped. When the two women sent off the letter, they had tears of laughter in their eyes thinking of the recipient's astonishment. By return mail I received a poem to my glory. I replied with a poem. The habit was formed, grandfather and grandson were united by a new bond. They spoke to each other, like Indians and the pimps on Montmartre, in a language out of bounds to women." [9] Next, he composed madrigals to a little invalid girl, rewrote La Fontaine's *Fables* in twelve-syllable verse and switched to comic-book prose with himself as the hero. The first story he completed was called *Pour un papillon* and was indeed the story of a butterfly expedition in the Amazon, with plot, characters and title plagiarized from an old magazine. "My mother was lavish with encouragement. She would bring visitors into the dining room so that they could surprise the young creator at his desk. I pretended to be too absorbed to be aware of my admirers' presence. They tiptoed out, whispering I was too cute for words. My uncle Emile gave me a little typewriter I didn't use and Madame Picard bought me a globe so that I would make no mistakes in laying out my globetrotters' itinerary. Anne-Marie copied out my second novel, *Le Marchand de bananes,* on glossy paper. It was shown around. Even my grandmother encouraged me: 'At least he behaves himself, and isn't noisy.' Fortunately, hallowed veneration was put off by my grandfather's displeasure." Charles had never approved of Poulou's "unwholesome reading material." He couldn't stand spelling mistakes and after a leafing through *The Banana Vendor* left the dining room. For a while, Poulou's literary activities became more or less clandestine. He wrote more complicated plots and poured everything he had read, good or bad, into the stories. "As a hero I fought tyranny. As Supreme Being I became a tyrant myself. I was harmless, I became wicked. What prevented me from plucking Daisy's eyes out? Scared to death, I told myself: Nothing. And pluck them out I did, as I would have plucked the wings off a fly. I wrote, with a beating heart, 'Daisy ran her hand over her eyes. She was blind.' and I sat there stunned, with my pen in midair. I had created an event in the realm of the absolute that exposed me, deliciously. I wasn't really sadistic and my perverse joy changed immediately to panic. I crossed everything out until it was illegible. The young girl would regain her sight, or, rather, she never lost it. But the memory of the flight of my imagination tormented me for a long time."

[9] *Ibid.*

* * *

The Institute for Living Languages was a success. The students were foreigners, mostly Germans, learning French by direct method. They paid well. Also, Schweitzer's textbook publishers brought out a new edition of the *Deutsches Lesebuch* every year. The arrival of the proofs during the family holidays was an annual event. Charles spread the galleys over the dining-room table and, at each printer's error, cursed between his teeth. As the threats of war rumbled closer during the summer of 1914, Charles was obliged to moderate his patriotic ardor. War with Germany would of course give Alsace back to France, but it would also put an end to German students and a good part of the livelihood of the now seventy-year-old breadwinner. The guns of August surprised the Schweitzer household in Arcachon and Charles decided they would stay there for the time being. Poulou started a new novel in a brand-new notebook, the story of Soldier Perrin who captured the kaiser, brought him across to the French trenches, where, in front of his whole regiment, he provoked him to a duel, threw him to the ground and with a knife at his throat forced him to sign a peace treaty that gave Alsace-Lorraine back to France. After a week, Poulou was bored with the story. When the family returned to Paris he was soon bored with the war, too.

The first year of the war was the happiest for the nine-year-old Jean-Paul. His young mother was all his. They rarely left each other, had their myths, odd expressions and ritual jokes. In public, they had their little collusions and were shy and afraid together. One incident would remain in Sartre's mind forever. "One day, on the quays, I came upon twelve issues of *Buffalo Bill* I didn't have yet. She was about to pay for them when a man approached, fat and pale and with anthracite eyes, a waxed mustache, a straw hat and that slick look that smart young men liked to affect then. He stared at my mother, but talked to me, 'You're being spoiled, kid, you're being spoiled!' First I was only offended; I resented such familiarity. Then I noticed the crazed look in his eyes and Anne-Marie and I were suddenly a single, frightened girl who stepped back. Put off, the gentleman walked off. I have forgotten thousands of faces, but that greasy mug I still remember. I knew nothing of lust and I couldn't imagine what this man wanted of us, but carnal desire was so manifest that, in a way, everything became clear to me. I had felt it through Anne-Marie; through her I learned to scent the male, to fear him, to hate him. The incident brought us closer. I would trot along with a hard gaze, my hand in hers, and feeling sure I was protecting her. Is it the memory of those years? Even now I love to see a too serious child talk gravely with his child-mother.

I like those tender, uncultivated friendships which are born far from men and directed against them. I stare for a long time at such puerile couples, then I remember I'm a man and look away."

It was no longer possible to evade the quesiton of Poulou's education. He had yet to spend more than one semester in any school and Charles swallowed his grudge and registered his grandson at the Lycée Henri IV, a five-minute walk from Rue Le Goff. After an entrance exam, the ten-year-old Sartre was placed in a sixth-grade class. The transition from teaching as a personal experience to classroom courses where everybody was taught at the same time was disconcerting but promptly cured him of his superiority complex. There was always someone else who answered faster and better than he. When he turned in inferior papers and Charles began to frown, Anne-Marie hastily asked for an appointment with Poulou's official teacher, who received mother and son in his bachelor apartment. She told the tall, lean, hooknosed teacher that her son's perception of things was better than his work showed. He had learned to read by himself, he wrote novels. When she ran out of arguments, she revealed that he was a ten-month child, as if the extra month in her womb meant he was better baked than others. The teacher, who was more sensitive to her charms than to Poulou's merits, refused to give him private lessons but promised to "follow up" on him. In class, Poulou imagined the teacher spoke only to him and a few kind words did the rest. Charles grumbled at the report at the end of the term but no longer thought of pulling his grandson out of school. Poulou finished the 1915–16 school year with good grades and the following year stopped getting special treatment.

At eleven, he had playmates for the first time. Schoolwork left him no time for writing and he lost interest in it. The school chums were mamma's boys like himself, boisterous and noisy but never far from their mothers' eyes. There were only boys and old men in Paris in 1916. Schools were not heated and curriculums were improvised. Max Bercot, a frail and tubercular boy, had already lost his father in the war and everybody had dead men in his family. The men who were not on the front were looked down upon and wanted their sons not to notice them. Paul Yves Nizan was a new boy in the class that year who immediately became Sartre's friend. Cross-eyed behind steel-rimmed glasses, Nizan was the only boy who spoke ironically about his parents. When he got mad, he stammered, but he had read a lot and wanted to become a writer.

In April 1917, Poulou's life was shattered—his mother remarried.

The stepfather was Joseph Mancy, a civil engineer and executive director of the Delaunay-Belleville Company, a car- and ship-construction business. Anne-Marie was going on thirty-five, Mancy was in his early forties. The marriage lifted a considerable burden from the shoulders of the now seventy-three-year-old Schweitzer and answered Anne-Marie's desire finally to leave her parents' home. Sartre would never mention Mancy in his autobiography but would later say he had felt betrayed by his mother's remarriage. "My mother certainly didn't marry my stepfather out of love," he would tell this biographer late in life. "He was a tall, lean man with a black mustache, furrowed skin, a big nose and handsome eyes. My mother's remarriage made me break off my inner relations with her. I felt she had betrayed me although I never told her that." The inner break saw the newlyweds take an apartment while Poulou stayed with his grandparents until the end of the term. The war effort was in high gear and during the summer of 1917 Mancy was appointed head of Delaunay-Belleville's naval construction and transferred to the Atlantic post city of La Rochelle. Wife and stepson followed.

The next years were to be the unhappiest period in Sartre's life. The break with his mother and his psychological differences with his stepfather added to the normal difficulties of adolescence and turned him into a surly near-delinquent. In school he slumped into mediocrity, remained an outsider and learned to fight. He realized his ugliness and, to impress classmates, systematically stole money from his mother's purse. His stealing was discovered shortly before his grandfather made a visit to La Rochelle. To show Poulou that thieving made him an outcast, Charles Schweitzer let a ten-sou piece fall to the floor. "As a well-brought-up kid I bent down to find the coin, but a stern gesture stopped me," Sartre would recall more than sixty years later. "With his knees creaking, my grandfather lowered himself to the floor to retrieve the coin. I was no longer allowed to touch money. I was totally excluded."

At eleven, Poulou lost what little faith had survived Charles Schweitzer's Catholic-baiting freethinking and his unpracticing grandmother's Catholicism. Joseph Mancy felt it was not his role to be the father Sartre had never had, but to exercise a distant if benevolent authority. In the evening he taught his stepson geometry and urged him to become a science teacher. When Sartre decided to go for a Ph.D. in philosophy it was not only because he thought philosophy would reveal eternal truths, but to contradict his stepfather.

As an adult Sartre managed to gain enough objectivity to find some saving grace in the man his mother had married. "In his own way, he was all right since after all I became what I wanted. I systematically opposed whatever he said or believed. I felt a lot of ambiguity in our relations. I had no filial sympathy for him; in fact there was between us a fundamental hostility although on the surface our relationship was correct and I was respectful and recognized his right to a certain ascendancy." In a foreword to a posthumous reprinting of *Aden-Arabie,* Paul Nizan's 1931 indictment of colonialism, Sartre would write that he had spent ten years "under the thumb of a civil engineer," while in a 1973 radio interview he would intimate that it was at the Delaunay-Belleville shipyards in La Rochelle that the notion of class struggle had first dawned on him.[10]

The 1918–19 school year saw him return to his studies and finish the year the first in his class in French composition, Latin and German. The reason for the top grades was also that his mother and stepfather promised him he could return to the Lycée Henri IV after still another year at La Rochelle's lycée for boys. In July 1920, he finished first in Latin, second in French and for the last two years before his *baccalauréat* returned to Henry IV, his friendship with Nizan and carefree room and board with Charles and Louise. At fifteen he suddenly became his grandmother's darling. He spent rainy afternoons playing the piano for her and, by himself, began to read Dostoevsky and Tolstoy. Nizan, who had more advanced literary tastes, made him discover Jean Giraudoux's clever novels about adolescence, André Gide's pagan values and the exotic sensuousness and urbane ingenuity of the writings of Valéry Larbaud and Paul Morand. On his own he discovered Francis Carco, the poet of Montmartre who, with a mixture of cynicism and sympathy, wrote about the criminals, pimps and whores of the Butte in such (later much-filmed) novels as *Jésus la Caille* and *Rue Pigalle.* During his last year at Henri IV, he discovered jazz and for graduation festivities was named head of pranks by his classmates. In June 1921, he passed the first half of the *baccalauréat* and the following year the second half, finishing his undergraduate studies one week before his seventeenth birthday. To show his approval, Charles took him on a tour of Alsace, including a visit to the Schweitzers' ancestral home in Pfaffenhofen.

Sartre began to write again that summer and composed a short story and the opening of a novel, both of which were published the following year in *La Revue sans titre,* a writers' magazine that lasted only four issues but managed to publish texts by Giraudoux, by Nizan and his classmate,

---

[10] Interview with Jacques Chancel, broadcast by Office de Radio-Télévision française (ORTF), February 3, 1973.

and future UNESCO president, René Maheu, plus a letter to the editor by future Prime Minister Pierre Mendès-France. *L'Ange du morbide* was set in the French Alps and told of an Alsatian schoolteacher and a tubercular patient who nearly coughs to death when he finally has enough courage to seduce her in the woods behind a sanatorium. *Jésus la Chouette* imitated the title of Carco's famous novel, but was meant to be a Balzacian study of provincialism. The story of a cowed college teacher, his pompous wife and overripe daughter who take in student boarders to supplement a shabby income, was actually inspired by one of Sartre's teachers in La Rochelle who couldn't control his classes and ended up committing suicide. The fragment published in *La Revue sans titre* was a first-person narrative of a new boarder's arrival at the teacher's home. Together with *L'Ange du morbide,* the opening chapters of *Jésus la Chouette* were the only pieces of Sartre's adolescent writing to survive.[11] The rest of the *Jésus la Chouette* manuscript was lost as were the numerous notebooks he had filled since he was ten.

Mancy was transferred back to Paris and took a cozy apartment on Montmartre where Sartre lived with his mother and stepfather during his preparatory year at the Lycée Louis-le-Grand before presenting himself for the Ecole Normale entrance exam. In October 1923, he was drafted but given the routine deferment until the end of his studies and for a six-month period had a violent falling-out with Nizan. The following June, he passed the Ecole Normale entrance exam—together with Nizan, Maheu and a new friend, Raymond Aron.

The four years at the Sorbonne teachers college were rich, happy years. "From the first day, the Ecole Normale was the beginning of my independence," he would tell this biographer in 1975. "I belonged to the youth of the period, a youth that was socialist-oriented, rarely communist-leaning, yet wasn't really politicized. We were not so much revolutionaries as anarchists, but on private points. Society at large didn't interest us. What was important was what you did with yourself." A teacher at Louis-le-Grand had characterized Sartre as "alert, guaranteed to succeed although vulnerable to his own overconfidence." This plucky facility continued into teachers college. He excelled in most subjects and was singled out by his philosophy teacher, yet had nothing of the pondered gravity of the class egghead. "He seduced everyone with his humor," fellow student Georges Canguilhem would remember. "He loved wisecracks and wasn't against provoking major disturbances." Together with Nizan, Canguil-

[11] Reprinted in Michel Contat and Michel Rybalka, *Les Ecrits de Sartre,* Paris: Gallimard, 1970; *The Writings of Sartre,* Evanston: Northwestern University Press, 1974.

hem, Pierre Guille and several others, he formed a screw-you inner sanctum that exercised its own intellectual terror.

Philosophy became a revelation when he read Henri Bergson's *Essai sur les données immédiates de la conscience* and his teacher had him do a dissertation on The Conscience of Duration. To Bergson, who was himself a former Ecole Normale student and, in the 1920s, was France's leading philosopher, duration was the essence of life. His antirational and very difficult concept of an instinctive life-force and creative evolution was linked with his account of memory. Duration, he proclaimed, exists in memory. Things remembered survive in memory and interpenetrate present things, making past and present mingle in the conscience. Action, Bergson believed, is what constitutes being.

"I was awestruck by Bergson and told myself, 'Philosophy is fascinating. Truths come tumbling out of the sky. The trick is to make more truths tumble out of the sky,' " Sartre would recall late in life. "With Descartes I believed that 'I think, therefore I am,' and in class I tried to start a discussion on 'What is a table?' Not the physical table, but the philosophical concept of a table."

His philosophy teacher gave him a special prize for his first essay. The recognition led Sartre to jot down—in alphabetical order like his future antagonist in *La Nausée*—his ideas on Art, Beauty, etc., and to read, also in alphabetical order, Joseph Conrad, Jules Laforgue, Hugo von Hofmannsthal, Nietzsche and Schopenhauer. The next year, he added Karl Marx, Sigmund Freud and Stendhal. He had difficulty understanding Marx and disliked Freud for trying to have it both ways—representing the unconscious as both a set of rigorous mechanistic determination and a mysterious finality—but liked Stendhal's blend of rationalism and romantic fervor.

When he was nineteen, Sartre encountered romantic fervor during a distant cousin's funeral in Thiviers and soon lost his virginity and, momentarily, his reason. She was Simone-Camille Sans, a much-courted twenty-three-year-old beauty who would later adopt the stage name Simone Jollivet. The daughter of a Toulouse pharmacist, Camille, as everybody called her, had cascading blond hair, blue eyes and an alluring figure. Deflowered by a friend of the family while still a child, she had since eighteen regularly kissed her parents goodnight and stepped out to spend nights at fashionable bordellos. An admirer of striking effects and fustian theatricality, she would arrange for elaborate settings to receive her clients, sometimes standing naked in front of the fireplace reading the *History of the French Revolution.* Her cultured mind, ravishing beauty and knowledge of men had Toulouse's town clerks and lawyers weeping on her pillow from sheer admiration. They showered her with presents and took her on trips when they didn't declare themselves ready to forswear home and family. When she fell in love herself, it could be with parts of a man's physique—a bony stark face, a pair of long pale hands.

For the funeral in Thiviers, Sartre had been rigged out in a dark suit and one of his grandfather's hats that came down to his eyes. Camille was stunned and thought he had the intelligent ugliness of Honoré de Mirabeau, the most formidable orator of the French Revolution. Despite her mourning veil, Camille had no trouble arousing Sartre's interest and the same week they stayed together for four days and nights until cousins and uncles found them and brought each back to a worried family. Camille was being courted by the son of a wealthy furnace manufacturer, but Sartre convinced her he alone could save her from provincial boredom and—as he told other ladies he met—urged her to trust herself, read a lot and become a writer. A week later, he was back at the Sorbonne and began a feverish correspondence with Camille, expounding his views about life and giving her a reading list that included Stendhal, Dostoevsky and Nietzsche. Six months later he visited her in Toulouse. Because he had very little money, he deprived himself of a hotel room and walked around town until midnight when the lights went on in one particular window above the pharmacy. This meant Camille had kissed her parents goodnight and he could come up. He left at dawn, dozing on park benches or in movie houses until the following midnight when, again, he would wait on the sidewalk opposite the drugstore for the beckoning light. By the fourth night, he was dropping with fatigue and Camille said, "Oh, go to sleep then; I'll read Nietzsche." When he woke up she recited from *Thus Spake Zarathustra*—generally the passage about man's will to overcome his baser urges.

In Paris, Sartre worked very hard, passing exams in psychology, sociology and logic. Together with Nizan, he supervised the translation and proofreading of Karl Jaspers' *Psychopathologie*. At the urging of Henri Delacroix, his philosophy professor, he began working on his thesis, The Imagination in Psychological Life. In September, Nizan dropped out of school to travel to Saudi Arabia and the British colony of Aden. If there was one thing that fascinated the post-World War I generation it was travel. They all dreamed of making tremendous journeys, of fraternizing with dockworkers in Istanbul, of getting drunk with pimps and white slavers in cesspools of iniquity and of discussing the meaning of life with Sufi masters in Samarkand or with holy men on the banks of the Ganges. Nizan would lose one year but that was a small price to pay.

To console himself between trips to Toulouse, Sartre took up school dramatics, acted in several productions and planned a stage adaptation of Jules Renard's novel about miserable childhood, *Poil de carotte.* For the end-of-semester dance, he borrowed all the money he could and had Camille come up from Toulouse. She made the expected impression at the university ball, but she was disappointed with Sartre's hotel accommodations for her and with the restaurants he took her to. He had gone to great lengths to get her a job in a stationery store, but she had no intention of selling envelopes for a living and soon returned to Toulouse. The next year after they had broken off, she came to Paris in style—with a wealthy, older friend she called her "enlightened lover" because of his taste in art—and promptly fell in love with Charles Dullin, the actor-director responsible for renewing French acting techniques and for introducing Luigi Pirandello to Parisian theatergoers. Camille had first seen Dullin play a king in a historical screen drama and now went to his Atelier Theater to see him in Aristophanes' *The Birds.* Dressed at her most dazzling, she spent several nights in the same front seat before asking for an interview. Dullin was by no means impervious to her admiration and soon had her set up in an apartment close to his Montmartre theater. From time to time she would tell him she had to visit her parents and would go to spend a week or two in Toulouse with her "enlightened" and often prodigal lover. The actor-director didn't investigate the situation too closely since he was himself still living with his wife.

Although school left Sartre little time to write, he managed to commit poetry, essays—one, *A Theory of State in Modern French Thought,* published in French, English and German in an international university review [12]—and one novel. *Une Défaite* was a fictionalization of his affair with Camille, although it was ostensibly inspired by Nietzsche's doomed love for Cosima Wagner in 1868, when the thirty-two-year-old illegitimate daughter of Franz Liszt and Countess Marie d'Agoult left her conductor husband to live with the fifty-five-year-old Richard Wagner, and Nietzsche was a brilliant twenty-four-year-old university professor. The novel was first entitled *Empedocles,* in honor of the philosopher-scientist-charlatan who called love the unifying principle of all things and supposedly died in 430 B.C. by leaping into the crater of Etna to prove he was a god. Sartre sent the manuscript to Gallimard, but the publishing house turned it down —"judiciously," Sartre would admit a decade later.

Together with Aron, Sartre was a witness at Nizan's marriage to Henriette Alphen on Christmas Eve, 1927. Sartre and Nizan had been close

[12] In *The New Ambassador/Revue universitaire internationale,* Paris, January 1927.

friends since they were eleven—so close that at the teachers' college they were sometimes called Nitre and Sarzan—and Nizan's marriage soon gave Sartre ideas. He commissioned his parents to ask for the hand of a young girl he had met while they were vacationing in the Massif Central region of south-central France. She was the cousin of one of his friends, the daughter of a general store owner. "She was nice and somewhat rebellious against the milieu she lived in," Sartre would remember. "We became engaged. When my grandfather heard about it, he became indignant, 'What, my grandson marrying a grocer's daughter!' "

The jolting experience of 1928, however, was neither a sentimental letdown nor a compensatory marital prospect, but flunking the written part of his Diplôme d'études supérieures. The year before Professor Delacroix had graded as "very good" The Imagination in Psychological Life, in which Sartre had researched the perception of the imagination since Descartes. For the Diplôme, Sartre now wanted to be original, rewrote his thesis and ended up fiftieth and last in the class. Everybody was stunned. The failure set him back one year—and again made him a classmate of Nizan—but it also taught him a lesson. "The thing to do," he would say later in life, "was to present a trite subject but in an original manner."

His thinking was already far away from the philosophy that was taught at the Sorbonne in the late 1920s. When the *Nouvelles littéraires* launched a "Survey of Today's Students," Sartre wrote a lengthy letter to the editor, saying his generation was alienated and out of touch with the attitudes and norms of the preceding generation. Calling Sartre's observations "remarkable," the magazine published long excerpts in its next issue. The idea of actually improving upon humanity was ludicrous, Sartre wrote. Man was a paradox and somewhat like a fortune-teller who can tell other people's future but not his own. "Everything is too weak; all things carry the seed of their own death. Above all, adventure—by which I mean the blind belief in a random yet inevitable connection between circumstances and events— is a fraud." [13] The text ended with a phrase that was to be much quoted: Comparing his own generation with the preceding one, Sartre wrote, "We are more unhappy, but nicer to get along with."

After the Easter recess when the real cramming began for the oral exams, Maheu one day brought along a girl who knew a lot about Leibniz. It was a Monday Simone de Beauvoir would always remember.

---

[13] *Nouvelles littéraires,* February 2, 1929.

CHAPTER

EASTER 1938

It was Gaston Gallimard himself who had come up with the title for Sartre's first published novel. Gallimard, who had a knack for titles, had found "Melancholia" inadequate and had not liked the author's alternate suggestion that the book be called "Les Aventures extraordinaires d'Antoine Roquentin" and published with a wraparound publicity streamer saying, THERE'S NO SUCH THING AS ADVENTURE. *La Nausée* (*Nausea*) [1] was an "also ran" on the 1938 spring list of the big publishing house, coming far behind *L'Espoir* (*Man's Hope*), André Malraux's big powerful novel about the still-raging Spanish Civil War.

For Sartre, the story of Antoine Roquentin was something he had lived with since his first teaching job in 1931. Its central idea was something he had lived with since his senior year at the Sorbonne—how to find salvation in creating imaginary worlds of formal perception. *La Nausée* is the diary of a man who is disturbed by the chaotic and glutinous quality of the real world and yearns for the predictable and accountable universe of Newtonian physics. The reviews were good, with Maurice Blanchot calling *La Nausée* an important and necessary book, but for Sartre the publication had been something of an anticlimax. Gallimard's formidable editor-in-chief, Jean Paulhan, had first turned down the "Melancholia" manuscript, then, at the insistence of Charles Dullin and Pierre Bost, the playwright

---

[1] *La Nausée,* Paris: Gallimard, 1938; *Nausea,* Norfolk, Connecticut: New Directions, 1949.

The author of La Nausée
GISÈLE FREUND

brother of one of Sartre's former students, reconsidered. Next, editor Brice Parain had suggested cuts to alleviate alleged tedium and crude language. Sartre had taken the manuscript to Grasset's but when this house also turned it down, he returned to Gallimard and made the suggested changes. He had dedicated the novel to Beaver and she had helped him with the revisions. The maddening thing of course was that Parain had turned down *her* novel.

Sartre lived with *La Nausée* since their first real separation when he had become a teacher in Le Havre and she had been appointed to a girls' lycée in Marseilles and they had almost gotten married. That had been in February 1931 when he had been advised that someone else had been given the Tokyo lectureship. Japan had been so many light-years away that they had both accepted the separation as mature and reasonable, but Le Havre was silly—so close and yet a twenty-hour train ride from Marseilles. Simone had panicked and he had proposed marriage because it would mean joint assignments. He had argued that the formality of marriage would not seriously affect their way of life, even if they considered it silly to submit to this particular custom. "We found it moral to behave in accordance with our convictions and took the unmarried state for granted," she would write in *The Prime of Life,* the second volume of her autobiography. "Only some very serious consideration could have made us bow to any conventional usage which we found repellent. But such a consideration had now, in fact, arisen, since the thought of going to Marseilles threw me into a state of great anxiety. In these circumstances, Sartre said, it was stupid to martyr oneself for a principle. Not for a moment, however, was I tempted to fall in with his suggestion. The task of preserving my own independence was not particularly onerous; I would have regarded it as highly artificial to equate Sartre's absence with my own freedom—a thing I would only find within myself. But I could see how much it cost Sartre to bid farewell to his travels, his own freedom, his youth—in order to become a provincial academic, now finally and forever grown up." [2]

They had found their lasting life-style in 1929 during the last free months before Sartre's military service. If the habit of setting up domicile in small Left Bank hotels was still a few years away, the optimistic living for themselves was there from those first October days when they met for breakfast in the Luxembourg Gardens and only left each other late at night, he to spend the night at his grandparents', she in the room she rented from her grandmother on the Rue Denfert Rochereau. From the

2 Simone de Beauvoir, *La Force de l'age,* Paris: Gallimard, 1960; *The Prime of Life,* New York: World, 1962.

beginning, they refused external limitations, overriding authority and imposed patterns. From the beginning, they never hesitated to disagree and to make up their minds in what they thought was the pure light of reason while at the same time creating their private fantasies. Pantomime and playacting took care of difficult or disagreeable situations as they turned dramas upside down, caricatured them and explored them in all directions. They called their relationship "a morganatic marriage" and sometimes played Monsieur and Madame M. Organatique, an unambitious, easily satisfied middle-class couple. Sometimes when Simone dressed up and they went to the movies on the Champs Elysées or dancing at La Coupole, they would be a wealthy American couple, Mr. and Mrs. Morgan Hattick.

They decided never to lie to each other. She had been used to a certain reserve but soon adapted to having her actions subjected to a scrutiny that was far more impartial than she had achieved herself. "The thought that Sartre was now an open book to me, as easily read as my own mind, had a most relaxing effect on me," she was to write. "Later I learned better. Since he concealed nothing from me, I thought myself absolved from any need to think about his problems." [3] She was to ponder the outer limits of "telling all" in *Les Mandarins* (*The Mandarins*) and he in *L'Age de raison* (*The Age of Reason*).

There were differences. She took setbacks badly, her face changed, she withdrew into herself and became stubborn and obstinate. Things had a way of getting him down, especially in the morning or when he had nothing to do, and he had a tendency to look like an elephant seal they had seen in the Vincennes Zoo. When he looked like that, she would tell him about the elephant seal and he would mimic the animal, rolling his eyes up, sighing and making silent supplication until they both laughed. Making fun of themselves would stay with them. He would call her "a clock in a refrigerator" and she said that "Sartre only associates with people who associate with Sartre."

She was less committed to literature than he. He believed the creative act meant assuming responsibility for the world, giving it something it needed; she felt turning away from the world led to creativity. She distrusted all pathos and liked hermetic poems, surrealist films, abstract art and puppet shows. He verbalized everything, placed more value in "emotional abstractions" than on feelings and could describe a landscape better than she. She liked Bach, he preferred Beethoven; but they both rejected psychoanalysis and Sigmund Freud as leading to the destruction of human free will. She felt personally affected by Virginia Woolf's reflections on

[3] *Ibid.*

language and the gulf between writing and life. He, too, believed that
writing had a way of imposing deceptive patterns upon truth. He thought
a writer could turn the gap to his advantage, while she felt a writer
should strive to narrow the discrepancy between the world and its artistic
recreation. He had a tendency to go off deep ends and she to puncture the
wilder flights of his imagination. She accused him of careless inaccuracy
but realized his exaggerations were often more provocative than her
scrupulous precision.

They both read prodigiously. She had taken out books from Adrienne
Monnier's lending library-bookstore in the Rue de l'Odéon since she was
nineteen and had begun to go across the street to Sylvia Beach's Shakespeare
and Company bookstore, where the frail-looking James Joyce showed up
in not too clean sneakers, and the expatriate Americans were to be found.
Her English was better than Sartre's and she read all of Virginia Woolf,
a vast quantity of Henry James, Rebecca West, Sinclair Lewis, Theodore
Dreiser and Sherwood Anderson. What struck *him*—in translation—was
John Dos Passos' new novel, *The Forty-Second Parallel,* because no one
in the novel was wholly self-determined but conditioned by his social
background.

Sartre ranked films as high as books. It was in a movie house that he had
discovered what he called the "fundamental necessity of art" and the concomitant contingency—it was a word he liked—of their own lives. Besides
his "trashy" comic books, he needed his weekly dose of cowboy and crime
movies and steered Beaver clear of all art films. "In *The Singing Fool*
Al Jolson gave such a contagiously emotional rendition of 'Sonny Boy'
that when the lights went up I saw, to my astonishment, tears in Sartre's
eyes," she would write. "He used to cry unashamedly in the cinema and I
regretted the efforts I had made to stop myself doing the same thing."

To be teachers was a necessary irritant, a way of earning a living that
had little to do with the central purpose of their lives, but they were con-
fident their respective literary vocations would be vindicated. What interested Sartre above all was people and what he wanted to write about was
subjective humanism, to apply reason to the problems of existence. This
was something he had stumbled on while proofreading the French edition
of Jaspers' *Psychopathologie.*

Nizan was an active communist, but politics bored Sartre and Beaver.
They counted on events to turn out according to their wishes without any
need for them to get involved, except by way of books. With Nizan they
ridiculed bourgeois values, but Sartre rejected the idea of one of Simone's
former classmates that he was himself a *petit bourgeois,* saying the label

was inadequate. As a communist, Nizan was more rebel than revolutionary and here Sartre and Beaver agreed. "We were anticapitalists yet not Marxists," she would remember. "We glorified the powers of pure mind and perfect freedom, yet we rejected the spiritual approach. Although our interpretation of man and the universe was strictly materialistic, we despised science and technology. Sartre was not bothered by these inconsistencies, and refused so much as to formulate them. 'When you think in terms of *problems,*' he told me, 'you aren't thinking at all.' He himself skipped from one conviction to the next without rhyme or reason."

One afternoon when they had been to see V. I. Pudovkin's *Storm Over Asia* in a Champs Elysées cinema with the Nizans and were walking back to the Latin Quarter by themselves, Sartre said, "Let's sign a two-year lease." He would be doing at least part of his army stint at Saint-Cyr, near Versailles. She could arrange to teach privately and also live in the Paris region during those two years, which they would spend in the closest possible intimacy. Afterward, he suggested, she should try to get a job abroad. They would live apart for two or three years and then join each other again somewhere. The separation he proposed caused her some agony, but it was well in the future and she had made it a rule not to worry about anything prematurely. There was no question to her of either of them actually taking advantage, during the two-year "lease," of those "freedoms" they theoretically had the right to enjoy.

In November, Sartre was off to his eighteen months of military service. With former philosophy classmate Raymond Aron as sergeant-instructor and Pierre Guille as fellow recruit, Sartre went through basic training and was assigned to the army's weather service. His specialty became wind-velocity reading. He hated it but in January 1930 was transferred to a camp near Tours, one hundred and fifty miles southwest of Paris. Together with a *chef de poste* and three other recruits he lived in a villa that had been turned into a meteorological station. When on duty, his job was to wave an anemometer every two hours and telephone the measured wind strength to a station somewhere else. The chief was a civilian who let the military personnel work out a schedule that gave each an extra week off every month, over and above their legal furloughs. Simone came down every Sunday— with an armful of books borrowed more or less legitimately from Adrienne Monnier's bookstore—and he made it to Paris every third week. In August, she took up residence for one month in a little hotel in Saint-Radegonde ten minutes from the weather station. On sunny days she spent the morning reading on the banks of a stream, lunched on a pack of biscuits and a bar of chocolate, then climbed the hill to meet Sartre a few yards from the station. They were too timid to go up to her room in broad daylight and made love al fresco. His grandmother Louise died at the age of eighty-one that summer, leaving him a small legacy that allowed him to take Beaver to a couple of decent restaurants in the Loire Valley.

Military meteorology allowed for a lot of free time and Sartre wrote a one-act play inspired by Pirandello and the beginning of a novel-length essay. *Epiméthée* featured Prometheus' brother Epimetheus preparing for his own burial. As in the Greek legend, Zeus sends Pandora down to Epimetheus to punish Prometheus for having given the human race the knowledge of fire and Epimetheus only realizes his mistake when she opens her box full of evil, toil and disease. In Sartre's update, Prometheus is an engineer, Epimetheus a practical joker and Pandora a beauty salon owner. As with most of his previous writing, the *Epiméthée* manuscript would disappear and Sartre only mentions it in passing in an interview nearly forty years later.[4]

Légende de la vérité was an attempt at mythmaking, the story of Truth. "Truth was not born first," it began. "The warring nomads weren't so much in need of truth as of pretty creeds. Who can say what is the truth in a battle?" Truth came before barter, artisans learned to use it and truth came into its own when people began to think about what they were actually doing. The Greeks invented truth with a capital T which allowed people to say that it isn't just because something exists that it is true. This led to democracy because it allowed humble folk to feel equal to the Great. Later, people learned to distrust solitary men and to say that anyone who did the work for several others was a subversive. This led to a peril that would prove fruitful—miracle workers were chased from the city and took up residence in deep forests and became the forefathers of a long line of profound men on whom nature bestowed its secrets. Full of bad faith, this riffraff went from town to town, pulling with them on a leash their terrible knowledge and extorting alms from people by letting them pull a little on the leash. These scoundrels were artists, writers and philosophers—the only people who really grasped living reality. When they died out, a certain apprehension persisted and a bold government sent out an expedition that discovered a profound inequality among men. And so on through swipes at enlightenment, politicians and colonialism in Africa to the birth of Probable. "One day I will sing the glory of this late-born son of Boredom and Truth. It will be a fable for grownups." With Nizan's help, the long opening chapter of *Légende de la vérité* was published in

---

[4] In *L'Avant-Scène Théâtre*, special Sartre issue, May 1968.

the last issue of *Bifur,* an avant-garde magazine with an unnerving taste for important writing, which had Joyce on its editorial board.[5]

Simone also started a novel. She had been impressed by Alain-Fournier's wistful *Les Grandes Meaulnes* (*The Wanderer*) which had fascinated the whole postwar generation of young intellectuals, and with British author Rosamond Lehmann for her intense writing on suffering women in love. Like Alain-Fournier and Lehmann, she tried to write on the borderlines of lucidity and lost wonderment and began the story of a young girl living in an old castle with a taciturn father, but who escapes to Paris after one day seeing three carefree young people. All sorts of adventures would happen in Paris, but Simone never got any further than the third chapter. She felt she was doing a school assignment and that she had only started it because Sartre had been adamant about her also becoming a writer.

Her vacuity and the thought that she was disappointing him made her furious at herself. She wondered whether adapting to someone else wasn't the surest way of losing that person. Her best friend, Zaza, had died in pathetic circumstances, the victim of meningitis and encephalitis after her mother had opposed her marriage to Jean Pradelle—not so much because he was an unworthy match but because he was Simone's friend. For a long time Simone was to feel she had paid for her freedom with Zaza's death.

The discovery of her own sexuality was also disconcerting. Separated from Sartre for days and even weeks, she discovered that her body craved his, that his physical absence actually could cause pain. She hated suffering and found her own physical appetites baffling. Worse, strange hands feeling her up in trains or on the métro could arouse sensations of shattering intensity in her. "I said nothing about these shameful incidents," she would write. "Now that I had embarked on our policy of absolute frankness, this reticence was, I felt, a kind of touchstone. If I didn't dare confess such things, it was because they were unavowable. By driving me to such secrecy my body became a stumbling block rather than a bond between us, and I felt a burning resentment against it." [6]

To make matters worse, Sartre began to hold Simone-Camille Sans up as an example of a girl who was doing something with herself. Simone wanted to meet this fascinating creature and one night went to see her play a barmaid in Armand Salacrou's *Patchouli* and thought she looked like an oversized porcelain doll. When they met, Simone had to agree that Camille did possess a peculiarly seductive charm, despite her heavy exotic jewelry that clinked when she moved. For Dullin, Camille planned to

[5] *Bifur,* June 1931.
[6] Beauvoir, *The Prime of Life.*

adapt the medieval Spanish tragicomedy *La Celestina* and she was also writing her own play, *L'Ombre*. Camille had portraits of Nietzsche, Albrecht Dürer and Emily Brontë on her walls and told Simone a woman should never have any difficulty catching a man. For Camille's next stage appearance, Simone took her sister and Fernando Gerassi, visiting from Madrid, along to the Atelier Theater and found her costume, makeup and dancing grotesque. Simone scored a point when Sartre had to concede that Camille's sleeping around with men she didn't love added up to a tedious self-debasement and a considerably meeker personality than would appear from the Camille legend.

But Simone herself would have to face the idea of sexual encounters with men she might not love since Sartre still planned to leave for Japan once his army stint was over. She decided also to find a teaching job abroad and wrote to Fernando, now back in Madrid with Stépha Avdicovitch. Someone told her about a possible opening in Morocco and one of Stépha's former admirers suggested she try the University of Budapest. She looked forward to taking fresh stock of herself and felt she would no doubt come to a conclusion about writing and *doing* something with herself.

The fear of the dreaded two-year separation suddenly melted away in February 1931 when Sartre returned to civilian life and was advised that someone else had been given the Tokyo lectureship. He was disappointed but the same week he was offered a substitute post, during the final term of the year, at the boy's lycée in Le Havre, the industrial port city on the Seine estuary one hundred and fifty miles northwest of Paris. Because it was so close to the capital, he accepted and even managed to smile when Beaver got her first assignment—a girl's lycée in Marseilles. But the school year lasted only nine months and with two days off and a convenient dose of flu she could get to Paris now and then. And there was still all summer. Her term would only begin October 2.

Stépha and Fernando came to Paris on a visit, excitingly telling Sartre and Simone how the Republic had finally been established in Spain. Stépha was nine months pregnant and they all celebrated the birth of her son at the Closerie de Lilas, Sartre's favorite Montparnasse hangout. Children were something Sartre and, above all, Simone would never have. She, especially, found they were sufficient to themselves and to each other and her own lack of affinity with her parents made her feel that she could only expect indifference or hostility from any children of her own. She didn't feel she was holding out against motherhood, but that it was not her natural lot in life.

Their love was deepening and becoming more demanding. They decided to revise their provisional "lease." They would allow for brief separations but not vast solitary escapades. "We didn't swear oaths of eternal fidelity, but we did agree to postpone any possibility of separation until the distant time when we reached our thirties," she would write. As she made her hero tell her heroine in *L'Invitée* (*She Came to Stay*), " 'It's impossible to talk about faithfulness and unfaithfulness where we are concerned,' said Pierre, drawing Françoise to him. 'You and I are simply one. It's true, you know, neither of us can be explained without the other.' " [7]

While Stépha and the baby stayed in Paris, Fernando returned to Madrid where he was a radio salesman with very little time for painting. Sartre and Beaver decided to go and see him.

It was their first real trip together and the first time either of them had been outside France. Seeing Spanish customs officials on the border made them feel they were entering a new and exotic world and as they got a room in a little *posada* in Figueras and walked about town after dinner they excitedly told each other, "We're in Spain!"

Sartre had converted the final remnants of his grandmother's legacy into pesetas and they spent an exciting summer traveling from Barcelona to Madrid, Toledo, Pamplona, Burgos and San Sebastian. "Like most tourists of our generation, we imagined that every place and town possessed a secret soul, some unchanging essential element that a traveler had to discover," she would write. "We knew that the key to Toledo or Venice was not to be found searching exclusively in the museums and monuments to the past, but in the here and now of light and shade, the crowds and characteristic smells of the place and its special dishes. This was what we had learned from Larbaud, Gide, Morand and Drieu La Rochelle. According to Georges Duhamel, the whole mystery of Berlin was distilled in the unique smell of its streets and Gide declared that to drink a cup of hot Spanish chocolate was to hold all Spain in one's mouth. So daily I forced myself to swallow cups of black, sauce-like liquid, heavily flavored with cinnamon." [8] In Madrid, Fernando put them up in his apartment and took them through the Prado where Sartre loved the grotesque paintings of Hieronymus Bosch but hated Titian's mastery. The Republic was still amazed by its own victory and in deep, gloomy cafés Spaniards discussed the future with impassioned rhetoric. In one café they were respectfully introduced to Ramón del Valle-Inclán, the elder statesman of Madrid's

[7] Simone de Beauvoir, *L'Invitée*, Paris: Gallimard, 1943; *She Came to Stay*, Cleveland and New York: World Publishing, 1954.
[8] Beauvoir, *The Prime of Life*.

literati whose novels and plays anticipated the theater of the absurd. Valle-Inclán was a proud, bearded, one-armed figure who would tell anyone who cared to listen just how he had lost his arm and make a different story of it every time.

They returned to Paris at the end of September with just enough time to say good-bye to their friends and to each other before Sartre headed for Le Havre and Beaver for Marseilles. Sartre had been to his lycée in Le Havre several times—in July to give a graduation day speech on the glory of movies [9]—and didn't dislike the big Channel seaport. Nor did he altogether dislike teaching, and many students would recall his classes with fondness. "He was nice, simple and astonishingly funny," Albert Palle would remember. "He took a lot of things seriously but his own profession was not one of them, and we had a kind of rapport with him that we had never had with any adult, a kind of rapport that had nothing to do with family or authority, but was a relationship stripped of the usual barriers." Jacques-Laurent Bost would illustrate the free rapport between teacher and students with the obscene rebuses they wrote on the blackboard before he came in, rebuses where the syllable "con" (cunt, fucking ass) was invariably pictured with a drawing of a man saying in a cartoon-strip balloon, "My name is Sartre." "So Sartre would come in and look at the blackboard and say, 'Gotcha,' and try to solve the rebus . . . On days when nothing went right he would look out over the class in stony silence and say, 'All these faces and not a ray of intelligence.' It sent a mortal chill through the room, but it didn't last long."

Teaching was loathsome in other ways to Sartre. He hated the necessary discipline, hierarchy and rules and as he settled down in a *hôtel-pension* near the railway station he keenly felt an abstruse and difficult "age of reason" was beginning for him. The start of his career was accompanied by indigence and the final rejection by several publishers of his full-length *Légende de la vérité.* The last money from his grandmother's inheritance was gone and he would henceforth have to live on his junior teacher's salary. Le Havre was gray, rainy and industrial, Simone was in Marseilles, the friends in Paris. He was lonesome.

Almost in desperation he threw himself into writing and frantic reading. "It was when I arrived in Le Havre with my scribblings behind me that I told myself, 'This is the moment to begin real writing,'" he would tell interviewers later in life. Contingency was something he felt deeply. His life was contingent insofar as it happened by chance, without known

[9] "L'art cinématographique," reprinted in *Gazette du Cinéma,* No. 2, June 1950; No. 3, September 1950.

cause and could never be foreseen. Each individual was fortuitous although in the end responsible for what he or she became. He began to write what he facetiously called "On Contingency," a lengthy and abstract meditation by a provincial scholar named Antoine Roquentin [10] and, after sitting and watching a chestnut tree in a square, wrote a poem about the tree and, in a long letter to Beaver, described his park-bench contemplation and "understanding" of what a tree was. When he showed her "On Contingency" during the Christmas holidays, she suggested that he give Roquentin some fictional depth and infuse the plot with some of the suspense they both enjoyed in detective novels. He agreed and, back in Le Havre, reworked the story.

The gradual transformation of the tale of Roquentin's from abstract meditation to a sweet-and-sour philosophical novel was also influenced by the books he discovered—Paul Valéry's Socratic dialogue, *Eupalinos ou l'Architecte,* and *Les Cahiers de Malte Laurids Brigge,* Gide's translation of Rainer Maria Rilke's only novel. *Eupalinos* intrigued him by its almost mathematical symbolism and *Die Aufzeichnungen des Malte Laurids Brigge* by its intense imagery and story of a solitary artist's torment in the midst of other people's poverty and misery. Since the story of Roquentin was cast in the form of a diary, Sartre began his own journal and, in *The Words,* would say that writing *La Nausée* was an act of exorcism. "I was Roquentin; I used him to show, without complacency, the texture of my life. At the same time, I was myself, the superior human being, chronicler of someone else's hell, a photomicroscope made of glass and steel bent over my own protoplasmic juices."

Simone's existence in Marseilles was concomitant and parallel, lived with an eye on the mailbox and the calendar. An hour after her arrival, she found a reasonable *pension,* breathed in the smell of tar and sea at the Old Port, mingled with the crowds along the Canebière and determined to transform her exile into a holiday. On Sundays and on days off, she went hiking from dawn to dusk and, with a Michelin map, systematically worked her way through the Mont Aurélien, Mont Sainte-Victoire and other sandstone peaks and gorges in the Rhône River delta. When her art-student sister came for a visit in November, she took her on a hike that had Poupette's feet in blisters and forced her to return, feverish and exhausted, to Marseilles on a bus while Simone trekked on.

Her students were interesting insofar as it was the first year in philosophy

---

[10] Sartrian scholars say he either found the name in Flaubert or in a lexicon of medieval French, where a *roquentin* was a sing-along made up of fragments of other songs and juxtaposed so as to produce an incongruous effect.

for all of them and Simone's own knowledge was still fresh. At twenty-three she still looked so much like a college girl herself that other teachers often took her for a *lycéenne*. When she began teaching ethics and gave assignments on labor, capital, justice and colonialism, she could see fathers' belabored arguments in her girls' papers which she demolished with passion. She got in trouble when on the subject of pain, she assigned Alexandre Dumas' *Traité,* which also discussed pleasure. Some parents complained and she was called down to see the headmistress, who finally dropped the matter. Most of her fellow teachers were old maids, and a married English teacher she would call Madame Tourmelin in *The Prime of Life* became a friend. Madame Tourmelin was thirty-five; her husband was recovering from tuberculosis in a sanatorium in the Alps. Both alone, the two teachers went to the theater, to dinner and on walks until once in Madame Tourmelin's apartment the older woman grasped Simone, kissed her passionately and told her to drop the pretense. Simone screamed No! and fled. In school the next day, Madame Tourmelin managed to say that she hoped Simone didn't really believe anything that had happened the night before. For the rest of the school year Simone managed never to be alone with the English teacher.

Georges and Françoise de Beauvoir came for a week-long visit that turned out to be pleasant, with Simone's father treating them to bouillabaisse at Isnard's, the best restaurant in Marseilles, and her mother coming along on an outing to Sainte-Beaume. A cousin also passed through, but Simone preferred her solitary state. She read Katherine Mansfield's *Letters* and found that she, too, was a romantically "solitary woman." She had too much time at her disposal not to start a new novel, but this time was fiercely critical of herself. To train herself she wrote out complete descriptions of restaurants where she was eating. "In my dealings with Sartre, as previously with Zaza, I reproached myself for failing to keep our relationship completely honest and for risking the loss of my freedom," she would write. "I felt that if I managed to translate this error into fictional terms I would be cleansed of it, redeemed even. For the first time I had something to say." Pursuing what she would call "the mirage of the Other," she invented two women protagonists and apportioned between them the two contrasting tendencies in herself—zest for life and the urge for literary achievement. Madame de Préaline was forty and, like Sartre's friend Madame Morel, possessed measured elegance, tact, reserve and although she was surrounded by friends, she remained in her own life a "solitary woman." Geneviève was twenty, endowed with a somewhat clumsy mind and given to heavy emotionalizing. She lived for the moment and lacked the psychological perspective to think or feel anything without reference to another person. She worshiped Madame de Préaline, who was in love with a man from whom fate kept her apart. Zaza was also in the novel, renamed Anne and married off to a conventional man.

The novel didn't really come together, Simone realized, because Anne's death was never explained and because the plot was detached from the context which contained its truth. "The most valuable thing about this apprentice work was the way I had handled the various viewpoints," she would write. "Geneviève was observed through Anne's eyes, which lent a certain air of mystery to her otherwise simple character. Madame Préaline and Anne were, in turn, presented as Geneviève saw them, and Geneviève was made aware that she didn't understand them very well. The reader was therefore invited to deduce a level of truth above and beyond her shortsightedness and did not have this thrust crudely at him. The pity of it was that despite this carefully worked-out presentation, my heroines were such inconsistent creatures."

Vacations were the best times. As soon as school was out, Sartre and Beaver would hop on trains to Paris, wait at each other's railway terminals, repair to a hotel and, if the vacation was short, see no one except Simone's sister. During longer recesses they saw their friends—Nizan was deep into politics in suburban Bourg, Dullin was staging Camille's play, *L'Ombre*. For the 1932 Easter recess they went to Britanny and, in an issue of the *Nouvelle revue française,* discovered Franz Kafka. In June, Sartre went to Marseilles and gave Simone the pleasure of falling in love with her cherished sites—the Old Port, the Canebière bistros, the Château d'If and the beaches at Cassis. The best news was that during the next school year she would teach in Rouen, the old Normandy capital sixty miles from Le Havre. They spent the summer revisiting Spain with a side trip to Morocco, which enchanted them. They were in Seville during General José Sanjurjo's unsuccessful coup against the Republic and on the way back stopped off in Toulouse, where Camille showed them around. *L'Ombre* had not been a success, but Camille was writing a novel, making both Sartre and Beaver jealous of her six-hour-a-day stamina.

Rouen was an hour's train ride from Le Havre—and an hour and a half from Paris—and Simone took a room at the Hôtel La Rochefoucauld where she could hear the reassuring whistle of trains and have breakfast at the Café Métropole. They got themselves Rouen-Le Havre railway-commuter passes and managed to spend at least one day together every week. The insipid and rainy Normandy landscape didn't inspire Simone to go hiking and her fellow teachers at the Lycée Jeanne d'Arc were, with one exception, even more annoying than her colleagues in Marseilles. The exception was Colette Audry, who was a communist activist on her days off. Colette also lived near the railway station and had furnished her room with rush mattings and burlap. On her bookshelves were the works of Marx and Rosa Luxemburg. She was not a member of the Communist Party but of a Trotskyite splinter group that believed a revolution against Joseph Stalin inside Russia was a possibility. Simone introduced Colette to Sartre and they got along well. Colette sometimes spoke about Simone Weil. Simone's former Ecole Normale classmate had become a university teacher at Puy-de-Dôme. It was said that she lived in a truck drivers' hotel and on the first of every month emptied her pay envelope on the table and let anyone take what he needed. More astonishing, Weil had acted as leader of a strike delegation and worked alongside railway workers without having herself kicked out of the university, apparently because her total commitment and her courage had impressed everybody. In comparison her own and Sartre's existence seemed safe. They distrusted classical French psychology and had only a limited faith in psychoanalysis. The communists condemned psychoanalysis but the Trotskyites embraced it eagerly. Colette and her friends interpreted their feelings and individual actions according to Freudian and Adlerian patterns.

Sartre and Beaver tried to work out a philosophy for themselves and he hit on the notion of *mauvaise foi*—the "bad faith" of lying to oneself in order to escape the responsibility of making choices. "We set ourselves to expose this dishonesty in all its manifestations—semantic quibbling, false recollections, fugues, compensatory fantasies, sublimations and the rest," she would remember. "We rejoiced every time we unearthed a new loophole, another type of deception. One of my younger colleagues was a goldmine of dogmatic opinions and violent moods in the teachers' lounge, but when I tried to talk to her privately, I found myself plunged into mental quicksand. This contrast disconcerted me, until one day light dawned. 'I've got it,' I told Sartre, 'Ginette Lumière is unreal, a sort of mirage.' Thenceforth we applied this term to anyone who feigned convictions or feelings which they didn't in fact possess; we had discovered, under another name, role-playing."

The best times were in Paris. Henriette and Paul Nizan invited them to stay with them, but Sartre and Beaver preferred the Hôtel de Blois in the Rue Gay-Lussac near the Sorbonne and the Luxembourg Gardens. Simone's sister, Poupette, had taken a secretarial job but she hadn't given up painting. An old student friend they were in contact with was Raymond

Aron, who was spending a year at the French Institute in Berlin studying Edmund Husserl's phenomenologist philosophy while at the same time preparing a thesis in history. When he came to Paris, they all spent an evening in a Montparnasse nightclub, ordering the house specialty—apricot cocktails. Pointing to his glass, Aron said, "You see, if you were a phenomenologist you could talk about this cocktail and make philosophy out of it." Sartre turned pale with emotion. Here was the idea he was groping for, to be able to describe objects just as he saw and touched them, and extract philosophy from the process. On the Boulevard St. Michel, he bought Emmanuel Lévinas' *La Théorie de l'intuition dans la phénoménologie de Husserl* and was so eager to get into the subject he began reading it in the street. His heart skipped a beat, Beaver would remember, when he found references to contingency.

Other occasions were less jarring. On one trip, Dullin let them sit in on rehearsals of *Richard III* and let them discover accents, rhythm and delivery and a director's skillful use of actors' virtues and shortcomings. Colette Audry's sister, Jacqueline, was a script girl and they were intrigued and flattered when Colette took them along to the film studio and let them watch an actor say "You wanted me, sir?" thirteen times. "We were always a little depressed when, at eight o'clock, we got to the Gare Saint-Lazare and boarded the train that would take us back to Rouen and Le Havre," Simone would write. "We would bury ourselves in the latest S. S. Van Dine, or some sanguinary thriller by Whitfield or Dashiell Hammett, whom the critics acclaimed as the pioneer of 'a new kind of fiction.' When I emerged from the station the town was already asleep. I would eat a *croissant* at the Métropole just before closing time and go straight back to my room." The Paris trips could lead to protracted arguments between them. Once they found themselves without a penny and no one to borrow from. Simone suggested trying the manager at the Hôtel de Blois since they were staying there every week. They spent an hour arguing, with Simone finally saying, "If he disgusts you that much, why should you care what goes on inside his head?" and Sartre replying that his own opinions about the man militated against borrowing money from him.

Lévinas' book had Sartre fascinated. He decided that the Lithuanian-born Lévinas, who was exactly his own age, gave only a formal and decidedly vague outline of Husserl. Sartre breathed a little easier when he found that contingency did not play any important part in Husserlian phenomenology. He decided to make a serious study of the now seventy-four-year-old Husserl who, until 1929, had been teaching in Freiburg and was still living in the Black Forest university town. Sartre wrote to Aron in Berlin for more information. By return mail, Aron suggested that Sartre succeed him as a research student at the *Institut français* in Berlin for the 1933–34 academic year.

In January 1933, the *Nouvelle revue française* began the serialization of André Malraux's *La Condition humaine* (*Man's Fate*), and they both followed, week after week, the story of individuals caught in revolutionary events. Although Malraux was only three years older than Sartre, he was somehow of the previous generation, already an effective voice on the left. His fiction was close to Sartre's ideals. Malraux's characters were "engagé" but at the same time solitary men. A new book that touched them even deeper was Louis-Ferdinand Céline's *Voyage au bout de la nuit* (*Journey to the End of the Night*). They learned whole passages by heart of the hallucinated account of the author's agonized descent into the sticky opacity of his own experiences.

Sartre and Beaver spent the Easter recess in London, walking for hours through Piccadilly, the City, Hamstead and Putney, eating in chophouses off the Strand or in Soho, spending hours at the Tate Gallery to stare at Van Gogh's yellow chairs and sunflowers and looking for vestiges of Shakespeare and Dickens in Old Chiswick. Movies were Sartre's obsession. He spent a whole day dragging Beaver around Whitechapel in pouring rain to find a little cinema where, according to one poster, *One Way Passage,* with Kay Francis and William Powell, was playing. She could not drag him through the British Museum, but he usually accommodated himself to her ideas and itineraries. When it rained and they didn't know where to take shelter, the absence of cafés disconcerted them and they were disoriented by the shabby taxis, the advertising graffiti, the tea shops and the ugly window dressings. They made side trips to Canterbury, which they found beautiful, and to Oxford, where Sartre was annoyed by the snobbishness of the English undergraduate. They got into an argument when, after twelve days in London, Sartre tried out his Husserlian phenomenology on the British capital and she found his summing-up omitted countless sides of the total picture. She recognized Le Havre in Roquentin's "Bouville," [11] feeling that Sartre was revealing the true essence of the place. On London, she said, he was dead wrong.

The application for the 1933–34 research scholarship at the French Institute in Berlin was accepted. Sartre was elated. It meant he would get away from teaching for a whole year. Berlin was not the most serene place to study philosophy, but almost everybody agreed that Adolf Hitler

[11] Literally, "Mudtown."

wouldn't last very long. Hitler had become Chancellor in January and with the February 27 burning of the Reichstag had managed to liquidate the powerful German Communist Party. French public opinion was disturbed by the Nazi policy toward German intellectuals. German scholars and artists, particularly those of Jewish extraction, went into exile, but Communist Party chief Ernst Thälmann declared Germany's fourteen million workers would never allow fascism to become a permanent solution and would never allow Hitler to lead them into war. When Hitler had Thälmann arrested, together with Bulgarian Komintern secretary-general George Dimitrov, and planned to try them for the Reichstag burning, Malraux organized a Thälmann Defense Committee and, together with German exile leader Willi Münzenberg, planned mock "countertrials" in Paris, London and Amsterdam. The majority of the French left, however, agreed with *Le Monde* commentator Henri Barbusse that Hitler could not restore the German economy, that the powerful German proletariat would gain the upper hand again and that the real threat was a panic on the right in France. In the National Assembly, socialists and communists continued to vote against French rearmament.

Sartre and Beaver were leftist but passionately apolitical. Politics, they felt, had nothing to do with their struggle. She would write in *The Prime of Life* that Sartre was vaguely tempted to join the Communist Party although his ideas, aims and temperament were against it, but he would repeatedly say that until 1939 he considered himself an individual whose existence had no relationship to the body politic. "I was the 'solitary man' who opposes society because he doesn't owe society anything and, most important, because society has no hold over him," Sartre would tell this biographer. "I had no political opinions and I never voted in any election. I listened to Nizan's political discussions but I also listened to Aron and to socialists. I felt my job was to write and that writing was in no way a social activity. I thought bourgeois were shits and didn't hesitate to say so on paper. *Nausea* is not *only* an attack on bourgeois mentality, but it is that, too. The novel is the literary consequence of the 'solitary man' idea which I didn't manage to escape until the walls came tumbling down in 1939."

During the summer, they made their first visit to a country they would come back to again and again—Italy. The Benito Mussolini government was staging a so-called Fascist Exhibition and in order to attract foreign tourists, the Italian railways offered 70 percent fare reductions. Taking advantage of this—"without scruple," as Simone would write—they crisscrossed northern Italy and spent two weeks in Florence. She was instantly captivated; Sartre was not. Blackshirts were everywhere and all walls were covered with fascist slogans. After nightfall no one was in the streets. In Rome, they decided to stay up until dawn. At midnight they were accosted by two Blackshirts in the Piazza Navona and told to go home to bed. They paid no attention. At 3 A.M. in the Colosseum, however, flashlights were shone into their faces and they finally returned to their hotel.

When Sartre arrived in Berlin in September, faculty and students at the Institut français told him Nazism was in its last throes. The students associated only with antifascist fellow students and intellectuals who were all convinced the Nuremberg Congress, where three hundred thousand brownshirted Nazis had paraded, was a temporary fit of collective hysteria. They considered antisemitism too stupid to merit serious concern. A tall, handsome, strapping young Jew and a small, kinky-haired Corsican at the Institute were always taken for the opposite of what they were and everybody joked about the inanities of racial politics.

Sartre settled in. The Institute offered him a freedom and camaraderie that he hadn't experienced since teachers' college. It also offered a quick and easy affair. She was the wife of another resident scholar—Simone would call her "Marie Girard" and say she was an attractive girl with a slow smile and a penchant for daydreaming, who in Paris had been around the Latin Quarter for ages. Sartre and "Marie" saw a great deal of each other. They agreed there was no future in their relationship but that its present reality was enough for them. During the Christmas holidays, he told her, he would return to Paris.

He also began to work.

Phenomenology was, in 1934, a movement trying to understand the way Man thinks and to redefine his relations with himself and the world. Totally outside the sphere of Anglo-American interests—Bertrand Russell was exploring analytical logic and the dominant force in American philosophy was a kind of modified pragmatism—phenomenology wanted to go back to basics by *describing* things—phenomena—without trying to explain or analyze them, and from this narrowed notion of thinking move forward to a new, more intuitive grasp of our sense of being. Phenomenology meant to stand back, to suspend all judgment and to try to grasp things and ideas with a kind of primal intuition. It meant to realize, as Husserl said, that we can intuitively imagine three or four things, even if we can "think" a thousand. With Descartes, it tried to ask, "What do we know for certain?" and with Kant to ask, "What form does knowledge take?"

Phenomenology rejected wholly rationalist metaphysics as being insufficient to account for the meaning of human existence, and was in return rejected by Marxists as a kind of crypto-idealism, making a spectator out of man instead of a deeply committed agent in the historical process. Phenomenology was not founded; it grew. Husserl was its fountainhead, an energetic little man with a goatee and steel-rimmed bifocals who had converted from Judaism to Protestantism, believed passionately that philosophy could be a science and, with a mixture of pride and sadness, liked to call himself "a perpetual beginner." Now seventy-five, he lived in active retirement from Freiburg University, working hard and fast on a series of lectures he was to give in Belgrade, and content to see his most promising student, Martin Heidegger, appointed his successor, even if for one aberrant year Heidegger embraced Nazism. Husserl was to live to be near eighty and, during the last years of his life, be exposed to various pressures because of his Jewish ancestry.

A trained mathematician, Husserl had not been satisfied with doing mathematics with fuzzy concepts and, in 1891, published *Philosophie der Arithmetik,* an attempt at psychological analysis of certain basic notions of mathematical logic. His book was reviewed by Gotlob Frege, the formidable founder of mathematical logic, who accused Husserl of confusing psychology and logic. Husserl was so impressed by Frege's objections that he stood the whole thing on its head and instead of psychoanalyzing mathematics tried to make philosophy into an exact science. By 1910, when he was teaching in Göttingen, he had worked out a "method" of carefully defining meaning and began to tackle "judgment." In painstaking studies, he narrowed the notion of thinking by eliminating sense experiences so as to open the way to an intuitive "givenness" of relations, essences and values. Something given is *contingent,* he would say; it is like this, a *fact,* but it could be otherwise. Facticity reveals the essence of something—the facticity of freedom is the fact that freedom is not able not to be free.

To distinguish between ordinary thinking and primary perception, Husserl developed a technique of "reductions" or "bracketing off" of judgments to purify a phenomenon of all factual ingredients and interpretations. The most important "reduction" was the phenomenological or "transcendental" one. Once we perform this reduction, he claimed, we discover the "transcendental ego" or "pure consciousness" and can begin to explore and describe a previously unsuspected realm of being—the essential character of awareness. All consciousness is consciousness *of* something, he said. In order to exist, awareness must be conscious of something other than itself. During the 1920s, when he became philosophy dean at Freiburg, Husserl developed some extreme views, maintaining, for example, that pure consciousness could remain even if the entire world were destroyed—an idea that science-fiction authors would toy with. Some phenomenologists thought this was a regrettable lapse into metaphysics and in the 1930s he backed off a bit to say pure consciousness was "correlative" to the world.

Sartre believed life must be grasped from within and saw in Husserlian phenomenology a powerful means of exploring the existence from within and, as a writer's tool, a way of describing this inner search of the imagination and emotions. He had come to phenomenlogy via Karl Jaspers, the Heidelberg phenomenologist who saw human existence as a clash between the individual's presence in the world and his desire for transcendence. What Sartre had liked in Lévinas' French presentation of Husserl was the rejection of rationalism as wholly sufficient to do justice to the immediacy of living. He felt phenomenologists had managed to thrust man back into the world, complete with his despair, suffering and revolt. He set about reading all Husserl and Heidegger—in German—while at the same time rewriting his novel about Antoine Roquentin in a more phenomenological perspective.

He found that Husserl hadn't gone far enough in "bracketing off" subjectivity from pure consciousness, that indeed Descartes' cogito—"I think, therefore I am" (*cogito ergo sum*)—which makes mind more certain than matter, should read, "I doubt, therefore I am," or even better, "I am aware that I doubt; therefore I am." Descartes, he claimed, confused spontaneous doubt, which is consciousness, with systematical doubt, which is an act. This led Sartre to establish the prereflective cogito as the primary consciousness. The very nature of consciousness is such that for it to be and to know itself are one and the same, he now wrote in "La Transcendance de l'ego," an essay that would only be published in 1936.[12] When I am aware of a chair, I am nonreflectively conscious of my awareness, but when I deliberately think of my awareness, this is a totally new act of consciousness.

He agreed with Husserl that consciousness is consciousness *of* something, but was increasingly intrigued by Heidegger's idea that the real question was the meaning of being. In *Sein und Zeit* (1927), Heidegger held that to discover this meaning no sophisticated theories about "substance" or "case" were necessary. What was needed was to investigate the tools people

[12] "La Transcendance de l'ego; esquisse d'une description phénoménologique," in *Recherches philosophiques*, Vol. 6, 1936–37, reedited in volume, *La Transcendance de l'ego, esquisse d'une description phénoménologique*, Paris: Librairie Vrin, 1965; *The Transcendence of the Ego; An Existentialist Theory of Consciousness*, New York: Noonday, 1957.

were concerned with, and their basic situation, aims and moods. When considered this way, Heidegger held that human existence is ultimately absurd. We are in a world we have neither made nor chosen. We alone, among all creatures in this world, have the ability to comprehend the past, to conceive of a future and to use our understanding to shape the present and influence destiny.

Sartre defended phenomenology against charges that it had wandered into idealism by saying that if the ego and the real world are both objects of consciousness, if neither has created the other, then this awareness guarantees a person's active participation in the world. Most important, he claimed that consciousness infinitely overflows the "I" that ordinarily serves to unify it, an idea that would later lead him to believe that we feel dread and anxiety when we realize that nothing in our past or discernible personality ensures our following any of our usual patterns of conduct in the future, indeed that nothing guarantees the validity of *any* of the values we choose. "Everything happens as if awareness constitutes the ego as a false image of itself," he wrote, "as if consciousness were hypnotized by this ego which it had established and become part of." This was a new way of expressing the idea of "bad faith" that Beaver and he had tried to pinpoint in semantic falsehoods, fake recollections and other sublimations that both they and other people used. Bad faith meant that awareness seeks refuge from the responsibilities of constant choice by pretending to be confined in an already established ego.

Sartre would always have a knack for translating complex metaphysical concepts into striking fiction and during the cold Berlin winter of 1933–34, when he wasn't busy with "Marie" or writing long letters to Beaver, he reworked his structures of consciousness into Antoine Roquentin's story. He had already decided that what happened to his hero was contingency— Antoine's life is *this* but it could be otherwise. He now gave his hero's progression toward illumination a precise framework. The collapse of the illusions that had held Antoine's life together could now become a demystifying tonic. Antoine could end up accepting that nothing justifies his existence, that if any justification is needed it is simply that that is the way it is. Sartre would rewrite his novel once more in 1936 and the draft he wrote in Berlin while reading Husserl would not survive. It was in this version, however, that he invented the Self-Taught as a caricature of traditional humanism, a grotesque homosexual who devotes his life to the systematic and alphabetical reading of all the books in the Bouville city library but ends up sinking into "bad faith" dishonesty.

* * *

Simone heard about "Marie" during the Christmas recess when Sartre came to Paris for ten days and by mid-February she was desperate enough to go to Berlin. It was the first time Sartre had felt the need to be with another woman. That he had needed to consummate the freedom was what hurt her. She invented a nervous breakdown to get away from her lycée and a doctor had readily prescribed two weeks' rest. It was very cold when she got off the train and Sartre had her walk from Kurfürstendamm to the Alexanderplatz while they talked. She knew that no such episode could destroy their relationship, but she needed his presence to be reassured.

Sartre didn't leave her for the next two weeks. He showed her kinky Berlin, bars for transvestites and beer halls that had standing room only from 11 A.M. on, and took her to the Café Romanisches, the intellectual hangout where the crowds of writers and artists were thinning out. They made a trip to nearby Hanover to see Leibniz's house and at the Institute he introduced her to the currency trafficking that both students and faculty were involved in. When Simone came face to face with Marie, the meeting proved almost anticlimactic and with some exaggeration she would write in *The Prime of Life* that there had been no feeling of jealousy on her part. "Yet this was the first time since we had known each other that Sartre had taken a serious interest in another woman and jealousy is far from being an emotion which is alien to me, or which I underrate. But this affair neither took me by surprise nor upset any notions I had formed about our joint lives, since right from the outset Sartre had warned me that he was liable to embark on such adventures. I had accepted the principle and now had no difficulty accepting the fact. To know the world and give it expression, this was the aim that governed Sartre's whole life, and I knew just how set he was on it." Francis Jeanson, her biographer and friend in the 1950s, would say she was less serene: "Yes, this woman has known jealousy; see for example the history of Sartre's relations with Camille, with Marie Girard, with Olga or with 'M.' " [13]

Olga came into their lives in a more insidious and lasting manner when Sartre returned to his post in Le Havre after the year in Berlin. She was Olga Kosakiewicz—Olga D. in Simone's autobiography—a former student of hers, the daughter of a reactionary White Russian father and an equally conservative French mother who lived forty miles from Rouen and let their daughter board at the same *hôtel-pension* as Colette Audry. A girl with a pale face and blond hair, the eighteen-year-old Olga was now a graduate student heavily involved in radical politics and the friend of a cluster of exiled Polish students who were either passionate Zionists or passionate

---

[13] Francis Jeanson, *Simone de Beauvoir, ou l'entreprise de vivre*, Paris: Seuil, 1966.

communists. When one day she asked Beaver what it really meant to be a Jew, Simone replied with absolute certainty, "Nothing at all. There are no such things as 'Jews,' only human beings." Long afterward Olga would tell her what an impression she had created by marching into her Polish friends' room and announcing, "My friends, none of you exist! My philosophy teacher has told me so." As Simone would admit, she and Sartre were sometimes deplorably prone to abstractions. Olga was making a half-hearted attempt at entering medical school and during the year Sartre was in Berlin, Simone had taken Olga to lunch once a week, both bemused and distracted by the young girl's vivacious personality, the stories of her Polish friends and her moody ups and downs. Olga had flunked the entrance exams and now spent all day and night walking, dancing, listening to music and having marathon discussions. The prosect of a second failure, with trouble from her parents sure to follow, made her absolutely miserable.

A new friend of Simone's whose irresistible clowning and classical records could make Olga forget her distress was Marc Zuorro, a lycée teacher with handsome Mediterranean features who wanted to be an opera singer but whose hairline was receding alarmingly fast. Marc was the kind of person it was hard to get mad at, although his practical jokes were of doubtful taste.

Sartre was hard at work at Le Havre and Simone spent most of her free time with him at his place in the old seaport, which both agreed was less depressing than Rouen. She liked the new version of Antoine's story but thought Sartre had overdone his adjectives and comparisons and he now intended to make a scrupulous revision of every page. In the meantime, however, Henri Delacroix, his philosophy teacher at the Sorbonne, wondered whether he would be interested in writing a book on his old thesis, The Imagination in Psychological Life. Professor Delacroix was now the editor of a New Philosophical series for a small publishing house. The idea interested Sartre and he abandoned Antoine Roquentin for nonfiction psychology, hoping to write the book quickly.

Suddenly, Nizan was in town, speaking to a communist rally and dressed in a carefully casual style. Everything about him spelled success. He had just spent a year in the Soviet Union and together with Malraux, Louis Aragon and the elder playwright Jean-Richard Bloch had made up the French delegation to the All-Soviet Writers' Congress, rubbing shoulders with Stalin and Maxim Gorky and now rhapsodizing over the Georgian wines, the "soft" sleeping cars and voluptuous hotels they had been treated to. With a casual tone, Nizan tried to suggest that this luxury reflected vast

general affluence in the Soviet Union. He said nothing of the Congress's
condemnation of Joyce, Proust and Dos Passos as "decadent" and "nihilis-
tic," but told them Yuri Olesha's expressionistic novel *Envy* was a fresh
approach to the conflict between the old and the new Russia, telling the
intertwined stories of a "new man" and his anachronistic brother with
equal sympathy and without attempting a "solution." "Sartre *is* Olesha,"
Paul insisted, gnawing his nails with some complacency. Sartre and Beaver
found Nizan most interesting when he talked about death. "Though he
never openly alluded to the fact, we knew how anguished he could be at
the thought of one day vanishing for all eternity; for days he would cruise
from one cheap bar to the next, drinking glass after glass of cheap red
wine to keep this terrifying prospect at bay," Simone would remember.
"He had asked himself whether the socialist creed might not somehow help
him and felt quite optimistic as to the prospect, but his lengthy question-
ing of young Russian communists had elicited a unanimous reply—in the
face of death, comradeship and solidarity were no help at all, and they were
all scared of death themselves." Nizan was publishing his third novel,
Le Cheval de Troie, in which Sartre appeared as Lange, a schoolteacher
and an anarchist who stalked through cobbled streets, his mind abandoned
in dark metaphysical speculation.

For Christmas, Sartre and Beaver did something new that she had "discovered." They went skiing in the Alps. Every morning and afternoon
they turned up at the same beginners slope, where a ten-year-old boy
showed them how to make turns. They loved the iridescent sun on the
slopes and every night trudged happily back to their *pension* to hot tea
and evenings of textbook reading. For the book commissioned by Professor Delacroix, Sartre felt he had to know about the nervous system.
They rang in the New Year in Montroc, high above the Chamonix Valley,
but 1935 was to be a year of crisis.

Sartre was thirty.

Thirty meant the end of youth. It meant taking stock and admitting
what he was—a provincial schoolteacher. It meant admitting that nothing
new would happen to him, it meant becoming aware of the vanity of
human endeavors. His books were being turned down and now the Felix
Alcan publisher decided to print only the first part of his essay on Imagination in Psychological Life. Beaver still had an absolute faith in his future,
but he had thrown himself so wholeheartedly into the business of being
young and living for today that he needed strong enchantments to keep
going. An experiment with drugs to probe deeper into consciousness be-

came one; Olga and a ménage à trois became another. Beaver didn't mind. What got her down and made her argue and plead and finally feel betrayed was the fact that he seemed to give in to his fears and delusions. He had no right to indulge such whims when they threatened their joint existence. To her, having a profession was a delight; to him it was something he took for granted.

Teaching, in which he saw his freedom finally founder, still meant liberation to her. For her his mere existence justified the world, but there was nothing she or anyone could do to perform the same service for him. "I could not have solved Sartre's actual difficulties for him," she would write. "I lacked both the experience and the skill that were needed to cure him of these temporary worries, but if I had shared his anxiety I most certainly would have been no help at all to him, so no doubt my anger was a healthy reaction."

The reading in the Alps about chronaxia—the minimum time a current must flow to excite nerve tissue—had been part of a phenomenological probe of intentional awareness and of the mind's capacity for conceiving nothing—a near impossibility if consciousness is consciousness *of* something. Sartre now took a marked interest in dreams, dream-induced imagery and anomalies of perception. Talking to Daniel Lagache, his teachers' college friend who had switched to medicine and specialized in psychiatry, he was told he should try mescaline, a new drug used in experimental psychology to produce hallucinations. If Sartre would come to Dr. Lagache's clinic at the Sainte-Anne Hospital in Paris and undergo a mescaline injection, he could observe the phenomenon in himself. The only side effect, Lagache warned, would be that Sartre would "behave rather oddly" for a few hours.

Simone spent the afternoon Sartre was at Sainte-Anne's with Madame Morel and Pierre Guille. When she phoned the hospital at the appointed hour, she heard Sartre tell her in a thick, blurred voice that her phone call had rescued him from a battle with several devilfish. When she got there, he told her everything had changed in the most horrifying manner, umbrellas had become vultures, shoes had turned into skeletons and faces had acquired monstrous characteristics, while behind him, just past the corner of his eye, swarmed crabs and polyps and grimacing Things. One of the interns, who had gone romping through flowery meadows when he had taken mescaline, was amazed at these reactions. In the train back to Le Havre, Sartre spoke listlessly and stared at a pair of crocodile-skin shoes Beaver was wearing, but the next day he was apparently himself again, talking about the experience with cheerful detachment.

A Sunday or two later, however, when Colette Audry came with Beaver to Le Havre, he was surly and distracted. The next time they were alone together, he explained that he had been in a state of deep depression and that his vision was distorted. He saw black spots, houses had leering faces, all eyes and jaws, and every clockface he looked at had the features of an owl. He knew perfectly well that such objects were in fact houses and clocks and no one could say that he believed they had eyes and gaping jaws, but a time might well come when he *would* believe it. One day he might really believe that a lobster was trotting along behind him. Another afternoon, when they were walking along railway sidings near Rouen, he suddenly said, "I know what's wrong with me. I'm on the edge of a chronic hallucinatory psychosis." For the Easter recess, they went to northern Italy and he seemed in the best of moods, but when they attended the Paris opening of an exhibition of Fernando Gerassi's paintings, he sat huddled in a corner, expressionless. Madame Morel thought he was overworked and sent him to see a doctor friend of hers who refused to certify that he needed legal rest. Prescribing an atropine stimulant, the doctor said the only things Sartre didn't need were idle moments and solitude. So he went on teaching and writing and, for distraction, began to go out with Bost and Albert Palle, two of his former students. Their presence, he said, protected him from crabs and assorted monsters. When Simone was busy at her school, Olga kept him company.

In July, Sartre's mother began to worry and he let himself be talked into joining her and his stepfather on a cruise of the fjords of Norway. For the shipboard fancy-dress ball, he borrowed a black velvet dress from his mother and a blond wig with pigtails and, he later told Simone, had an American lesbian follow him all night. Dressing in drag became his specialty when they all entertained each other in Olga's room in Rouen and Marc sang, Bost struck matches with his toes and a girl named Gégé belly danced.

Determined to have Sartre snap out of it, Beaver summoned him to join her on an active vacation in southern France. Her therapy was the Cevennes mountains. Up at dawn and packing hard-boiled eggs and country sausage for lunch, they followed the gorges of the Tarn River, climbed Mount Aigoual and walked for miles over limestone plateaus. They got lost among the "false keeps" at Montpellier-le-Vieux and to get back down made a hair-raising descent, clambering from rock to rock. Pierre Guille joined them with a girl friend for more hiking, paddling on the Tarn and riverbank trout and crayfish barbecuing. One evening when they drove into a village near Albi in a packed bus in pouring rain, Sartre suddenly declared he was tired of being crazy and returned to his normal self. Much later, they learned the mescaline trip could not possibly have provoked the depression. Doctors they spoke to felt the drug session had furnished him with certain hallucinatory patterns and that the actual cause was overwork and exhaustion. Sartre himself would say, "The deep cause of my neurotic problems, I think, was the difficulty I had accepting that I was growing up. It was a kind of identity crisis."

That year, Sartre's grandfather died. The Schweitzers' longevity was indeed proverbial. He lived to be ninety-two. His nephew Albert, who would receive the Nobel Peace Prize in 1952, would live to be ninety.

Simone's taking Olga under her wing began when they returned to work. Olga had skipped the medical-school entrance exams altogether and had spent a sleepless week walking around Rouen and dancing at the Royal every night before returning to her parents, haggard and carrying a stray epileptic cat. Her parents wanted to send her to a boarding school and in a state of defiant defeatism she turned to Simone. Nine years younger than her former philosophy teacher, Olga possessed an impetuous, whole-hogging streak that Simone found disarming. Olga was "real," never faked her emotions and surrendered herself with enthusiasm to her pleasures. She would go on dancing until she passed out from sheer exhaustion and she had an indiscriminate appetite for people. In Simone, Olga recognized her own hatreds and rejections overcome, a grownup woman who traveled and understood people, someone who had attractive friends and had blazed her own trail.

With Sartre's encouragement, Simone wrote to Olga's parents and when she was invited to visit them, actually persuaded them to let her take charge of their eldest daughter. If Olga had shown little appetite for the natural sciences, she had been good in philosophy and it was agreed she would study hard for a diploma with special coaching from Simone and Sartre. Simone settled her ward into a room at her own *hôtel-pension* in Rouen and Olga seemed to enjoy her new studies. Abstract speculation, however, held little attraction for her and fear of failure, indolence and attendant guilt made her defeatist again and she stopped trying. Simone swallowed her disappointment but as a dropout Olga began to bloom. As a student she had been sulky; now she lived enthusiastically from day to day, dragging Beaver and Sartre to cafés to hear an all-female orchestra or a gypsy violinist or to play poker. For Olga the present was enough and words of definition, limitation or anticipation seemed wholly irrelevant.

Simone didn't mind Sartre's growing interest in Olga; she much preferred to see him angle for Olga's emotional favors than slump into another depression, especially since he apparently had no intention of giving any kind of physical embodiment to the relationship. Their infatuation with this "mere gamine" amused some of their friends and annoyed others and, Simone would write, could only be explained in terms of the loathing that the adult world aroused in them. "Rather than compromising with that, Sartre had plunged into neurosis, and I frequently told myself, weeping, that growing older meant falling into decay. Day by day I found myself reminded of my own relative maturity when compared to Olga. The fact that we too pursued the cult of youth, with all its rebellious upheavals and intransigent emphasis on freedom, made no difference at all. This was why we loaded her with values and symbols. She became Rimbaud, Antigone, every *enfant terrible* that ever lived, a dark angel judging us from her diamond-bright heaven. She did nothing to provoke such a metamorphosis herself; on the contrary, it irritated her, and she hated the fantastic character who had usurped her place, but she was powerless to prevent herself being absorbed. We admired the way in which she lived unreservedly for the moment. But our own first consideration was to build a future for her and for us. From now on we would be a trio rather than a couple. We believed human relationships are a matter of constant fresh discovery and that no particular kind is a priori either especially privileged or impossible—this one seemed to have come about by itself." [14] When Simone realized Sartre had become Olga's lover, she found it impossible to take his opinions and tastes casually anymore since they outlined a system of values that contradicted her own. As she would tell Francis Jeanson, "There is something absolutely valid and true in jealousy. If A lives something with B and B begins to live the same thing with Z, A will obviously feel excluded; something common has been broken, something irreplaceable that he has lived with B." [15] The "trio" would give Simone the theme for her first novel anyone would accept for publication, *She Came to Stay*. For Sartre, it would be Olga's husband who would suggest what was to become his most famous play, *Huis clos* (*No Exit*).

Simone had continued to write—out of loyalty to her past and because Sartre pushed her. She had behind her two long novels she now found to have little more than promising opening chapters. They had discovered William Faulkner with the French translations of *As I Lay Dying* and *Sanctuary* and had marveled at the infinite symbolic overlay the author managed to give to perfectly realistic novels. Simone felt she should discipline herself to write brief stories where fantasy and shoddy romanticism

[14] Beauvoir, *The Prime of Life.*
[15] Francis Jeanson, *op. cit.*

would be banned, where she wouldn't try out plots she couldn't believe in, or unfamiliar backgrounds, but where she would restrict herself to people and things she knew. As a title she borrowed, somewhat ironically, *Primauté du spirituel* (*Divine Ascendency*) by Jacques Maritain, the Christian philosopher who fought Bergsonism with neo-Thomist theology. In the first story she retraced the slow atrophy of a young girl, timidly reaching out but overwhelmed by the mysticism and intrigues of her parochial school, actually the story of a Cours Désir classmate. The second narrative was a study in "bad faith," the account of a fellow teacher in Rouen who made herself into an emancipated woman of such shimmering possibilities that two of her bedazzled students got into trouble imitating her. Written in Faulknerian interior monologue, the tale ended with the teacher renouncing her false identity for the benefit of the girls in trouble. The third story was yet another attempt at reviving Zaza, whose untimely death as a victim of bourgeois rectitude Simone could not forget. Called Anne Vignon this time, the character was not entirely to her author's liking however. The last story was a satirical retelling of her own teenage crisis and emancipation and ended with the heroine making up her mind to look the world straight in the eye. It was written in the first person and, thought Simone, was the best thing she had ever done.

Sartre was also hard at work and 1936 saw the publication of his first book. The Felix Alcan publishers chose to call his essay *L'Imagination*. The 162-page volume was not the book Sartre had wanted and over the next four years he would rework the parts Alcan had rejected and, in 1940, have Gallimard bring out *L'Imaginaire, psychologie phénoménologique,* to which *L'Imagination* would eventually stand as an introduction of only cursory importance.

Fiction was really what kept him busy during this year when Hitler reoccupied the Rhineland, France elected a leftist Popular Front and Spain plunged into civil war. First came Antoine Roquentin. The third version, written during the early spring, took on an eerie dimension as Sartre wrote in his mescaline trip, his depression and a visit he and Simone had made to a madhouse. Sartre now called the novel *Melancholia*—after Dürer's brooding and enigmatic 1514 engraving.

Melancholia was submitted to Gallimard's reading committee by Nizan, and Sartre plunged into a short story. He called it *Erostrate* (*Herostratos*), after the youth of Greek mythology who, to gain immortality, set fire to Artemis' temple in Ephesus.

Gallimard's answer was a turndown.

For the 1936–37 school year, Sartre was offered a job teaching a preparatory class at teachers' college in Lyons, but when Simone was promoted to
the Lycée Molière in Paris, he preferred to take a post in Laon, the old
Roman town midway between Paris and the Belgian border. By train it
was about the same distance from Paris as Rouen.

Without Olga, they spent their summer vacation in Italy. After ten days
in Rome they went to Naples and were shocked by naked, scabby infants
and slums with beatific Virgin Mary statues at every street corner. While
Beaver hiked to Amalfi and Sorrento, Sartre had fun on his own. A young
man he met in a bar invited him to see *tableaux vivants* reenactments of
the erotic frescoes in the Pompeii ruins and for a modest sum, Sartre sat
alone in a mirrored salon watching two women, one with an ivory phallus
in her hand, mime erotic postures. He declined the madam's offer to retire
with either of the two performers, but told Simone that what had delighted
him was the sense of utter alienation he had felt sitting there in the garish
room surrounded by his own mirrored reflections while the two women
performed an act that to look at was at the same time comical and banal.
He wrote a short story about it, *Dépaysement,* rewrote part of it as *Nour-
ritures,* where he tried to create a *Nausea*-like feel for obscene flesh.

They got back to Paris as Léon Blum's leftist coalition backed off sending
arms to help its sister Popular Front in Madrid and instead called on
Britain, Germany, Italy and the Soviet Union to join France in a nonintervention pact. The Spanish Civil War was instantly a burning topic. Like
most left-leaning Europeans, Sartre and Beaver saw the great issue of
democracy vs. fascism at stake in the elected Spanish government's attempt
to subdue an armed coup. "Blum's neutrality was all the more disgusting
in that Hitler and Mussolini were openly supplying the rebels with both
men and material," Simone would write. "The first bomb dropped on
Madrid, on August 28, was released by a German plane. We had great
admiration for Malraux and his squadron, who had volunteered for service
with the Republic, but how could they possibly face up to the Nazi air
force single-handed?" When Francisco Franco's rebel troops closed in on
Madrid, Fernando Gerassi said he could no longer bear to stay in Paris
and resolved to go off to fight.

Sartre and Beaver returned to their classrooms. Finally a teacher in Paris,
Simone moved into a hotel in the Rue de la Gaîté, a busy shopping and
entertainment street two blocks up from Boulevard Montparnasse. She
vaguely toyed with the idea of getting an apartment but setting up house
terrified her. Besides, Sartre was as determined as ever to keep clear of
anything that might weigh him down and didn't want to own so much as

a bed or a table. Poupette had given up her secretarial job, had a first exhibition of her paintings behind her and was living on Montparnasse with Francis Gruber, who together with Bernard Lorjou and André Marchand were expressionist painters adopting Picasso's cruel anger of *Guernica.* Fernando and Stépha lived nearby with their now four-year-old son. Marc Zuorro was teaching at the Lycée Louis-le-Grand and lived in a hotel around the corner from the Dôme. Bost was at the Sorbonne teachers' college, living in a room in the apartment of his playwright brother on Place St.-Germain-des-Prés. Charles Dullin and Camille—she had taken the stage name Jollivet—lived farther away, on Montmartre, currently rehearsing Shakespeare's *Julius Caesar,* adapted by Camille and with Dullin playing Cassius.

It was unthinkable to leave Olga behind in Rouen. Her parents were opposed to her leaving Normandy so she went to Paris without their permission. She got a room at Simone's hotel and for a while had a job serving tea in a combined cafeteria, bookshop and record store.

Twice a week Simone picked up Sartre at the Gare du Nord when he got off the train from Laon, where his students, he said, "are the sons of hefty farmers who know that a penny is a penny and a bull is a bull." Their new hangout was the Dôme, where, thanks to Poupette and Gruber, they began to be able to put names on some of the faces. There was Ilya Ehrenburg, the stocky, bushy-haired one-man outpost for Soviet arts and politics, *Izvestia* correspondent and acquaintance of Stalin. There were the expatriate Russian painters, Ossip Zadkine and Moise Kisling, and a handsome Swiss with searching eyes and a wiry mop of hair, Alberto Giacometti. As sidewalk café spectators, Sartre, Beaver and Olga found the women more interesting than the men, women artists and artists' women, models, minor actresses, pretty girls, all of them, more or less, kept by somebody. After a while the word got around that Sartre and Beaver were civil servants and comparatively well off. "So very often a drunk or a hard-up type or a professional cadger came up and begged a five-franc piece from us, feeling obliged, in return, to spin some long, lying yarn," Simone would remember. "Chronic fantasy flourished in this setting. All these exiles, failures, daydreamers and left-behinds made a change from our previous provincial monotony."

They had always lived in bistros, eaten in cheap restaurants and Simone did most of her writing in cafés. Setting down her thoughts in notebooks in her fast schoolteacher's longhand, she liked to order her *café-crème* and at a marble-top *guéridon* with a Suze ashtray to spend the next hours writing in the midst of people, smoke and noise. Sartre and Olga often wandered through the streets until dawn when Olga was liable to turn sulky and to irritate him. Sometimes she wandered alone for hours in a state of chronic boredom, sometimes she drank and lapsed into gloomy fantasies. Besides Sartre and Beaver, Olga knew only Marc and Bost, who had become inseparable friends, going to concerts and movies together. Marc's singing career was not getting anywhere and his defeats, plus Bost's rejections of his homosexual advances, brought the ménage à trois to an end. Marc had given the key to his room to Bost so he could go and listen to his records whenever he wanted. One evening when Marc came home and heard faint music and voices coming from his room, he peeked through the keyhole and saw Olga and Bost locked in an embrace. Wild with jealousy, he stalked the cafés all night until he found Beaver working at a table at the Dôme and with tears in his eyes told everything, including his repressed love for Bost.

Suddenly the kisses of the two nineteen-year-olds made everyone snap out of it. Even Beaver had despaired of finding a solution to the triangular labyrinth. Sartre, she would write, "showed himself a good loser." To console Marc, Sartre and Beaver took him skiing with them on their Christmas holiday. He was scared stiff of the gentlest hill and had them give in to letting him share their room. In the bleak three-bedded chalet room in Chamonix, he lay crying half the night, describing aloud Bost's youth and unconscious cruelty.

Back in town, they went to the rehearsals of *Julius Caesar*. Dullin was an old friend of Gaston Gallimard. Together with cofounders Gide and Jean Schlumberger, Gallimard had been a supporter of the founding of the Vieux Columbier Theater where Dullin had staged early Paul Claudel plays that, with some trepidation, the new publishing house had decided to publish. Dullin now wrote a letter to his old friend and asked him to personally read the rejected *Melancholia* manuscript, an initiative that coincided with Pierre Bost dropping in on Gaston Gallimard to put in a supplementary good word.

Little Bost—as they called Jacques-Laurent to distinguish him from his playwright (and soon to be famous screenwriter) brother—wanted to go and fight for Republican Spain and asked Sartre to see if Nizan and his communist contacts could get him across the now closed border. The request became a phenomenological question for Sartre. In theory, individual freedom of choice should always be respected, but if something happened to Little Bost he, Sartre, would feel directly responsible. When he finally did mention it to Nizan in the most casual manner, Nizan put Bost in touch with Malraux, who asked the teachers' college student if he could handle a machine gun. What the Republic needed, said Malraux, was trained men, not raw recruits. Little Bost stayed home.

In early 1937, Beaver came down with a pulmonary congestion that caused one collapsed lung and had her in and out of consciousness in an intensive care unit for forty-eight hours. Little by little she came around. Her mother visited her every morning, Sartre every afternoon when he wasn't in Laon, and Poupette, Olga, Madame Morel and Little Bost took time out to sit with her. When she left the hospital at Easter, her doctor prescribed a three-week rest in the sun and she chose to go to Provence.

Sartre wrote her daily and one day could report that he had been asked to make an appointment with Paulhan. On the appointed day, the Gallimard editor-in-chief told him it had all been a misunderstanding. When he had turned down *Melancholia,* he had meant that the manuscript was not suitable for serialization in the *Nouvelle revue française*—better known by its acronym *NRF*. "But it's an admirable piece of work," added Paulhan. "Your book will certainly be accepted." [16]

It was not the end of the tribulations of Antoine Roquentin. Editor Parain claimed the legal department demanded cuts in Sartre's description of Bouville's honest citizens, in Roquentin's encounter with Anny and in a scene with two maids at his hotel. When Parain was through with the manuscript, Roquentin no longer had "a hard-on," his "little gray balls" had become "little gum balls" and the scene with the maids had disappeared altogether, but Sartre's aggressive and mocking tone had been improved. In the meantime, Paulhan bought two of Sartre's short stories and created a minor sensation publishing *Le Mur* (*Three Who Died*) in the July issue of *NRF*. *Le Mur* was an "absurdist" story of three men facing the firing squad in the Spanish Civil War. It was inspired by Sartre's moral dilemma of whether to help Little Bost go to war. In scatological language, *Le Mur* painted vivid images of mental alienation, sexual aberration and "bad faith." When Gide read it, he dropped a note to Paulhan calling it "a masterpiece." Wrote the elder statesman of French letters: "I haven't been so pleased in a long time over anything I have read. Tell me who is this new Jean-Paul? It seems one can expect a lot from him."

After a summer in Greece where Sartre and Beaver took Little Bost along, Sartre was finally appointed to a Paris lycée. "No more train journeys, no more hanging around on station platforms," Simone would write in *Prime of Life*. "We moved into a hotel that Sartre had discovered while

[16] Beauvoir, *The Prime of Life.*

I was convalescing in Provence. I had a divan and bookshelves and a really comfortable working desk. I often worked at home now. Sartre lived one floor above me; thus we had all the advantages of a shared life without any of its inconveniences." [17] The "hôtel meublé" was in the short Rue Cels behind the Montparnasse cemetery, three blocks from the Dôme.

While Poupette typed up Simone's *Primauté du spirituel* so Sartre could give it to Parain with his warmest recommendations, Paulhan published *La Chambre,* dealing with the locking up of a girl in a concealed attic, a theme Sartre would return to again.[18] In October, Gaston Gallimard decided Sartre's novel would be called *La Nausée* and be published in the spring. Success emboldened Sartre, not only for himself but for Beaver. One evening when they were sitting at the Dôme discussing her writing, he told her she was too timid. "Look," he suddenly said with vehemence, "why don't you put *yourself* into your writing? You're more interesting than all these Renées and Lisas." Although the idea of putting her raw, undigested self into a book at first scared her, she began a story of a girl she named Françoise after her mother, but whose emotional makeup was her own. Writing in a style she borrowed from Dos Passos, she tried to suggest the sort of deceptive trickery young girls so readily adopt to acquire status and gave Françoise a friend, Elisabeth, who was not Zaza but one of Simone's fifteen-year-old students, a provocatively self-confident, pretty girl Françoise could only find overwhelming.

Sartre was writing philosophy, a four-hundred-page treatise on phenomenological psychology which he called *La Psyché,* but was obliged to put it aside for the mundane pleasures of giving interviews for the March 1938 publication of his novel and, when *La Nausée* became a handsome success, for an anthology of short stories that Paulhan pressed him to finish. Sartre's first-ever interview was with Claudine Chonez, a poet-journalist who in her verse also tried to express worlds beyond reality. He told her that in the next novel, Roquentin would be mobilized and, in war, make the voluptuous discovery of free choice, only to return home ready to commit a totally gratuitous act. "Naturally he rapes a woman and makes someone else commit a crime. A gratuitous act is always directed against the betters of society, usually carried out in areas which society considers reprehensible. And yet, isn't it also a profound moral reconstruction of the individual, a true resurrection, progressing from nausea to ardor, from suicide to a taste of life, a unique, irreversibly free life?" [19] There was

---

[17] *Ibid.*
[18] In *Mesure,* January 15, 1938; *Mesure* was a Gallimard quarterly.
[19] In *Marianne,* December 7, 1938.

never to be a "Son of Nausea" and Sartre scholars would eventually wonder whether he was pulling his interviewer's leg or expressing the thematic core of his big wartime novel, *Les Chemins de la liberté* (*Roads to Freedom*).

The gratuitous act was something that fascinated both Simone and Sartre. Always avid readers of newspaper accounts of sensational crimes, of murder mysteries and detective novels, they had been impressed by the 1934 trial of a young man who had murdered a taxi driver and in court explained he had had no money to pay his fare. In their minds, "l'acte gratuit" was closely connected with the notion of responsibility for justifying someone else's existence. Simone tried to come to grips with it in her new piece of fiction and Sartre was elaborating on the phenomenological idea that most human beings try to conceal their freedom from themselves by a variety of deceits, the most typical being the belief in some form of psychological determinism.

They went skiing at Mégève, reading Malraux's *L'Espoir* in the train back to Paris "with an excitement that far outstripped any purely literary emotion." The winter had brought a lull in the Spanish war and it was not impossible that the Republic might stave off the fascist onslaught. Franco was quarreling with Germany, while the hard-pressed Republicans' political moderation allowed a new rapprochement with the wobbly French government which had followed the collapse of Léon Blum's Front Populaire. There were even reports of British initiatives for the withdrawal of both Italian fascist battalions and of the International Brigades.

In January they attended the rehearsals of Aristophanes' *Plutus,* very freely adapted by Camille, with Dullin playing the lead and Darius Milhaud composing a special score. In March, *La Nausée* came out. With the exception of Robert Brasillach in *L'Action française,* the reviews were excellent. Most critics underlined the conviction with which Roquentin's visionary periphery was depicted. In *Ce Soir,* the Communist Party's new evening paper, Nizan wrote that if it wasn't for the fact that Sartre was not interested in moral dilemmas, he could be called France's Kafka. The most penetrating critique appeared in the colonies, in *Alger républicain,* the sixteen-page newssheet published in Algiers. It was signed by a twenty-five-year-old journalist who had left the Communist Party because he didn't like its attitude toward Arabs—Albert Camus. Gallimard had printed 4,100 copies of *La Nausée* and it sold so well that a 3,300-copy second printing was ordered.

La Nausée was a book of its time and an advance notice of the kind of sentiment the European novel would express during and after World War II. Joyce, Jean Cocteau and the surrealists had questioned the apparent order of things with the hunch that another, more mysterious and subtler, order existed. The war would simplify the question and make novelists wonder whether, beyond the crude need to lie, to conform and to get along, *any* order existed, thereby making literature serve not so much as a means of revealing the secrets of life as a sounding board for soul searching and the clearing away of illusions. Roquentin was a man of his time, stripping away reassuring illusions in order to discover the void of the self deprived of disguises. On his own he *is* nothing. Sartre shared with Evelyn Waugh a certain nihilism and an aversion to a life decorated with irony and pride. With Georges Bernanos, whose Catholic faith he didn't have, Sartre shared a scorn for the lying to oneself and with Malraux, he agreed that if man *is* nothing he can only justify himself by *doing,* but whereas Malraux felt action would save man from despair, Sartre believed man would have to be saved from his own uselessness. Kafka had introduced the notion of life being essentially absurd and Céline, Malraux and Bernanos had already sketched man as lonely and forsaken. Sartre—and very soon Camus—made a break with metaphysical hope and religious or historical transcendence.

It was a deliciously busy spring. Besides the full-time teaching at Lycée Pasteur and rewriting and editing the short stories for publication, Sartre was becoming a literary critic, reviewing Faulkner's *Sartoris* and, with great enthusiasm, Dos Passos' *1919*. But Gallimard turned down *Primauté du spirituel*. And so did Grasset. As the Easter recess was approaching and they had decided to go to Algeria, Simone took the rejection "in a fairly cheerful mood."

They didn't get to Algeria. Just before the holidays, Simone had a relapse that kept her in bed several days. Sun and the great springtime outdoors would do her good, however, and they decided they still had time for a tour of the Basque country. The actual border was closed but they found a charming hotel in Itxassou three miles from Spain. Their room had a tree as an annex, with a ropewalk leading to it. A platform had been built in the tree high among the branches. While Beaver roamed the neighboring hills, Sartre sat working in the tree house.

CHAPTER

CHRISTMAS 1940

THE PLAY was called *Bariona*. Ostensibly, it was a "mystery play" about the birth of Christ although everybody in the Stalag soon got the message. There was the Roman overlord Lelius using the census of all Judea to press for higher taxes. There was the collaborator Levy Publicus and the Judean chieftain Bariona who has his villagers renounce sex so as to deprive the occupiers of a new generation of slave labor. And there were the Three Kings, with the author himself in blackface playing Balthazar, stopping Bariona from dashing to Bethlehem to murder the newborn King, and, in the last act, transforming him into a resistance fighter so as to let Joseph, Mary and the Child slip through Herod's dragnet. The play had some sharp lines—Bariona saying the country had been agonizing since the Roman occupation—but the kommandant thought the Romans stood for the British occupying various French overseas territories and it was standing-room only for the Christmas Eve show. To accommodate everybody in the camp, repeat performances were staged December 25 and 26.

The camp was Stammlager XII D—Stalag in the abbreviated German fashion—at Trier, sixty miles southwest of Koblenz, and *Bariona*[1] was the result of theological discussions with fellow prisoners-of-war, including a fiery Father Page who believed that any political system that reduced

---

[1] Published in limited private edition, Paris: Atelier-Copies, 1962; reprinted in Michel Contat-Michel Rybalka, *Les Ecrits de Sartre, op. cit.*

men to slaves was an insult to divine will and that God was so much in favor of freedom that He preferred to see men free rather than flawless. Sartre had spent long monotonous days with Father Page and two Jesuit chaplains. He had told them about Heidegger and had engaged in eschatological discussions on predestination and free will. Father Page believed in an unremitting humanity of Jesus Christ and maintained that the Virgin Mother had not given birth miraculously, but that the Saviour had been born in the filth of a stable and in the pains of all childbirths. Sartre agreed with Father Page. Christianity, he felt, had no meaning if it didn't load all man's miseries on Christ's shoulders. "By my writing a mystery play certain people seem to have thought I was going through some sort of spiritual crisis," Sartre would say more than twenty-five years later. "That wasn't the case. What united me with the POW chaplains was a common hate of Nazism. The Nativity seemed to me to be a subject that could unite both Christian and atheist POWS and it was understood that I could write what I wanted." [2]

Simone spent a joyless Christmas in her cold room in an occupied Paris settling into eerie helplessness. The last letter she had received from Sartre had been one of the long "unofficial" ones, smuggled out by a work party and simply mailed from a Trier streetcorner mailbox. Half of Europe was under Hitlerian rule and the mails functioned with impeccable punctuality when it came to sending letters from the Reich to occupied territories. Besides telling her that he was busy rehearsing a play he had written for Christmas, he had intimated that he would be home soon. The date of his return apparently depended on nothing but his own say-so. Was he thinking of escaping? She imagined bloodhounds in pursuit and sentries firing, but the letter mentioned a forthcoming repatriation of various civilians. He was not a civilian of course, but maybe he had finagled some clever assignment or something.

Sartre had been a POW for almost six months. Without ever firing a shot, he had been taken prisoner on his thirty-fifth birthday, June 21, 1940, together with hundreds of thousands of others as France's disintegrating armies retreated and Marshal Henri Philippe Pétain's government signed Hitler's armistice terms. Not all had been as lucky. Nizan had died on the front on May 23 when General Erich von Manstein's armor had outflanked the Maginot Line and the French government had scrambled out of Paris for Bordeaux.

Nobody could have imagined any of this just two years ago.

[2] "Le théâtre de A jusqu'à Z: Jean-Paul Sartre," *L'Avant-Scène Théâtre*, No. 402–403, May 1 and 15, 1968.

Sartre and Beaver had returned from their Basque Easter vacation paying little attention to the "Czech crisis" and the war jitters that flared up again. With most of their friends, they had believed it all depended on Russia. The question had not only been whether the French government would honor its commitment to Czechoslovakia but whether the Soviet Union would. When Foreign Minister Georges Bonnet had put that question to Soviet Foreign Commissar Maxim Litvinov, he had been told Russia would if France would. Then in June, British Prime Minister Neville Chamberlain had made off-the-record remarks to the effect that neither Britain nor France nor probably Russia, would come to the aid of Czechoslovakia and *The London Times* had suggested the Prague government should grant self-determination to the Sudeten Germans.

Sartre and Beaver spent the summer of 1938 in Morocco. Sailing from Marseilles to Casablanca in a second-class luxury liner, they crisscrossed the French protectorate from Meknes to Marrakesh and went as far as Ouarzazate on the edge of the Sahara, where the hotel owner went around coughing up his lungs and gave them a graphic description of a recent typhus epidemic. Every day at noon the Ouarzazate hotelkeeper made a free distribution of boiled rice to local urchins with appalling diseases and hideous deformities. Squatting in the hotel courtyard around several huge bowls and dipping into the rice with bare hands, the kids kept time so that no one could take unfair advantage.

During the September days when Hitler was on the brink of invading Czechoslovakia and World War II was only avoided when Premier Edouard Daladier and Chamberlain met the Führer in Munich, Sartre was alone in Paris writing the review of Nizan's new novel, *La Conspiration*. Like everyone else, Sartre felt France had no stomach for another bloodletting like the Great War, but he also agreed it was impossible to go on appeasing Hitler. "I was pro-Munich and anti-Munich with equal sincerity," he would remember. "I was completely torn apart."

Together with Olga, Simone was spending the last week before school hiking the hills above Nice. If Marc Zuorro was still sulking, Olga had remained a friend. Through the auspices of Sartre and Beaver, she and her kid sister, Wanda, had joined Dullin's acting classes at the Atelier. Olga had spent part of the summer with Little Bost who was now doing his military service. At the Gap post office on September 25, Simone found a general-delivery telegram from Sartre awaiting her. The political situation was worsening, he said. On the train back to Paris she blamed herself for her blind optimism. When she reached the capital, newspaper headlines at the Gare de Lyon terminal announced the call-up of a million men.

A week later, things seemed to calm down again. Hitler was only threatening.

Both Beaver and Sartre returned to what she would call their "obsessional preoccupation" with their own affairs. She was teaching only sixteen hours a week now and began a new novel. So did Sartre.

Simone's story was their own augmented by murder; the story of an intellectual couple for whom it has always been unthinkable that they should ever stop loving each other. And yet, talented, unconventional and restless, Françoise and Pierre constantly feel the need for new people. It is because of this that a young, beautiful girl comes between them. With various important transpositions, Pierre was Sartre and Françoise herself. Pierre is an innovative stage director and Françoise his alter ego and theatrical jack-of-all-trades, den-mother for insecure actors, late-night typist of new lines of dialogue, critic and essential support to Pierre's talent. She allows him a central and sovereign position in her life and pays the price—losing her definition of herself. The young girl is Xavière, full of irresponsibility, esctasy and pouting guile. One day when all three are together, Françoise feels herself "exiled" from them, and tries to draw on her own resources for self-support. In vain, for she is without features and individuality. Someone else is stealing the world from her, invading her personality and disfiguring her inner self. To shatter the spell, Françoise kills Xavière.

Simone sent the first one hundred pages dealing with Françoise's childhood to Brice Parain. The editor felt these pages didn't measure up to *Primauté du spirituel,* which he had turned down. Sartre agreed with him and Beaver decided to throw out her heroine's past, including her meeting with Pierre and the eight years they had spent together. Instead she began the novel on the eve of the premiere of Pierre's new production of *Julius Caesar.* Sartre suggested that to emphasize the importance Françoise attaches to the happiness she and Pierre have built together she should give up something for his sake in the first chapter. That allowed Simone to introduce an actor whose youth and charm might tempt Françoise. Later, when Xavière has fallen for the actor, betrayal can be expunged with murder—Françoise surreptitiously turning on the gas range in Xavière's room during a final confrontation. Simone wanted an ending in accordance with Sartre's and her belief of free, lucid choice. Xavière has taken sleeping pills to calm herself and bolts her door, making Françoise realize that everybody will think Xavière's death is an accident or a suicide. Françoise tells herself she might one day tell Pierre, but even he will only know what she did from the outside. Her act belongs totally to her. By turning on the gas and—once outside in the corridor by failing to turn off the gas main—Françoise has made a deliberate and open-eyed choice that seems to mean she will again conquer her own self.

Sartre was also writing about a clear-eyed individual. His hero was an ineffective intellectual, Mathieu, and the time was now, September 1938. Mathieu will discover events bigger than himself and realize that war *can* happen. His immediate predicament, however, is to find money for an illegal abortion for Marcelle. Abortion was something Beaver and Sartre had experienced although it would be decades before she, along with a hundred other prominent Frenchwomen, would say so publicly in a feminist campaign to change the country's archaic abortion laws.

In the meantime, *Le Mur,* dedicated to Olga Kosakiewicz, came out in January 1939. *Wall: Intimacy,* as it would be titled in English, contained five short stories about failure—tragic or comical failure, all sympathetic but gloomy accounts of the various mechanisms by which people remain trapped in boredom, abstractions and delusions.[3] Besides the title story about Pablo facing the firing squad, the volume included *La Chambre, Herostratos* and two new stories—*Intimacy,* an account of a woman's hatred of her own body—and *L'Enfance d'un chef,* the reflection on a man's escape into contemplation. "All these escapes are stopped by a wall," Sartre wrote in a publicity release for the book. "To run away from life is still to be alive."

When he wasn't working on the story of Mathieu, which he now called *Le Chemin de la liberté (Road to Freedom),* he became a critic and in the February issue of the *NRF* wrote an essay on fiction that provoked quite a stir. Ostensibly a review of François Mauriac's 1935 novel *La Fin de la nuit,* Sartre's piece in effect declared that Mauriac was not a writer, saying a character's point of view in a novel must exclude any knowledge or notion outside that point of view and that all narrative technique added up to metaphysics.[4] In another magazine, he reviewed the translation of Vladimir Nabokov's doppelgänger crime novel *Despair*[5] and in yet another review wrote a phenomenological text about the human face.[6]

During the spring, Beaver and Sartre began to forsake Montparnasse and the Dôme for the more staid Saint-Germain-des-Prés quarter and the Café Flore, the hangout for film and theater people and a crowd not

---

3 *Le Mur,* Paris: Gallimard, 1939; *Wall: Intimacy,* New York: New Directions, 1969.
4 "François Mauriac et la liberté," in *NRF,* February 1939.
5 "La Chronique de J-P Sartre," in *Europe,* June 15, 1939.
6 "Visages," in *Verve,* Vol. 2, July–October 1939.

wholly bohemian nor wholly bourgeois, dropouts spending their days venting their blues with blasé aphorisms and girls, as Simone would say, "with sad mouths and shifty, restless eyes." The Flore had its own mores and its own folklore and Jacques Prévert, the renegade surrealist poet and screenwriter, was the god and oracle of the place. Everybody worshiped the poetry and the movies he wrote and did their best to copy his language and attitude. Simone and Sartre also liked his dreamy, somewhat inconsequential anarchism and his cheerful onslaught on the "official," the pompous and the dehumanized. They were especially impressed because he had written the screenplay of their favorite movie, *Quai des brumes*. Prévert was now doing another script for Marcel Carné.

It was Olga who took Simone to the Flore the first time. As an understudy, Olga had been noticed by Dullin and was now a dedicated drama student at the Atelier, attending all possible classes and studying mime under Jean-Louis Barrault. Together with Louis Jouvet, Dullin was starring in Maurice Tourneur's filmization of *Volpone*. Whenever Dullin saw Simone he talked warmly of Olga's talent. Her first acting was in Barrault's stage production of Knut Hamsun's *Sult* (*Hunger*).

Events bigger than themselves forced Sartre and Beaver to live in the present. On January 24, Franco's armies were in the suburbs of Barcelona and almost half a million Republican soldiers and civilians fled to the French border. A month later the government of the Republic fled into French exile, leaving its mangled armies and a starving Madrid at the mercy of the fascists. On March 13, Hitler marched into Czechoslovakia and three weeks later Mussolini invaded Albania, giving Italy a springboard for an attack on Greece. As Premier Daladier assumed emergency powers and France and Britain began talks with the Soviet Union on a "triple alliance" to prevent Hitler from overrunning Poland, Sartre and Beaver made an Easter-recess trip through Provence, he reading Heidegger and she scaling still snow-capped mountains above Digne.

Like others, they tried to grasp the overall pattern and realized that their attitudes, theories and ideas were no longer enough to explain the political situation. Their friends were becoming politicized and increasingly pinning their hopes on the Soviet Union, mistrusted and deliberately discarded from European affairs by Britain and France for more than a decade and now asked to join the Western Allies to stop fascism.

What to think? After the collapse of Republican Spain, Colette Audry lost all hope and said anything was preferable to war. Sartre replied, "No, not anything." He convinced Simone that war was now a certainty but couldn't explain how anyone had allowed events to get this far. Their reassessment of the political situation forced them to realize a few things about themselves. As college teachers with over nine years' tenure, they were financially secure. They had no children, no responsibilities, spent their money capriciously and contrived to ignore their economic position. They were bursting with good health and because they didn't mind unorthodox traveling had seen as much of the world as most wealthy people.

Simone recovered her natural optimism during the early part of the summer when everybody read and commented on Marcel Déat's editorial, "Why die for Danzig?" in *L'Oeuvre* and the second round of talks with Stalin began. If the Soviet Union would line up with France and Britain, Hitler would hesitate to go to war; if he did go to war, Russia's military power, together with that of the West, would defeat him. Madame Morel invited Sartre and Beaver to spend part of August with her in her villa at Juan-les-Pins, the chic Basque resort, and Simone joined Fernando and Stépha Gerassi in Nice for two weeks' hiking before meeting Sartre in Marseilles. They were having a drink at an Old Port sidewalk café with Little Bost on furlough when they saw Nizan stroll by with an enormous rubber swan under one arm. He, Henriette and the kids were sailing to Corsica that evening and, he told them confidentially, the Triple Alliance pact would be signed. His views of the situation were very different from those he expressed in his columns in *Ce Soir,* but he was a big shot in the Communist Party and, they theorized, was obviously privy to top secrets. They wished each other a pleasant summer and Nizan left them with his swan under his arm.

Sartre and Beaver spent gorgeous weeks in Juan-les-Pins, eating breakfast on Madame Morel's terrace, watching waterskiers skimming over the blue surface of the bay, writing, reading and, in the early afternoon, going to the beach where Sartre tried to teach Beaver to swim. They were still in Juan-les-Pins August 23 when the news of the German-Soviet nonaggression pact suddenly changed the whole balance of power in Germany's favor. The Western democracies had dragged their feet on the Triple Alliance pact for five months. Nazi Foreign Minister Joachim von Ribbentrop flew to Moscow with a proposal that offered the Soviet Union the advantages of staying out of any war. In twelve hours, he reached agreement with Stalin.

Sartre and Beaver left Juan-les-Pins feeling depressed, and decided there was no hurry to get back to Paris. They went to Carcassonne aboard a train packed with soldiers summoned back from leave. They would have liked to talked to Nizan now. Stalin's about-face was hard to swallow for the communists and caused many fellow travelers to ask for a painful revision of the broad leftist alliance. Léon Blum was sure the French Communist Party would be torn apart, but the Daladier government suppressed *L'Humanité* and *Ce Soir* when the two communist dailies expressed lukewarm support of Stalin's realpolitik, thus rescuing them from profound embarrassment and opening to them the vast advantages of going underground.

They returned to Paris to prepare for the school year. People were divided. Conservatives had little desire to fight fascism, which they secretly preferred to any Popular Front, and now the right was joined by the millions of communists who felt betrayed by Stalin and resented the harassment by police, the courts and the government. Workers and the middle class had little confidence in the Daladier administration and couldn't follow the reason why it was necessary to fight for Poland after having deserted socialist Austria and Czechoslovakia. The general opinion was that there would be very little fighting and that, in any case, France was safe behind the Maginot Line fortifications.

They were at the Flore at 1 A.M. on September 2 when the British-French declaration of war went into effect and World War II began. General mobilization had been ordered since midday and Sartre's draft instructions ordered him to report in Nancy within twenty-four hours. A hard-faced woman sat sobbing to herself. A waiter observed that it looked like the real thing this time, but the crowds still seemed cheerful. "I've given up trying to think altogether, but I still have a headache," Simone wrote in a diary she had begun the day before. "There's a gorgeous moon rising above Saint-Germain-des-Prés making it look like a country church. Everywhere, underlying everything, a feeling of unfathomable horror." [7] They tried to sleep for a couple of hours, before Simone accompanied him to the Gare de l'Est for his 7:50 A.M. train to Nancy. "We sit down outside a café, and Sartre repeats that as a weatherman he won't be in any danger. Then he's gone. I walk back to Montparnasse. A wonderful autumn morning, the fresh smell of carrots and cabbages along the Boulevard Sebastopol."

Sartre joined the 70th Division at Essey-les-Nancy convinced it would be a short war. Poland was crushed by the overwhelming might of the German army in one week, but France, with eighty-five divisions facing an enemy with little more than a covering force, did little in the West to keep its commitment to Warsaw. Britain did no more. Its small contingent of two divisions didn't reach the "front" until September 26. After a perfunctory "Saar offensive" by nine French divisions, all was quiet on the

[7] Beauvoir, *The Prime of Life.*

western front as France settled into the "phony war." After induction and processing, Sartre was sent to Sector 108, which, in school kids' cipher, he managed to tell Simone was Brumath, a town ten miles north of evacuated Strasbourg and eight miles west of the Rhine River "front." In his first letter from his weather station, he told her he was getting on with his work—*Le Chemin de la liberté*. As he wrote in a letter to Paulhan, his job consisted of sending up balloons and watching them through a pair of field glasses. "This is called 'making a meteorological observation.' Afterward I phone the battery artillery officers and tell them the wind direction. What they do with this information is their affair. The young officers make some use of intelligence reports; the old school just shoves them into the wastepaper basket. Since there isn't any shooting either course of action is equally effective. It's extremely peaceful (I can't think of any branch in the armed forces that has a quieter, more poetic job, apart from breeders of carrier pigeons, assuming that there are any of them left nowadays) and I'm left with a large amount of spare time, which I'm using to finish my novel." [8] Boredom was becoming a problem for the two million troops along the "front." By loudspeakers and large signs the Germans chided the frontline French about "dying for Danzig" and blamed the British for the whole thing. "Don't shoot. We won't if you don't!" Often French troops would hoist a crude sign of their own signifying OK. Sometimes Wehrmacht troops across the river would cheer soccer games played by Frenchmen on their bank of the Rhine.

In October, Simone began an elaborate scheme to try to see Sartre. Since safe-conducts were not issued to girl friends or wives for frontline visits, she invented a sister dying of bone cancer in Marmoutier near Strasbourg. A fatherly clerk at her local police station took down all her information but it was another two weeks before she was called back. In the meantime school began—with gas mask and air raid drills—and, as foreigners, Stépha and Fernando were suddenly in trouble.

On October 30 her pass was ready. Getting a doctor to declare her ill for the following week, she was off to Nancy on the same train Sartre had taken two months earlier. At the Nancy army headquarters she mingled with Alsatian farmers who wanted to go home and harvest. She was issued a military *laissez-passer* authorizing her to go to Marmoutier—via Brumath —for twenty-four hours.

She got to Brumath at 4 A.M., the only person getting off the train, and spent the next hour trying to find a room and to locate Sartre. Helpful

[8] *Ibid.*

soldiers who happened to be Parisians also, banged on the shutters of one hotel with their rifle butts without results, but half an hour later the large blond hotelkeeper of the Ville de Paris gave her an ice-cold bedroom where she slipped between freezing sheets for one hour's sleep.

In his letters Sartre had mentioned a Taverne du Cerf where he ate breakfast at a long wooden table, but when she got there the two young women in charge brushed off all her questions with, "Ask at headquarters." Jotting down "You forgot your pipe in the Taverne du Cerf" in a hand-writing Sartre would recognize, she went to a big modern brick building and asked one of a group of soldiers to deliver her message. "Must be one of the guys in the office," the soldier said, promising to get her note to Sartre. She went back to the Taverne du Cerf to wait. Suddenly, Sartre's figure came down the street in the dawn light. "I recognized him at once from his walk and his pipe and his size, though he has grown a horrible scrubby beard which makes him look simply awful," she wrote in her diary.[9]

They spent an hour in her freezing room before he had to get back. At 11 A.M., however, he joined her again, clean-shaven, but at 1 P.M. she was told in Alsatian that the room was now for a lady who had traveled a long way to see her husband at the front. Alone, Simone managed to get a gendarme at city hall to give her safe-conduct an extension—largely be-cause he seemed impressed by the Paris stamps. Sartre, in the meantime, managed to arrange accommodations for her at the place where he was quartered although not with him. When he had told his "landlady" his wife was coming she had said in a shocked voice, "But you aren't married," and he had had to amend it to "my fiancée." Beaver stayed another two days, reading the first hundred and eighty pages of his novel, and eating in the gloomy Taverne du Cerf where all lights were covered with blue paper. She showed him her diary and listened to the soldiers' rumors, some saying it would all be over by Christmas, others believing that it was really a "diplomatic" war where there would be no fighting. "The nearer you get to the front," she wrote, "the more intangible the war becomes." Sartre walked her as far as the railway yard under a great starry sky, then he vanished into the night. Her trip back to Paris was long and uneventful except for a big Alsatian who, when she stretched her legs toward him on the bench in the overstuffed compartment, said, "This is the first contact I've had with a woman in twelve weeks."

The long winter dragged on. Sartre wrote to Beaver every day, obses-sively, about the progress of his book. "Since I have overcome my inferi-

[9] *Ibid.*

ority complex vis-à-vis the Far Left, I feel a freedom of thought that I've never had before, vis-à-vis phenomenology also," he wrote on January 6, 1940. Three days later, new doubts assailed him. Rereading the five notebooks he had filled with his novel disappointed him. In February he was given a one-week furlough and hurried to Paris to give his manuscript to Parain. But in March he told Simone he would give the story of Mathieu and Marcelle and their friends, Ivich, Boris, Brunet and Daniel, a vast flashback introduction showing them all ten years earlier. In mid-April this "repair job" was almost finished and he could write to her about a sharp captain right out of officers' school coming for an inspection tour: " 'And this guy who looks as if he's about to collapse, what does he do?' I didn't look as if I were collapsing but I looked like I always do when I work. 'A personal work, Captain.' 'What kind of personal work?' 'Writing.' 'A novel?' 'Yes, sir.' 'What kind of novel?' 'That's a little long to explain.' 'But is it a book where women get fucked and husbands are cuckolded?' 'Of course.' 'Very good. You're really lucky to be able to work like that.' " All of which led Sartre to buy fresh bread for everybody's evening chow.

In early April as Germany overran Denmark and Norway, Sartre was given a special furlough to go to Paris and receive the Prix du Roman populiste for *Le Mur*. Gallimard was finally publishing *L'Imaginaire*. On May 1, a fellow weather-station recruit going to Paris on furlough brought Simone the near-finished manuscript of *L'Age de raison* (*Age of Reason*) as Sartre now called the first volume of what he considered would be a multivolumed worked of fiction for which he put the overall title in plural, *Les Chemins de la liberté* (*Roads of Freedom*). In an accompanying note, he told Beaver she had full power to "cross out, obliterate, and erase anything you care to but to write me back about more substantive passages that don't work," and to get the manuscript to Parain as soon as possible for forwarding to Gaston Gallimard and Paulhan.

Ten days later, the lull was over. On Friday, May 10, the Luftwaffe struck airfields in northern France and German armor crossed the borders of Holland, Belgium and Luxembourg. In two days seven German panzer divisions pierced the "impenetrable" Ardennes and began rolling toward the Meuse and the Sedan. By May 16, the Allies had suffered their first disaster causing panic in the high command and consternation in Paris. Three weeks later, General Erwin Rommel's armor had swept across northern France to the English Channel. The Luftwaffe hammered the ragged remnants of Allied armies standing at Dunkirk while Britain desperately set up a rescue mission to get more than three hundred thousand men across the Channel.

On June 4, the outskirts of Paris were bombed and the Exodus—the fleeing of the civilian population ahead of a German army soon catching up with them—began. Olga's parents begged her and her sister, Wanda, to come home to Normandy and they did so, a few hours before Stépha and Fernando made a dash for the Spanish border with the idea of slipping through secretly and making their way to the United States or Mexico. On June 10, Simone packed her essentials—including all of Sartre's letters—and together with the father of one of her students plus two of his employees set out by car for Chartres. She ended up at Madame Morel's villa near Nantes without her luggage. While trying to phone the Morel residence from the Angers railway station overflowing with refugees, she checked her things at the left-luggage counter. When she returned for her suitcases they were gone. The letters Sartre had written her since 1929 would never be found.

Most of the numerous guests who had descended on Madame Morel were in favor of fleeing to Juan-les-Pins. Simone was convinced Sartre was already a prisoner and to her it seemed pointless to escape south. Besides, her lycée had technically been evacuated to Nantes. One evening someone shouted from a truck, "They've reached Le Mans." The following morning the villagers fled by pickup truck, horse-drawn carriage, bicycle or else vanished across the fields. French soldiers walked through town and an officer in a car told Madame Morel they were trying "delaying tactics" along the Loire River. A few soldiers without helmets or rifles came down the highway followed by a column of tanks. Then, after an explosion shattered the plate-glass window of a restaurant across the street, the Germans marched through by tanks, trucks, artillery and field kitchens. A detachment stayed and in the evening villagers crept back into their houses and the cafés opened. The Germans paid for their drinks and for the eggs they bought from the farms.

On June 13, Prime Minister Winston Churchill flew to Tours to prop up the demoralized Paul Reynaud administration, but the next morning the Germans marched into Paris while, in Bordeaux, the Reynaud government collapsed. The next day the eighty-four-year-old Marshal Pétain went on the radio and, "with a heavy heart," announced he had asked for armistice terms. Four days later, Sartre was taken prisoner in Lorraine.

Simone heard the conditions of the armistice traveling back toward Paris with a Dutch family who had ten liters of gasoline in their car. She had convinced herself that Sartre might have returned to Paris and that, in any case, she would be able to pick up news about him. The Dutchman ran out of gas a hundred and ten miles from Paris. Together with two other women she got a lift from a German truck going as far as Mantes, thirty-odd miles from Paris. It was horribly hot under the gray tarpaulin where people sat crowded on suitcases and gasoline cans. Nauseous with heat and gasoline smells, Simone vomited over the tailgate. When a German offered her food, she shook her head. At Dreux they saw a few shell holes. The long procession of refugees trailed on.

The landlady at Hôtel du Danemark in the Rue Vavin had thrown out whatever Simone had left behind, but she gave her a letter from Sartre dated June 9. After she washed up, she went out to telephone and ran into her father. They had a sandwich and a beer together. He told her the Germans were very polite and that it was highly unlikely that POWs would be released before the end of the war. He had heard there were camps at the outskirts of Paris where the POWs were starving on a diet of "dead dog." Occupied France, he told her, would be assimilated into Germany. In the evening she went over to the apartment on the Rue de Rennes to see her mother. The war had surprised her sister, Poupette, in Portugal and in all probability she would find herself exiled for the duration of the conflict. When Simone left her parents at 8:30 her mother told her to get back to Rue Vavin in a hurry because of the curfew. "I don't think I have ever felt so utterly depressed as I did during that walk back through the deserted streets, under a stormy sky, my eyes burning, my head on fire, and the one thought in my mind was Sartre, literally and physically starving to death," she wrote in her diary.

She got the first letter from him July 11, a penciled note in an open envelope saying he might be home before the end of the month, that he was well treated and that that was all he was allowed to say. She breathed a little easier, broke off her diary and settled down to waiting while slowly picking up her daily existence. A new school year would begin.

The trains were running again and brought Olga back to Paris. Charles Dullin and Camille were back after various adventures. Simone found her table again at the Dôme and the sight of young Germans in gray became so common it hardly struck her as odd. More nauseating was the reading of Le Matin and La Victoire with self-righteous apologies for Germany, the signs "Out of Bounds to Jews" appearing in certain shop windows and Vichy Radio denunciations of "renegade Jews" who had left France in the lurch. At her lycée—as in all French schools—she was made to sign a document affirming upon oath that she was neither a Freemason nor a Jew. She found it repugnant to put her name to this but no one

refused. Ration cards appeared at the end of September and in October
the Vichy government published its "Jewish statute" debarring all Jews
from public affairs. At Gallimard's she learned from Parain that the *NRF*
would begin to publish again. Paulhan had refused to edit the magazine
under German control so Pierre Drieu la Rochelle would take over. More
important, Parain told her that Nizan had been killed in the battle for
Dunkirk. The last time she and Sartre had seen Nizan was in Marseilles,
when he had shuffled off with his huge rubber swan. Henriette and the
children, Parain told her, had fled to America.

Other letters from Sartre arrived saying the conditions in the Stalags
were far from intolerable. Rations were short but Sartre was getting on
with his writing. He had made numerous friends and found his new way
of life intriguing. She did not dare believe it. Sometimes she told herself
he would appear the next minute, smiling and walking toward her with
that quick step of his. At other times she felt it would be three or four
years before she would see him. Hitler had not sustained a single defeat,
London was being bombed and Nazi troops might cross the Channel. The
United States still refused to budge and the Soviet Union remained in-
active. One day, however, they would surely intervene and one day Hitler
would be beaten, but this implied a long war and a long separation. A
letter from Sartre gave her the address of a fellow prisoner of his who
had been repatriated. She went to see this man who confirmed that life in
the POW camps was indeed bearable.

She decided to begin writing again. If everything was doomed, the
hours spent writing didn't matter anyway, she told herself. And if one
day the world, her life and literature would again mean something she
would surely reproach herself for months and years wasted. She also began
to read Hegel and found solace in losing herself in the perspective of Historical Necessity. To get back to the here and now, she rediscovered Sören
Kierkegaard and began to read him with passion. Kierkegaard put the
will before reason and argued that, in regard to man, no one should be
too scientific. Science, which deals with what is general, can only touch
upon things from the outside, Kierkegaard said. What was needed was
to recognize "existential" modes of thinking in order to grasp a situation
from the inside. She wondered if she couldn't make the confrontation of
the individual and the universal the theme of her next novel.

The theaters opened again and since cinemas played only German
movies or fourth-rate French slapsticks, Simone enjoyed being invited to
the rehearsals of Dullin's revival of *Plutus*. Olga had a minor part in the
Aristophanes play and, with her sister Wanda, was cast in Dullin's next

production, Ben Jonson's *The Silent Woman*. Simone was on her way out of the Hôtel du Danemark for the dress rehearsal when she found a note in her pigeonhole from the wife of one of Sartre's fellow prisoners. The slip of paper gave his address as Krankenrevier Stalag XII D. When somebody translated Krankenrevier as meaning sick bay she was sure he had typhus. She rushed across Paris to see the woman, who reassured her. Her husband and Sartre had wrangled crafty jobs at the camp hospital, where, among other things, they had heated barracks. Simone made it to the theater by the end of the first act.

The missives that followed—both the form letters and the longer, "unofficial" letters mailed from Trier—told of discussions with Jesuit chaplains about the Mystery of Virgin Birth and rehearsals of a play Sartre had written for Christmas.

IV

FALL OF 1946

STARDOM HAD ITS PRICE. Every other magazine in the world was writing about existentialism and tourists were making pilgrimages to the Flore and the Deux Magots in the hope of catching a glimpse of the two mandarins and the new in-crowd. Existentialism was something Juliette Greco sang in the new Saint-Germain-des-Prés boites. Existentialism was, with *haute couture,* France's newest export item, called everything from a protest movement for those who couldn't make up their minds to raunchy chic and "excrementialism." Existentialism was *La Nausée* translated into thirty languages and Simone's *L'Invitée,* now called "one of the masterpieces of metaphysical novels." It was Albert Camus' *Mythe de Sisyphe* and the Sartre doublebill at the Antoine—*Morts sans sépultures (The Victors),* dedicated to his American mistress, and *La Putain respectueuse,* which *Le Figaro* suggested that the government ban. In the United States, *The Respectful Prostitute* had censorship problems in Chicago (in Moscow they put a happy ending on the one-act play and bashfully retitled it *Lizzie McKay*). In the first issue of *Les Temps modernes,* the magazine they had founded, Sartre had tried to explain everything and Simone had followed up with a four-article series that was now coming out in book form at Nagel's because Gallimard couldn't print it fast enough.

Since his return from America, Sartre had a private secretary, Jean Cau, a young man who rather than going to the Sorbonne Ecole Normale

Existentialist guru, 1947
ROGER-VIOLLET

preferred to try and cope with Sartre's wild appointment schedules. Celebrity had a way of crashing in on them faster than Cau could answer Sartre's new telephone in his and his recently widowed mother's new apartment. When Simone wasn't correcting galleys at Nagel's or sitting on the Gallimard reading committee, she was soothing egos at *Les Temps modernes*— affectionately named after Charlie Chaplin's comedy they had loved so much before the war.

They never had a moment alone. Together, Sartre and Beaver had been to Rome to discuss a screen adaptation of *No Exit*. He took amphetamines in order to finish his speech for the opening session of the United Nations Educational, Scientific and Cultural Organization (UNESCO). Their refusal to play roles often laid them open to the strongest attacks. Naïvely, perhaps, they had not changed their life-style. *Liberté de l'esprit* wrote that by day right-of-center authors were casting longing glances toward the Flore and by night dreaming about Simone. Another weekly didn't hesitate to publish the confidences of a young girl who claimed Sartre had lured her to a hotel to have her sniff a camembert and when a *Samedi Soir* journalist badgered Simone into agreeing to an interview by saying he would write about them anyway, his article turned out to be a trashy indictment. Simone didn't so much mind being called the "grande Sartreuse" or "Notre Dame de Sartre," but certain looks men gave her made her realize a lady existentialist was obviously considered a dissolute woman. "We both led such independent lives that it was impossible to think of our relationship as a classical example of free love," she would write eighteen years later in *La Force des choses,* the third volume of her autobiography.[1] Thirty years later, Sartre would say that they eventually got used to being called seducers of the young or worse. "I was stunned. I had never thought that possible, but after all I have always been attacked by the right people, I mean the people I despise."

Not quite. They were distressed at finding themselves vilified by the communists. Party philosopher Henri Lefebvre accused Sartre of being a gravedigger and a decadent and two other Marxists accused him of leading the young astray, a notion the Catholic *La Croix* echoed when it called "atheist existentialism a more serious threat than eighteenth-century Rationalism and nineteenth-century Positivism." More ponderously, Hungarian thinker György Lukacs, who specialized in Marxist analysis of western literary modes, called existentialism the diseased reaction of a

---

[1] Simone de Beauvoir, *La Force de choses,* Paris: Gallimard, 1963; *Force of Circumstance,* New York: Putnam, 1964.

fetishized capitalist conscience unable to see its way out of its own gloom.[2]

If Sartre actually enjoyed it all, Simone was somewhat dazed. She didn't mind the fuss about the two of them or her name being dropped in newspaper columns. Sartre was more famous than she, but, as she would write, "because he meant so much to me I couldn't be jealous and also because it seemed to me quite justified. I didn't even regret not being entitled to more fame." [3] Money was a *moral* problem. She realized Sartre would have a lot of it and tried to discuss their new responsibilities. "In fact, we evaded them," she would remember. "Sartre had never taken money seriously. He loathed counting and had neither the time nor the inclination to turn himself into a philanthropic institution, besides which, there is something unpleasant about charity when it has been carefully thought out. He gave away most of what he earned but as chance dictated—to friends, to people he met, to people who wrote and asked."

"Dolores V" was a darker cloud in Simone's sky. Sartre had met this young New Yorker on his first trip to America as a correspondent for *Combat* and *Le Figaro* and had gone back a second time for three months to be with her. After the second trip, he had talked a lot about this woman, whom Beaver would call "M" in her autobiography. "At present their attachment was mutual, and they planned to spend two or three months together every year. So be it; separation held no terror for me. But he evoked the weeks spent with her in New York with so much cheerfulness that I became uneasy; so far I had supposed him to be attracted mainly by the romantic side of this adventure; suddenly I wondered if M were more important to him than I was. In a relationship that has lasted for more than fifteen years, how much is a matter of habit? What kind of concessions does it imply?" [4] She felt she knew her own answer but not his. The way he described Dolores, she shared completely all his emotions, his irritations and his desires. When they went out together she always wanted to stop or go the same instant as he, and Simone wondered if this meant Dolores and Sartre were together at a depth that she had never achieved with him. They were leaving for lunch with Lucienne and Armand Salacrou when she asked him who meant the more to him, Dolores or her. He answerd that Dolores meant an awful lot to him, "but I'm with you." She understood this to mean that he was respecting their

[2] György Lukacs, *Existentialisme ou marxisme*, Paris: Nagel, 1948.
[3] Beauvoir, *Force of Circumstance*.
[4] *Ibid.*

"lease" and that she shouldn't ask him for more than that. "Such a reply put the whole future in question," she would write. "I had great difficulty shaking hands, smiling and eating and I saw Sartre watching me uneasily. I pulled myself together but the luncheon seemed endless. In the afternoon, Sartre explained himself. We had always put more faith in behavior than in words, which was why instead of long explanations he had invoked the evidence of a simple fact. I believed him." It was understood that while Simone toured the United States on her combined travel-lecture tour, Dolores would come to Paris.

It had been difficult, too, five years ago when Sartre had been released from the POW camp. It had been a comedy of errors that March evening in 1941 when she had returned from dinner to find a note in her pigeon-hole in the Hôtel du Danemark in Sartre's handwriting saying he was at the Café Trois Mousquetaires. She had run all the way up to the Rue de la Gaîté. Nobody. When she had collapsed on a bench a waiter had handed her a piece of paper. Sartre had been waiting for two hours and was now taking a stroll to calm himself. He would be back shortly. They had never had any difficulty before when they got together after an absence, but that evening and the next several days he seemed a stranger to her. He talked a different language, the language of the camps, and he was full of moralistic self-righteousness. Did she buy anything at the black market? When she said a little tea occasionally, he said that was too much. She had been wrong to sign the paper stating she was neither a Freemason nor a Jew. He had always asserted his ideas, not to mention his likes and dislikes, in the most dogmatic fashion, but his ideology had been liquid. "I had been prepared to find him full of convictions and plans for the future and bursts of bad temper, but not armored with principles," she would write.[5] He had managed to get home through a subterfuge, passing himself off as a civilian, but life in the camp had been a tight-knit fraternity with everyone rejecting compromises and concessions. It was with some regret that he slowly abandoned the clear-cut simplicity of the camp for the improvised ingenuity of people living in an occupied territory.

He gave her yet another surprise that evening. He had come home not to survive, but to *act*. She was taken aback. They were isolated, powerless. Fascism was triumphant everywhere. Nazi Germany ruled Europe from Norway to the Mediterranean, from the Atlantic to the Black Sea, its Japanese ally was landing in China, while Italy, the third member of the Axis, mopped up Greece and in Africa plunged into Somalia and Libya. The Soviet Union, the hope and focal point of so many progressive pas-

[5] Beauvoir, *Prime of Life.*

sions, occupied the Baltic states and was preparing to sign a nonaggression pact with Japan, while in the United States Franklin Roosevelt was starting his unprecedented third term by only cautiously leading his country away from traditional isolationism toward alignment with Great Britain. At home, the doddering father-figure Pétain and his Premier, Pierre Laval, not only resigned themselves to knuckling under but by emulating Hitler's regime tried to curry enough favor with the dictator to have him go easy on France. Collaborators—they liked to call themselves mere realists—were increasingly out in the open and part of everyday life.

First, Sartre had to have himself legally demobilized, something that was possible only in Vichy France, the "free zone" under Pétain's rule not actually occupied by Germany. He was ready to bicycle down to the "border," sneak across to get his civilian papers, then sneak back into German-occupied France when he learned that the Paris University administration didn't look too carefully at returning teachers' papers. Sartre got his job back at the Lycée Pasteur and after a surreal meeting with an inspector-general of schools—where neither said anything outright—he understood he would teach an entrance class for the Ecole Normale at the prestigious Lycée Condorcet the following year. Life on the home front, as Beaver had said, was artful dodging and understanding things not spelled out.

The organizing took place in Simone's room, with duly demobilized Merleau-Ponty and Little Bost plus a handful of Merleau-Ponty's teachers' college philosophy students taking part. Dominique Desanti, a fiery co-ed and Marxist, suggested organizing attacks on notorious demoralizers such as Marcel Déat who had invented the "Why die for Danzig?" formula and now extolled the New Order in the German-controlled press. None of the others felt qualified to make bombs, however, and until further notice it was agreed they would limit themselves to anti-German propaganda. They would gather information and try to mimeograph news leaflets and pamphlets.

They discovered other groups existed, including one headed by Alfred Péron, a boyhood friend of Sartre's who was acting as a British intelligence agent. "Intergroup" meetings were soon held on school grounds and in the Luxembourg Gardens.

If all nascent resistance groups wanted the defeat of Nazi Germany, their ideas about the future were not the same. The communists, who were the first to really fight, wanted if not an outright Marxist France at least a Popular Front after the war. Sartre's boyhood friend was leaning toward the partisans of General Charles de Gaulle, who from London called on his country to continue the struggle, reminding them that "overseas

France"—nearly half of Africa, Indochina, the Caribbean islands—was not in enemy hands, that most of the navy was safe in Algerian and Moroccan ports, that whole divisions had made it across the Strait of Dover with the British and that England was fighting on. With Churchill's support, de Gaulle had constituted a "France libre" government-in-exile.

Sartre and his little group found it hard to think all the way to Germany's defeat, but they believed they should think of the future. "If the democracies won, it would be essential for the left to have a new program," Simone would write. "It was our job, by pooling our ideas and research, to bring such a program into being. Its basic aims could be summed up in two words—though their reconciliation created enormous problems—which also served as the name for our movement: Socialisme et Liberté." Sartre agreed that one of the Marxists could alternate with him or another noncommunist in the group in writing the inflammatory editorials in their underground newssheet.

In June Hitler's attack on the Soviet Union, the largest country and the largest enemy he could find, not only had French communists breathing easier again, it also had them beginning the first real resistance. Through Dominique Desanti, Sartre put out feelers to the communists but ran into a wall of mistrust. Besides their innate leeriness of intellectuals, the communists found anyone who had conned his way out of German imprisonment highly suspicious. Soon, they began to circulate rumors that Sartre had been released in order to work for the Germans as an agent provocateur.

In July, Simone's father died. Georges de Beauvoir had been operated on for prostate trouble and at first was believed to have made a good recovery. Months of undernourishment had weakened him, however, and the onset of tuberculosis saw him die in a few days. He was sixty-three. Poupette was in Portugal and Simone tried to be both his daughters during the final moments. "He did not struggle. I was amazed at the peaceful way he returned to nothingness. He had no illusions, either; he asked me if I could, without causing my mother distress, see to it that no priest attended his deathbed and she did, in fact, conform to this wish." [6]

Gallimard functioned at a low-key pace and the *NRF* appeared again under the editorship of Pierre Drieu la Rochelle, but the leading authors had left for the slightly more tolerable Vichy "free zone" and had congregated on the Riviera, several of them house-sitting magnificent villas for wealthy foreigners who had found it prudent to put more distance

[6] Beauvoir, *Force of Circumstance.*

between themselves and Europe's new masters. As the summer vacation approached, Sartre and Beaver decided to bicycle down to the Côte d'Azur —a twelve-hundred-mile round trip—and perhaps to canvass some of the more formidable names for Socialism and Liberty. While in the zone Sartre would also try to obtain his legal demobilization papers.

Near Roanne, fifty miles northwest of Lyons, a woman in black agreed to take them "across" for a reasonable fee and the same night they trudged behind her across fields and through woods until she suddenly announced they were over the border. They quickly got to a nearby village and to the local inn full of people who had also just slipped across. They tried to sleep on mattresses in a room where six people and a wailing baby were already settled down for the night.

Intellectual Paris was on the Riviera—the men mostly with ladies who were not their wives. André Gide was in Nice, Roger Martin du Gard in Cap Ferrat and André Malraux—with Josette Clotis, the mother of their newborn son—at an English couple's villa at Roquebrune Cap-Martin. In Marseilles, Sartre and Beaver got Gide's address from a former Léon Blum campaign worker who didn't think much of Socialism and Liberty. They pedaled off toward Nice.

Square meals were hard to come by but overripe tomatoes were everywhere. After a lunch on grapes, bread and wine in a ditch near Porquerolles, Simone went biking along the Grand Langoustier road while Sartre stayed put in a café working on the opening dialogue of a "Greek play." The idea stemmed from his enthusiasm at seeing Jean-Louis Barrault's production of Aeschylus' *Supplices,* starring himself, Jean Marais and Alain Cuny and with Olga Kosakiewicz in a minor part. During rehearsals Olga had asked Barrault how to go about getting a starring role, and he had replied the best way was to get someone to write a play for her. Sartre had thought he should be the playwright. *Bariona* had been something of a hit in the Stalag, so why not? The play he began in the café in Porquerolles while Beaver scaled the hills was, like Aeschylus' tragedy, about the house of Atreus of Greek legend. "Almost all his new ideas took a mythical form initially," Simone would write, "and I imagined he would soon eliminate Orestes, Electra and the rest of their doomed family."

They caught up with Gide in Grasse as Simone had a flat tire and settled down at the town fountain to repair it. The seventy-two-year-old Gide was nervous when they walked into a café and Sartre began to talk about an underground press. Suspiciously eyeing the other customers, Gide had Sartre move with him to different tables three times. There was noth-

ing Gide felt he could do except refer Sartre to Pierre Herbart, with whom
Gide had visited the Soviet Union and who was also a friend of Malraux's.
When Sartre mentioned he had an appointment the following day with
Malraux, Gide hoped he would stumble in on a Malraux in a good mood.

Sartre was neither the first nor the last intellectual eager for action and
commitment to seek out the forty-year-old Malraux who, in the Spanish
Civil War, had shown how a man of letters could intervene energetically
and intelligently and try to be more than a camp follower in revolutionary
events. But fascism had triumphed in Spain and during the summer of
1941 Malraux felt tired after a decade of political action that had led
nowhere. "Do you have arms?" was his pragmatic question to would-be
guerrilleros. Roger Stéphane was one young, energetic journalist who had
found his way to Roquebrune to ask for help and instead had gotten an
earful of Malrucian geopolitics. Other budding *maquisards* included Francis Crémieux who showed up to offer Malraux the leadership of a fledging
if not yet totally organized "secret army" in the Pyrenees, and Emmanuel
d'Astrier, aristocrat and diplomat who had married the sister of a Soviet
commissar. To both, Malraux wondered aloud whether they weren't just
playing boy scouts. What he was interested in, he said, was meeting "serious people"—like some of the British intelligence officers now being para-
chuted into France.

For their first meeting with Malraux, Sartre and Beaver were passably
impressed by the splendor of the villa and the Chicken Maryland exquisitely prepared and served by Luigi, the Italian butler who had come with
the house. Malraux heard out Sartre, but said that, for the time being at
any rate, all action would not only be dangerous but absurd. As Malraux
had told Stéphane, he saw the outcome of the war in terms of who had
the edge in technology. Although Nazi Germany was triumphant on all
fronts—steamrolling into the Ukraine and dashing through North Africa
toward Egypt while subjecting England to the relentless blitz—Malraux
said the German forces were already beyond their peak and that Germany's
defeat would mean a victory for the Anglo-Saxons "who will colonize the
world, France included." To Sartre, he said it was only a matter of time
before the United States would be sucked into the conflict. For the time
being, he counted on Soviet armor and American bombs to win the war.

After visits with Colette Audry in Grenoble and Madame Morel in
Nantes, they reached Paris to ponder bitterly on Malraux's words on premature action. Sartre's boyhood friend Péron had been arrested and deported as had a student of Simone's. And yet neither they, nor the Socialism
and Liberty group, had yet managed to *do* anything. Sartre felt the risks

totally out of proportion with what could be achieved. "Hitherto we had been lucky; none of our members had been bothered by the authorities," Simone would recall, "but Sartre could now see just what risk, and to no purpose, the continued existence of Socialism and Liberty would mean to our friends. All through October we had interminable discussions on this subject—or, to be more precise, Sartre argued it over with himself since I agreed with his view that to make yourself responsible for someone's death out of sheer obstinacy is not a thing to be forgiven." Quietly, the Socialism and Liberty movement was abandoned.

There was always the writing. As Sartre began to teach at the Condorcet and Beaver returned to her classes at the Lycée Molière, he took her ménage à trois novel to Brice Parain while plunging into his Greek play. He had managed to say quite a lot about occupation, collaborators and resistance fighters in *Bariona* and felt the story of Orestes, Electra and the usurped rule of Argos offered just as rich possibilities for comments on the current situation. He had finished *L'Age de raison,* although he realized it could not be published until after the war, and Simone also started a novel about the Resistance that she knew could not see print until after the end of the Occupation. But they had decided to conduct their lives as if ultimate victory was a certainty. In December, when the United States entered the war, that victory seemed a little more likely, even if the Japanese gained some shattering victories in the Pacific.

One book that *could* be published, Sartre was told by Gallimard, was a philosophical treatise. Since the Stalag, Sartre had had in mind to write a systematic presentation of his philosophy of being and during the winter of 1941–42, when life became much harder, he began *L'Etre et le néant* (*Being and Nothingness*). His basic positions had not changed and in the new volume he planned to enrich and elaborate on the important themes scattered in essays, articles and short stories. He would also consider such concrete problems as love, hate, sex, the trap of bad faith and the crises of anguish.

The winter brought the first real resistance against the Germans, even though the retaliation was merciless and for each member of the Reichwehr killed, the Gestapo shot fifty French hostages. In November, grenades were thrown into restaurants and hotels occupied by Germans and when railway sabotage began on the Paris-Brittany main line three men picked up at random were shot. In Bordeaux the ratio was 50-1 when a German major was found dead in the street.

Sartre and Beaver had a new friend—and new responsibilities. The friend was Alberto Giacometti. The sculptor had become infatuated with one of Simone's former students, Lise, who, together with Little Bost and Olga and Wanda Kosakiewicz now were more or less the financial charges of Sartre and Beaver. Lise had decided to leave the man she was living with but refused to return to her parents; Little Bost was struggling along in dire poverty, and roles were few and far between for the Kosakiewicz sisters, who now adopted the stage names Olga Dominique and Marie Olivier. It was not the last time that young people would live off Sartre and Beaver.

They had moved to the Hôtel Mistral in the Rue Cels behind the Montparnasse cemetery because some of the rooms there came with gas ranges. As the cost of strange meats served in fourth-rate restaurants began to skyrocket, Beaver borrowed pans and dishes and began to cook all their meals herself. "I had little natural liking for domestic chores and in order to adapt myself to the situation I had recourse to a familiar proceeding— I turned my culinary worries into a full-blown obsession, and stuck to it for the next three years," she would write. "I watched while coupons were clipped from my ration book and never parted with one too many. I wandered through the streets rummaging behind dummy window displays for unrationed foodstuffs, a sort of treasure hunt that I enjoyed. What a windfall if I stumbled on a beet or a cabbage! The first lunch we had in my room consisted of 'turnip sauerkraut.' " [7]

The "family" also institutionalized a custom dating back to the days in Rouen. Friendships were fragile and highly subtle arrangements and were best cultivated à deux. When Beaver was chatting in the Flore with Olga or Bost, when Sartre and Wanda went out together or when Lise and Wanda were having a tête-à-tête, none of the others would dream of joining their table. People found this ridiculous, but to them it was both obvious and natural.

A new book that impressed them deeply when it came out in July 1942 was L'Etranger (The Stranger) by Albert Camus. a young pied-noir, or Frenchman from Algeria. The twenty-eight-year-old actor-director-playwright had finished his novel in 1940 and sent it to Malraux in Roquebrune for possible recommendation to Gallimard. Malraux had been unable to put down the story of Patrice Meursault, who kills an Arab on a beach in apparent self-defense, "because of the sun," and who, because of his indifference and his incompetent lawyer, is condemned to

[7] Ibid.

death. Malraux sent the novel to Gallimard with a one-word recommendation, "Important!"

When Sartre and Beaver read the book, they felt it had been a long time since any new French writer had moved them so strongly. *L'Etranger* was like an echo of *La Nausée* and Meursault a blood brother of Antoine Roquentin. Like Antoine, Camus' outsider reaches a state of happiness because he refuses to subscribe to meaningless social rituals. In early 1943, Sartre reviewed *L'Etranger*.[8]

Sartre finished *Les Mouches (The Flies)* and had Jean-Louis Barrault read the play. The message was contemporary—people should throw off their guilt and assert their right to freedom. The hero is Orestes, returning as a young man to the Argos he had been smuggled out of as a child when his mother's lover, Aegisthus, killed his father, Agamemnon, and usurped the throne. The Argos Sartre's Orestes returns to is filled with big flies and the inhabitants live with guilty consciences for having welcomed a criminal as their king. As in Aeschylus, Orestes and his sister Electra avenge their father by killing their mother, Clytemnestra, and Aegisthus, but instead of being judged by the Furies at Delphi, Orestes discusses man's freedom with Zeus, saying human life begins on the far side of despair and that the reign of gods is coming to an end. In the end, while his sister knuckles under to tradition, Orestes says No to Zeus' offer to sit on his victim's throne and instead stalks out of Argos with the shrieking Furies flinging themselves after him.

Barrault wanted to stage *Les Mouches* until Sartre told him Olga Kosakiewicz had to play Electra. Barrault didn't think it was possible to stage the play with an unknown leading lady, so Sartre turned to Charles Dullin, who had a higher opinion of Olga's acting abilities. At Camille's urging, Dullin had taken over the Sarah Bernhardt Theater, but his productions— Camille's own play, *La Princesse des ursins,* and a Lope de Vega comedy— were financial fiascos. *Les Mouches* would be an expensive production since it demanded Greek costumes and sets plus a fairly big cast. Dullin agreed to stage *The Flies,* but everybody would have to be patient at least until the next season.

Simone had called her novel about Pierre, Françoise and Xavière *Légitime défense* and, with the reservation that Françoise was perhaps an unlikely murderess, Parain thought it worth publishing. Paulhan still had to approve and kept the manuscript for a long time.

Sartre was working on *L'Etre et le néant,* usually at the Flore, which

[8] "Explication de L'Etranger," in *Cahiers du Sud,* February 1943.

was warmer than the rooms at the Mistral. A massive attempt at construct-
ing a full-scale existential theory, *Being and Nothingness* was in many
respects an amplified restatement of the doctrines of Heidegger. It went
beyond phenomenology in its analysis of structures of consciousness but
retained Heidegger's pessimism that only by contemplating their nothingness can human beings be inspired to create their own destiny. To act is
to make choices and man is *condemned* to be free, Sartre argued. The
core of his morality was contained in his famous sentence, "Existence
precedes essence," by which he meant that a person's life isn't the result
of his or her personality (essence) but of a series of free choices that are
never really completely justified. Human beings are absolutely responsible
for their choices but their existence is not the result of these choices.

The notion of "Other" occupied a quarter of the book. How we are
perceived by another consciousness—that is, as an object—was something
that had fascinated both Sartre and Beaver for years. It is before the
Other, Sartre now argued, that we are *guilty*—guilty of making him or her
an object, guilty because we consent to this alienation and because we inevitably cause the Other to feel the same thing. We cannot live without
making an object of the Other, that is, we cannot live without doing violence to his or her subjectivity.

In June, Simone and Sartre were told to come around to Paulhan's
apartment. Paulhan wanted to know if her stage director hero in *Légitime
défense* was really Dullin, but once the small talk was over he told her
the book would be published in the spring. She had spent four years on
the novel and felt immensely relieved. Her legalistic title wouldn't do,
however, and after turning over various words and phrases she suggested *L'Invitée*.

Sartre wanted to continue working on his philosophy during the summer, but Simone dragged him on a bicycle tour of the Pyrenees, with
Bost tagging along for part of the trip. They were told that it was particularly easy to slip into the Vichy Zone in the Basque region so they put
their bikes on the train with them to Sauveterre-de-Béarn in the Pyrenees
foothills, where a guide, also on a bicycle, took them along a narrow
country road and after half a mile told them they were there. When
Sartre stayed in a country inn for a day's work or slumped into a meadow
for a couple of hours with his writing pad, Beaver and Bost pedaled on
to take in the sights. At Foix, Bost left them to join friends in Lyons before returning to Paris. He got caught trying to get back into German-
occupied France and spent two weeks fretting and fuming in a prison in
Chalons. Sartre and Beaver bicycled to Marseilles, where food was scarcer

than the year before, and returned by train half-starved to Madame Morel's villa near Nantes, where, after the first meal, Sartre passed out and stayed in bed for three days.

When they returned to Paris, the "family" had been increased by one— Bourla, Lise's boyfriend. An eighteen-year-old Spanish Jew who had been in Sartre's class at the Lycée Pasteur the year before, Bourla was the son of an important businessman and thought he had no need to be afraid of the Germans. If ever he got into trouble, the Spanish embassy would intervene. "We found him quite delightful," Simone would remember. "He approached the world in a clumsy, childish, excited fashion, with inexhaustible enthusiasm. He was tearing through Spinoza and Kant and intended to become a philosophy teacher." Bourla and Lise moved in together at the Hôtel Mistral, where he shared everything with her, his chocolate ration, his sweaters, the allowance he got from his father, not to mention the extra money he pinched at home.

They spent Christmas at Madame Morel's listening to British Broadcasting Corporation (BBC) reports of the Battle of Stalingrad. By March 1, 1943, Stalin could announce "the beginning of the massed drive of the enemy from Soviet lands." France's German-controlled press made no attempts to conceal the fact and now exhorted people to save the existing Europe from the "Bolshevik menace" instead of beseeching them to help build a new Europe. The underground was being organized and intellectuals were catching up with Sartre's idea of two years earlier. Members of the communist intelligentsia invited him to join a Comité National des écrivains (CNE). He asked if they wanted a spy in their ranks but they assured him they knew nothing about the rumors they had circulated at his expense in 1941. Presided over by surrealist poet Paul Eluard, the CNE held boring meetings, which Sartre attended. He also contributed to the clandestine *Lettres françaises* newssheet. The CNE was only for published authors and since *L'Invitée* had not yet come out Simone was not invited.

Dullin kept his promise and in the spring of 1943 began rehearsing *The Flies* at the big Sarah Bernhardt Theater. In addition to directing the play, Dullin played Zeus, with Olga Dominique as Electra. The neocubist sculptor Henri-Georges Adams created the sets, masks and statues in a bold and aggressive style. The rehearsals were long and tough. Like Olga, Jean Lannier, who played Orestes, lacked experience and Dullin lost his temper several times. At the dress rehearsal Sartre was standing in the foyer when a dark young man came up and introduced himself—Albert Camus.

Les Mouches was a moderate success and ran for twenty-five performances. Most critics passed over the political implications. Twenty-five
years later, Sartre would remember it in a homage to Dullin. "My
speeches were overlong. Without a word of reproach or without initially
advising me to make cuts, Dullin made me understand, in talking to the
actors, that a play is the opposite of an orgy of talk—the smallest number
of words irresistibly strung together by an action that cannot be changed
and a ceaseless passion." [9]

Simone was tempted to try her hand at a play but stuck to the novel she
knew could only be published after the Liberation. Unexpectedly she had
more time on her hands. Lise's mother was furious because her daughter
had left a highly suitable lover to live with Bourla and asked Simone to
use her influence to get Lise back to her previous suitor. When Simone
refused, the lady accused her of corrupting a minor. Before the war the
affair would probably have gone no further but the Vichy administration
took a different view of morals charges and at the end of the academic
year, Simone was expelled from the Paris school system.

She was not unduly upset. She had been teaching for twelve years and
was beginning to tire of it. She needed to earn a living, however, and
managed to get a job as a producer at the national radio network. Working
for the government radio did not automatically mean being branded a
collaborator by the growing Resistance movement. It all depended. The
program Simone produced was a reconstruction of traditional festivals,
from the Middle Ages to modern times, complete with speech, music and
background effects. The Middle Ages was "safe" not only in radio but in
film, with Marcel Carné directing the immensely successful *Les Visiteurs
du soir* and Jean Delannoy *L'Eternel retour,* the latter a retelling of the
Tristan-Isolde legend. The screenwriter of *Les Visiteurs du soir* was
Jacques Prévert (and Jean Cocteau wrote *L'Eternel retour*). Prévert
still presided at the "cinéastes' table" at the Flore and one day introduced Delannoy to Sartre. Would Sartre like to write for the movies?
Delannoy wondered, after lamenting the quality of the scripts they
received at the Pathé studios. Sartre would love to. As of September
1943, schoolteacher-philosopher-author-playwright Sartre could add part-
time screenwriter to his credits. The first script he turned in was called
"Typhus" and was based on the impressions he and Beaver had had in
Ouarzazate in Morocco in 1938. The retainer was sizable and, he told

Simone, if everything went well he, too, would give up teaching within a year.

Gallimard published the 724-page *L'Etre et le néant* in its Bibliothèque des idées collection during the summer. Dedicated "Au Castor" ("to Beaver") the weighty philosophical treatise passed almost unnoticed and not, as its American translator would have it, "attacked as absurd, then admitted to be true but obvious and insignificant, finally to be seen so important that its adversaries claim that they themselves discovered it." [10] In 1945, however, the existentialist craze gave the Sartrian *magnum opus* more attention than any philosophical work in modern times and for the 1945 reprint Gallimard listened to its author and agreed to a publicity wraparound, WHAT IS IMPORTANT IN A VASE IS THE VOID IN THE MIDDLE. With *L'Etre et le néant* Sartre emerged as a full-fledged ontologist of human existence, after the war to be reviewed and commented on by the world's leading philosophers from Bertrand Russell to György Lukacs. *L'Etre et le néant* would generally be associated with Sartre's 1946 attempt at a simplified restatement of his central doctrine, *L'Existentialisme est un humanisme,* the arresting and thorough presentation of atheist existentialism—as opposed to Kierkegaard's or Gabriel Marcel's Christian existentialism. *Being and Nothingness* says that human existence must be seen in a constantly fleeing reality and with man himself constantly changing. Written in a dense, technical language, the treatise says that we must give our life both meaning and direction individually. We are only the sum of what we do with ourselves. To be is to choose—freely. This freedom cannot be denied or rejected; man is condemned to be free, which explains the metaphysical anxiety that makes him realize both the Nothingness he comes from and the uncertainty of the choices that allow him to aspire to Being. Those who are frightened by this truth will try to seek protection by rationalizing the world. In this the man of science is at one with the religious believer. Both are trying to escape from reality. For Sartre they are both mistaken. The world is neither as science sees it, nor as religions portray it.

Both Sartre and Beaver tried to express the notion of Other in new fiction, he in a play he wrote in a few days and first called *Les autres (The Others);* she in *La Sang des autres (The Blood of Others),* as she called the new novel.[11] "My new hero, Jean Blomart, did not insist, as Françoise

10 Jean-Paul Sartre, *L'Etre et le néant,* Paris: Gallimard, 1943; *Being and Nothingness,* New York: Simon & Schuster, 1956.
11 Simone de Beauvoir, *Le Sang des autres,* Paris: Gallimard, 1945; *The Blood of Others,* New York: Knopf, 1948.

had done in *L'Invitée,* on remaining the one sentient personality when confronted with other people," she would write in *Prime of Life.* "He refused to be a mere *object* where they were concerned, intervening in their lives with the brutal opacity of some inanimate thing." Her heroine this time was a dying woman, Hélène. Originally, Simone had not wanted to involve Blomart and Hélène with the Resistance but when she began writing the novel in October 1943 she realized guerrilla attacks and reprisals would give the underlying theme coherence and forward momentum. Ironically, the novel's publication in 1945 made it into a "Resistance novel."

Sartre was also working for posterity—on the second volume of *Les Chemins de la liberté*—but temporarily dropped it to write *Les autres.* Olga Kosakiewicz had married an industrialist from Lyons, Marc Barbezat, who also published at his own expense an elegant semiannual periodical called *L'Arbelète (The Crossbow).* Marc wanted his wife to have a thorough grounding as an actress and upon hearing how *Les Mouches* had come into existence, suggested that Sartre write a play for his wife and his sister-in-law, something, in other words, that Marc Barbezat could underwrite. The idea intrigued Sartre, especially the limitation of very few characters. As Sartre would remember it he wanted none of his three friends to have the advantage over the other and felt none of them should ever be offstage, because the actor who would be in the wings would think the others were stealing the show. He and Simone had spent more than one night in bomb shelters and he thought of a similar situation—a group of people locked up together and getting on each other's nerves.

Published in *L'Arbelète* as *Les autres,*[12] the play's definite title became *Huis clos,* the legal French term for "behind closed doors."[13] Besides a bellboy introducing the characters to each other, Sartre settled on a diabolic trio, a man and two women, each guilty of bad faith, locked up together in a drawing room in hell and becoming trapped in an eternal vicious circle. The three are the coward Garcin, the lesbian Inez and the babykiller Estelle. To while away eternity Garcin loves Inez who loves Estelle who loves Garcin . . . until that most famous Sartrian line, "L'enfer c'est les autres (Hell is other people)." "That line has always been badly understood," Sartre would tell this biographer. "People think I mean that our relationships with others are always poisoned. What I mean is that our relationships are always twisted, always spoiled and perverted. But other

[12] *L'Arbelète,* Lyons, No. 8, Spring 1944.
[13] Jean-Paul Sartre, *Huis clos,* A play in one act, Paris: Gallimard, 1945; *No Exit,* New York: Knopf, 1947.

people are also what is most important in ourselves; without someone else none of us can understand himself. The three characters are of course dead since they are in hell and I wanted the public watching the 'living dead' on the stage to realize that to surround yourself with judgments and actions you can do nothing about, is also to be a living dead. I wanted to show, ad absurdum, the importance of free will, that one action can be changed by another. Whatever the infernal circle we live in, I think we are free to break out of it. And those who don't break out remain where they are *also* by free choice. They create their own hell voluntarily. The play is about relationships that get rusty and fossilize and about freedom— freedom as a barely suggested flipside."

Sartre suggested that Camus direct *Huis clos* and play Garcin. Camus loved the theater and *No Exit* broke the ice the first time they met at the Flore. The first rehearsal took place in Simone's room-plus-kitchenette at the Hôtel de la Louisiane in the Rue de Seine, where she and Sartre had moved after a summer in central France that combined tourism with scavenging for fresh food. Those present included, besides author and director, Olga, Wanda and R. J. Chauffard, a former student of Sartre's who would play the bellboy.

The Camus that Sartre and Beaver met in 1943 was a tall, skinny and talented jack-of-all-trades who had expressed *his* turning-thirty blues that year with *The Myth of Sisyphus,* representing man as Sisyphus in hell, compelled to roll a big stone up a steep hill, but before reaching the top, the stone would always roll down and Sisyphus had to begin all over again. It is necessary to go through two stages—to accept that you live in an absurd universe and then to fight against this acceptance, Camus argued in this essay that would be translated into eighty-five languages in less than ten years. "This malaise, this incalculable letdown when facing the image of what we are, this 'nausea' as a contemporary writer has called it, also is the Absurd."

Camus was a reader for Gallimard and deeply involved in clandestine activities, engaged in the editing, printing and distribution of the underground paper *Combat.* But he was also a breath of fresh air and Algerian sunshine. Camus hated Paris, was halfway through a second marriage and made no secret of the fact that he loved his own success. The son of an Alsatian father who had died in World War I, when Albert was one year old, and a Spanish mother, the novelist-essayist-playwright-journalist-un-derground-newspaper editor had behind him a dirt-poor childhood in Algiers, illuminated only by the hot North African sun. He had been in

France only since the end of 1942, suffered recurring attacks of tuberculosis and hated the cold, rain and gloom so much that he made an inhospitable and dirty Paris, a rainy Amsterdam and a sinister Czech village images of prison and exile where pale hard bodies longed in vain for light. North Africa was a veritable "patrie intérieure" to him and his attachment was not only to the sunbaked land but to its people—not the Arabs, but the insouciant *pieds-noirs,* the "white trash" whose society lacked culture but was also without fake values. "I sometimes entertain the crazy hope that without knowing it these barbarians are perhaps modeling a culture that will give man's grandeur its true face," he wrote.[14] His tragedy was that in the long Algerian war of the 1950s and 1960s his *pieds-noirs* would be on the wrong side of history, the last French colonialists, in the end hated by the majority of Frenchmen. His personal absurdity was to feel morally responsible for Arab society without being able to belong to it, to be the die-hard "conscience-stricken paternalist liberal" when everybody who was progressive in France, including his old friends Sartre and Beauvoir, had already come down on the side of Arab emancipation. He was to die in a car accident in 1960, two years before Algeria's independence.

Sartre would remember the Camus of 1943 as "a funny guy with a streak of Algiers thug in him," afraid of wading too deep into discussions but a true friend. Simone would remember him as a great charmer, "the product of nonchalance and enthusiasm in just the right proportions." Camus had left his wife in Algiers and had become an editor at Gallimard, a job he would hold until his death. Simone let him read the *Blood of Others* manuscript and was touched by his reaction. "It's a fraternal book," Camus commented and she thought that if fraternity can be created with words, writing was worthwhile.

With decent restaurant meals almost nonexistent, Simone took to entertaining in her room-with-kitchen at the Hôtel Louisiane, helped by Little Bost and by Louise Leiris, the poet Michel Leiris' wife, who had her ways with butchers to sometimes get extra meat. Simone's table could seat eight without too much difficulty and the dinner guests usually included, besides Sartre and kitchen-helper Bost, Camus, who brought the bottles, the Leirises and Jeanine and Raymond Queneau. The Leirises, who often reciprocated with dinners in their vast Quai des Grands-Augustins apartment, were the most intimidating new acquaintances. With his shaven skull, formal clothes and gestures, Michel was more

14 Albert Camus, *L'Envers et l'endroit;* Paris: Gallimard, 1937.

Albert Camus
RENÉ SAINT-PAUL

than an anthropologist, a brilliant representative of a "literature of confession" and a former surrealist who could tell the tallest yarns about André Breton, Louis Aragon, Max Ernst and Salvador Dali. Louise— Zette, to her friends—was more than the manager of the gallery of her brother-in-law, Daniel-Henry Kahnweiler. Kahnweiler was a German national and an art dealer who, together with Ambroise Vollard, had discovered Cubism in 1913 but had never been very lucky with the authorities of his country of origin or his land of adoption. He had been in Italy when the First World War broke out and to avoid incarceration in France as an enemy alien or service in the kaiser's army had spent the war years in Switzerland. He had been authorized to return to France in 1920 only to discover his property confiscated, some eight hundred canvases by his painters, from Pablo Picasso and Georges Braques to Juan Gris and Derain. In the Second World War, the German army had got to Paris before Kahnweiler had been able to make it to Switzerland and since 1940 he lived hidden in the Leirises' apartment overflowing with Picassos, Matisses, Miros and some of the most beautiful paintings by Gris. The Queneaus were the Leirises' best friends. Raymond was a native of Le Havre, an erudite encyclopedia editor, grammarian, philosopher and historian of mathematics as well as a creative writer and a humorist who used phonetic spelling, incorrect grammar and "pictograms" to capture the flavor of the spoken language. He never showed off but minted his knowledge into a stream of anecdotes, quips and repartees while his wife fired off embarrassing home truths and non sequiturs of her own.

It was Simone's first real encounter with married women of her own age. She was a good listener and began to realize how wrong she had been in seeing the sometimes vexing questions facing married friends such as Camille, Olga or Colette Audry as individual rather than generic problems; how wrong she had been in sticking to abstractions. The war had showed her how wrong she had been back there with Olga and her Jewish friends in Rouen when she had maintained there was no difference between Aryan and Jew, but she had not felt there was a specifically "feminine condition." Now she met a number of women who, in different circumstances and with various degrees of success, all had the identical experience of being their husbands' wives—dependent individuals. Her own situation was very different from that of Jeanine Queneau, Zette Leiris or Simone Prévert, but she began to take stock of the difficulties, deceptive advantages, traps and obstacles that most women encounter in marriage. "I also felt how much they were both diminished and enriched by this experience," she would write in *Prime of Life* about her first reflections on the feminine condition. "The problem didn't concern me directly, and as yet I attributed comparatively little importance to it; but my interest had been aroused."

The Leirises knew everybody and, at the Flore one evening, introduced Sartre and Beaver to Picasso and Dora Maar, his tall Yugoslav companion who always came in with their equally tall dog. A little later when Picasso had written *Le Désir attrapé par la queue* (*Desire Caught by the Tail*), a playlet in the 1920 avant-garde vein, and Leiris proposed a public reading of it, Camus directed it, Sartre played Round Head, Dora Maar was Fat Misery, Leiris Big Foot and Simone The Cousin. Picasso brought along an enormous chocolate cake and Simone met the psychiatrist Jacques Lacan and his actress companion Sylvia Bataille as well as Lucienne and Armand Salacrou.

On her "evenings," Simone managed to serve bowls of green beans and heaped dishes of beef stew. They listened to the BBC and shared the anxieties and hatreds of the war, telling themselves the defeat of Nazi Germany was imminent. New Year 1944 marked the turning of the tide, they were sure. The Germans were on the defensive. They had been forced out of Africa by U. S. and British troops. Soviet armies had launched massive counterattacks and were gathering momentum all along the front while the Allied air forces had conquered the skies and were devastating the Rhineland and Hamburg. In France, the Resistance was blowing up German trucks and sabotaging rail lines.

They also talked about the future. The postwar era would be *their* battle. They agreed they couldn't help construct a postwar France hostile to what they believed in, but neither could they reimpose ideas whose time was no more. Like everyone else, they felt tomorrow should not be a return to the world before 1939 and in their talks they came to feel that perhaps an era was drawing to an end, that tomorrow would belong to America and the Soviet Union. The question was not so much to hold stubbornly to obsolete dreams as to prevent the emergence of ideas they condemned. Their relationship to the communists was of capital importance, they felt. They wanted to be effective without losing their individuality. None of them felt ready to knuckle under to party dictates, but they wondered if a coherent left was possible without the communists. What was best, to remain aloof from the postwar politics or, if need be, to join the Party?

In principle, Gallimard agreed to underwrite the cost of a new literary magazine—under Drieu la Rochelle the *NRF* was too hopelessly compromised as a collaborationist magazine even to retain the title. Sartre would be the director of the new review and they would all sit on the editorial board. Gallimard also proposed a philosophy series, with Simone, Camus, Merleau-Ponty and Sartre as its editors. In Paris, the Occupation authorities no longer plastered warning notices on walls but did post photographs and names of twenty-two "terrorists" executed on March 4. Sartre continued to go to meetings at the CNE and the Comité national du théâtre, scaring the wits out of Simone if he was late getting back from any of these clandestine sessions.

Everybody knew everybody else at the Hôtel de la Louisiane. Lise and Bourla occupied a large studio a floor below Simone and Sartre. A floor above them lived actor-singer-writer Marcel Mouloudji, a frail Parisian Arab, with his girl friend, Lola. The other residents were all Café Flore regulars.

One morning as Sartre and Beaver were walking into the Flore, Mouloudji caught up with them. He was frantic. Lola and Olga Barbezat had been arrested. The two girls were not involved in the underground but they had been picked up with friends who were. With Sartre's help, Mouloudji and Barbezat tried every approach they knew to obtain their release. They did not succeed but received assurances that neither of the girls would be deported. In April, Bourla was arrested—on one of those few nights he wasn't with Lise but sleeping at his father's place. His father was living with a blonde who at once got in touch with a German called Felix. By the time Lise learned about the arrest, Felix had promised to save both father and son for a consideration of four million francs. Bribing a prison guard, he got a note to Lise from Bourla, a few words on a scrap of paper saying they had been handled roughly but trusted Felix to see them through. One morning Felix told the blonde that all internees at the Drancy political camp northeast of Paris had been deported to Germany but that he had managed to arrange for his two protégés to be left behind. In the afternoon, Simone accompanied Lise to Drancy. In a café near the suburban station they were told a number of sealed trains had left during the night, but when they walked up to the barbed wire, they made out two distant figures gesturing toward them. Bourla pulled off his beret and waved it excitedly, revealing a close-shaven head in the process. Felix could obviously be trusted.

Before her arrest, Olga had sometimes visited a mad homosexual convict whom Cocteau had discovered in prison and whom he maintained to be the greatest writer of his age. At any rate, that was how Cocteau had described the thirty-three-year-old Jean Genet to a police court judge ready to sentence the poet, with nine previous convictions for theft, desertion, pimping and other felonies. Abandoned by his mother to the Public Assistance and branded a thief by his foster-parents at ten, his career as burglar and pickpocket had taken him around the world. He had taken up reading in prison and Barbezat intended to publish some of his poems and an extract from his novel, *Notre Dame des fleurs* (*Our Lady of the Flowers*) in *L'Arbelète*. When they read the prose excerpt, Sartre and Beaver were impressed. In May, Genet was out of prison and one afternoon when Sartre, Beaver and Camus were at the Flore, he came over and said, "You Sartre?" Genet stayed only a minute, but came back on other occasions. "Hard he certainly was; an outcast from the day he was born," Simone would remember. "He had no reason to respect the society that had rejected him, but his eyes could still smile. Conversations with him were easy; he was a good listener and quick to respond. You would never have guessed he was a self-taught person; judgments and prejudices were sweeping and he had the unself-conscious attitude typical of people who take a cultured background completely for granted."

No Exit went into rehearsal in April with a new producer, a new director and, with the exception of Chauffard, a new cast. Olga's arrest had made Sartre abandon the whole idea and Camus, too busy with *Combat,* had also bowed out, but Annet Badel, who had just bought the Vieux Colombier Theater, wanted to produce the play and assigned Belgian actor-director Raymond Rouleau to direct it. Badel double-billed the one-acter with *Le Souper interrompu,* a "Parisian" comedy by the late Paul-Jean Toulet. The premiere was May 27. Camus' date was the actress Maria Casarès, currently rehearsing *his* play, *Le Malentendu* (*Cross Purpose*), the absurdist story of a man returning unrecognized after many years to his mother and sister who have taken to killing and robbing lonely travelers and who murder him too because an old servant refuses to tell who he is. It was not the easiest time to produce plays. British and American planes were systematically bombing suburban railway yards every night, power failures were frequent, no métro ran after 10 P.M. and the number of performances was reduced. The reviews—all good—only appeared June 4, two days before the Allied landing in Normandy.

The days that followed seemed like one long holiday. Parisians were happy and expectant. But the battle was hard. It took the Allies three weeks to capture Cherbourg. Olga and Lola were released. Lise demanded that Felix get a message through to her from Bourla, but he never brought one. She persisted and asked for a certain ring she had given Bourla and which he always carried with him. No ring appeared either. She asked for the exact whereabouts of the POW camp. It took days of persistent nagging to extract the truth from Felix—father and son had been killed some time ago.

They went to the premiere of *Le Malentendu*. They had read the play earlier and told Camus they much preferred his *Caligula*. Despite Casarès' fine performance, *Cross Purpose* was a flop. During the intermission, Sartre and Beaver watched the reviewers, telling themselves that any day now these critics would be thrown out, together with their collaborationist papers. Simone had also finished a play, *Les Bouches inutiles* (*Useless Mouths*), started three months earlier, but it was hard to concentrate on writing. In mid-July, one member of the CNE network was arrested and managed to get word out that he had confessed certain names. Camus advised Sartre and Beaver to move. They stayed a few days with the Leirises—hidden with Kahnweiler and the scores of paintings—then made their way by train and bicycle to Neuilly-sous-Clermont, forty miles north of Paris where they got rooms in the combined village hotel-grocery. The BBC announced "fire bombings" of Hamburg and sabotage broke out all over the Paris area. In southwestern France, the retreating Germans made summary executions of suspected saboteurs and civilians—on June 10, thirteen hundred persons, mostly women and children, had been burned alive in Oradour; in Tulle eighty-five "refractory elements" were hanged from the balconies along the main street. On June 26, de Gaulle landed in Normandy to establish a new government on French soil.

Zette and Michel Leiris came out and spent an afternoon in Neuilly-sous-Clermont, telling them of summary executions of even uniformed Resistance fighters. On August 11, the Americans were on the outskirts of Chartres, fifty-six miles southwest of Paris, and Sartre and Beaver packed their bicycles, suddenly afraid of being cut off from Paris. The main highway was out of the question as German troops were supposedly retreating there so they pedaled furiously under a blazing sun down backroads. A few trains were still running from Chantilly. They stowed their bikes in the baggage car and chose a compartment about halfway back for the thirty-mile run to Paris. The train traveled a few miles, went through a station, then stopped. There was the roar of a plane overhead and the clatter of machine-gun bullets. They flung themselves on the floor and, when the attack was over, followed everyone else into the ditch. The casualties were all in the front of the train. As someone said, the plane had been aiming at the locomotive.

As a precaution, they checked into a hotel a few yards down the street from the Louisiane and met with Camus who told them the Resistance leaders were in agreement on one point—Paris should liberate itself. There was no power and no gas, food was unavailable—Sartre and Beaver lived on a few pounds of hoarded potatoes and spaghetti—and all police suddenly disappeared, presumably into hiding. On the afternoon of August 18, Simone saw German troops moving down Boulevard St. Michel while passers-by whispered, "They're pulling out," but the Germans were still arresting and deporting people and the swastika was still flying over the Sénat. When she went to bed she thought, Perhaps tomorrow.

The next day the Préfecture de Police was liberated—from the Leirises apartment Simone saw the Tricolor fly from the roof mast. The City Hall, the Gare de Lyon and the majority of public buildings were in the hands of the insurgents. On the Pont Neuf, a detachment of Forces françaises de l'Intérieur (FFI) jumped out of a truck and fired on a German convoy. The next morning the swastika was still flying over the Sénat. Sartre was at the CNE headquarters, Simone with Zette. Camus and his men took over the printing presses and editorial offices abandoned by the collaborationists and *Combat* and *Libération* went on sale in the streets. Rumors flew that the Germans had agreed to retreat to spare the city or that they had mined Notre Dame and most of the city to blow it all sky-high. A week later, the Germans were still there.

For the new above-ground *Combat,* Camus asked Sartre to write a running commentary on the insurrection. The first piece was published in the August 22 edition. "I am only telling what I have seen," ran the first line —something of an overstatement as the eyewitness account was a pooled report of what both Sartre and Simone had seen. From August 29 on, the piece ran daily, describing the geography of the insurrection, the hopes, fears and excesses. The series ended, September 4, with the description of the crowds greeting General Philippe Leclerc's 10th Division entering the city via Porte d'Orléans and rolling down Boulevard Raspail to Montparnasse. "Never has an insurrection fraternized in this fashion with an army, never has anyone seen civilian combatants armed for guerrilla warfare and sniper action march under the same acclamations as these impeccable soldiers and their chiefs. The crowd hailed them all, half understanding the double character of this patriotic and revolutionary march, feeling all the promises contained in this extraordinary ceremony but also that the point was not only to chase the Germans out of France but to begin the harder and more enduring combat for a new order." [15] De Gaulle

[15] In *Combat,* September 4, 1944.

marched down the Champs Elysées with Sartre watching from a balcony
in the Louvre while Olga, Simone and the Leirises went to the Arc de
Triomphe. At the City Hall, die-hard Vichyites opened fire from rooftops
scattering thousands on the square below. Unlike German soldiers, Vichy
Frenchmen couldn't give themselves up; they preferred to die in desperado
suicide missions. That night at the Leirises, Sartre and Beaver saw their first
American, staring incredulously at his uniform, but the most fascinating
place in town was Camus' madhouse office. Everybody was there, from
Ernest Hemingway, who had proceeded to liberate the bar at the Ritz, to
André Malraux in a self-styled FFI uniform and Spanish Civil War-style
black beret, miraculously just out of Gestapo hands in Toulouse. Malraux
told them Drieu la Rochelle had tried to commit suicide.

Irresistibly, they were all sucked into politics.

Theoretically, the creation in 1943 of the National Resistance Council
had brought all partisans and guerrilla organizations under de Gaulle's
authority, but with the liberation of Paris—it would still be nine hard
months before the collapse of Nazi Germany—the "new tomorrow" began.
So far, de Gaulle had only had enemies to the right, the Vichyizing grande
bourgeoisie, which had largely ignored his siren calls from London for
armed uprising and open revolt. Now, however, his support shifted back
toward the right-of-center, toward that majority of Frenchmen who expected him to safeguard French society. For them this career soldier with
his general's stars and taste for authority began to emerge as the law-and-
order savior who, once the enemy had been driven from the national territory, would know how to disarm the millions of communists and fellow-
traveling maquisards.

The communists had fought hardest and suffered the heaviest in the
four-year resistance against Nazi Germany and they wanted the postwar
tomorrow to be commensurate with their sacrifices. The one million other
leftist partisans were generally anticapitalists out of indifference to money
and out of contempt for Vichy and for everything that reminded them of
prewar politics. By January 1945, two tendencies became apparent. A
number of leaders wanted to realize the old dream of a French labor party.
Others sought to bring de Gaulle onto their side through a broad-based
middle-of-the-road alliance while still others were keeping their options
open.

All of this was discussed intelligently and passionately in *Combat* as
Paris settled into its new freedom and as the Allied "drive to the Rhine"
bogged down in the fall and, by Christmas, Hitler launched his major and
carefully calculated Ardennes counteroffensive. Sartre and Beaver contem-

plated the future with some confidence. It was out of the question to return to the political insouciance of the prewar years. They hated all the little self-deceptions they had practiced before the war and agreed verbal protest was no longer enough. The thing was no longer just to *be,* but to *do,* not to stand aloof or, as intellectuals with long training in philosophy, to make abstractions or to contemplate meanings. Sartre's experience as a prisoner of war had taught him solidarity and loosened his contradictions, and the failure of Socialism and Liberty had given him a lesson in realism.

But the communists didn't like him. At the time of Socialism and Liberty, they had started the rumors that he had been freed from the Stalag in order to act as an informer. In the CNE, they had wanted unity and had accepted him, although an obscure pamphlet had blacklisted him together with Montherlant as a reactionary. A large minority of the French people were behind the Communist Party and Sartre wanted to be *with* them, but not *of* them. For one thing he was too independent; but above all, there were serious differences between him and the Marxists. To a Marxist, he was a well-meaning bourgeois because he believed in the phenomenological intuition. To him, Marxism failed to preserve the full dimension of man. He had no intention of abandoning his ideas—the concepts of interiority, of existence and of man's free choice, and he hoped communist ideologues would admit the values of humanism and indeed help him to try to tear humanism from the clutches of the bourgeoisie. He felt there was room enough on the left for sympathizers like himself, people whose role could help bridge the gap between the intellectual *petite bourgeoisie* and the Party intellectuals, people whose role would combine support and criticism.

The first months of euphoric freedom seemed to support this optimism. The communists supported the de Gaulle government with "national unanimity." Their leader, Maurice Thorez, returned from his wartime exile in the Soviet Union to tell the workers it was their duty to revive industry, to be patient and for the time being to refrain from all claims. That Camus was hostile to the communists seemed a subjective quirk of little importance since he was defending the same position as they were, and communist sympathizer Sartre totally approved *Combat*'s political line. But the communist weekly *Action,* directed by a group of young men surrounding Francis Ponge, suddenly attacked Sartre, calling existentialism a diversion from the class struggle. Ponge agreed to let Sartre answer his critics,[16] but six months later published a vicious attack by Henri Lefebvre, who feigned not to hold it against Sartre "to have been the disciple of the Nazi

[16] *Action,* December 29, 1944.

Heidegger" but accused him of idealism, of subjectivism and of being the maker of a war machine directed against Marxism.[17]

In November, Sartre got tired of party squabbling and asked Camus to send him to America as a correspondent. What he wanted, Sartre told Camus, was a new perspective. Sometimes he felt France had come out of the war a fifth-rate power and that Paris' getting through unscathed had duped them all, that they were living in the dying capital of a tiny country, and that a radical change had come with the Liberation. The exiles were coming home with fresh points of view. Raymond Aron had spent the war in London editing a French-language magazine that the Gaullists hadn't always liked. Romain Gary told stories, too, about the French in London. *L'Arbelète* published a collection of texts by unknown American authors— Henry Miller, Horace McCoy, Nathanael West.

On the stage, *Huis clos* was revived and Sartre and Beaver took their wartime novels to Gallimard, he the first two volumes of *Les Chemins de la liberté;* she *Le Sang des autres.* The Paris school system reinstated Simone, but she had no intention of going back to teaching. Her essay, *Pyrrhus et Cinéas,* came out and was well received and she began a historical novel, *Tous les hommes sont mortels* (*All Men Are Mortal*), going to the library every morning to research the story of Emperor Charles V and his éminence grise Mercurino Gattinara. Badel agreed to produce *Les Bouches inutiles* and Michel Vitold, who had played Garcin in the original *No Exit,* to direct Simone's play.

They spent New Year's with Francine and Albert Camus, who were living in Gide's apartment, and on January 12, 1945, Sartre left for the United States via military plane. He was one of six French journalists invited by the Office of War Information to report on the American war effort. To qualify Sartre, Camus had agreed to let *Le Figaro* share *Combat*'s "special envoy." Civilian mail service had not yet been reestablished between the United States and France and the only news Simone could get from him was by reading his newspaper accounts in *Combat* and *Le Figaro.* She would have loved to get out of France too and suddenly got her chance. Another returnee was her sister. During her four years in Portugal, Poupette had married Pierre Lionel, now the attaché at the French Institute in Lisbon and editor of a French-Portuguese review. Lionel invited her on behalf of the Institute to come to Lisbon and give lectures on the Occupation and Simone rushed to the cultural relations offices of the Foreign Ministry and demanded a travel permit. It wasn't easy, but everybody promised to do their best.

* * *

[17] *Action,* June 8, 1945.

Sartre loved America but for his journalistic debut committed the blunder of writing about the 1942–43 in-fighting among the Pétainist and Gaullist French in Washington and New York. The U. S. government had recognized the 1940 Pétain regime—and its Washington embassy, until the Allied invasion of North Africa in November 1942 when de Gaulle's French Committee of National Liberation became the recognized provisional government of France. After describing the hearty welcome extended to him and the five other Parisian newsmen, Sartre's first dispatch tore right into the hornets' nest. Quoting unidentified sources, he told how big business and the State Department had bankrolled *Pour la victoire,* a newssheet, he alleged, that caused a lot of harm to the French cause.[18] The next day, *The New York Times'* Paris correspondent picked up the *Figaro* story and blamed fellow correspondent Sartre for attacking the foundations of Franco-American friendship.[19] Hastily, Sartre wrote a letter to the editor, blaming the Paris *Times*man for misquoting him and reassuring the *Times'* readers that he had no intention of jeopardizing Franco-American friendship. In a later dispatch, he was back, attacking the New York Frenchmen who had backed the General Henri Giraud faction and the Pétain regime.

His crowd in Manhattan were old friends, the transplanted Montparnasse bohemia and local artists. Besides Stépha and Fernando Gerassi and his Ecole Normale fellow student Claude Lévi-Strauss, Sartre was introduced to Breton, Masson, Fernand Léger, Max Ernst and their friend Alexander Calder. The sculptor David Hare introduced him to Dolores V whose lover he became after two nights' courtship. The stranded bohemians were cautious. As refugees in a country rallying in war, their expression of politics was low-keyed and he was surprised to be told that certain American intellectuals were afraid of totalitarianism coming to the United States and even more flabbergasted when a Ford Motor Company public relations man cheerfully referred to World War III with the Soviet Union. When one of Sartre's colleagues had objected that there was no common frontier between America and Russia and had asked, "Where will you fight?" the PR man had replied, "In Europe."

The State Department had put up the sextet at the Waldorf-Astoria, where Sartre's lumber jacket and the others' equally shabby wartime clothes caused something of a sensation. Many things disconcerted Sartre, but he was moved by the crowds in New York. He felt the American people were better than the system, as he tried to say in his reports. His first piece for *Combat* said Americans had never been richer, followed by in-depth ac-

18 *Le Figaro,* January 24, 1945. Sartre's cable was dated January 22.
19 *The New York Times,* January 25, 1945.

counts of the contrasts between rich and poor, the scales of values, American conformism, the isolationism vs. intervention debate and the Roosevelt Administration's industrial reforms. One article was devoted entirely to the Tennessee Valley Authority and what it would mean to postwar social politics.

Before a flight to Los Angeles and a visit to the Hollywood war machine, they were taken to Washington and on March 10 admitted to see President Roosevelt for a brief interview. To the six Frenchmen, the dying President told of his love for their country. "What strikes you first of all is the profoundly human charm of the long face, both delicate and hard," cabled correspondent Sartre. "What is visible on the face is a kind of generous warmth, something open and forthcoming, curiously blended with the almost ferocious harshness of the jaw." [20]

Hollywood was uneventful except for a meeting with Henriette Nizan, who was earning a living writing French subtitles on Twentieth Century-Fox releases while her kids were fast becoming Californians. The visit resulted in *Combat* pieces about the unionizing attempts by the trade guilds, about war movies, Mexican filmmaking and an upbeat roundup hailing the birth of "a thinking man's cinema."

Sartre spent more and more time with Dolores but managed to write about patriotism, "new towns," the American Federation of Labor, the absence of monuments to the past and, more critically, about race. ONLY FEW BLACKS HAVE TIME FOR DREAMING ran one headline. "There seems only to be one solution to the black problem—and it won't be tomorrow—and that is for the American proletariat, black and white, to realize its common interest. All progress in America depends really on the evolution of its blue-collar workers." [21] He was in New York with Dolores on May 7, when President Harry Truman went on nationwide radio to announce victory in Europe.

Sartre returned to Paris with as much foodstuff and clothes as he was allowed only to learn that Simone had been in Portugal, that his stepfather had died, Francine Camus had given birth to twins, Drieu la Rochelle had finally managed to kill himself and Robert Brasillach, who had panned *La Nausée,* had been tried and executed for his glowing apologia of fascism during the war years. Anne-Marie was grief-stricken. Her marriage to Joseph Mancy had lasted almost thirty years. To console her, Sartre agreed to live with her. He was fast becoming, if not wealthy, at least rich enough to buy a vast apartment at 42 Rue Bonaparte, a stone's throw from the Flore. His sixty-three-year-old mother occupied the main part and he kept

20 *Le Figaro,* March 11–12, 1945.
21 *Le Figaro,* April 23, 1945.

a big room as his study although he never spent much time there. When he got a telephone installed and Cau became his secretary, Sartre had Cau spend at least half the day at the apartment, answering the telephone, replying to letters and keeping Mme. Mancy company.

Drieu la Rochelle's suicide, at the age of fifty-three, was lamentable, but Brasillach's execution, at thirty-six, was shocking. Drieu had been obsessed by decadence but also troubled by a tormented sexuality and he was not the only intellectual driven toward authoritarianism by the putrescence of prewar politics. There was no excuse for the brilliant Brasillach's unrestrained enthusiasm for Nazism, nor even his attachment to L'Action française, but his execution by firing squad—the only death sentence carried out of the Liberation purges of French writers—was deeply shocking, even to Resistance writers like Sartre, Camus and Malraux. Few authors had embraced Nazism but several had sufficiently sponsored the collaborationist cause to pay with imprisonment and ostracism. The seventy-seven-year-old Charles Maurras, who had founded L'Action française and headed prewar fascism in France, was condemned to death but pardoned because of his age. Jean Giono's anarchic pacifism led to his imprisonment for several months, while Céline's antisemitism and shadowy collaboration saw him flee to Germany with the receding Wehrmacht and, after the collapse of the Third Reich, to prison and a six-year exile in Denmark.

For Simone, Lisbon had been both exhilarating and disturbing. The government of strongman Antonio de Oliveira Salazar had offered all its sympathy and a certain amount of help to Germany, but with Hitler's defeat, it was attempting a rapprochement with France. It was as a result of this policy that Simone's lecture had been authorized. She was well paid and she went on a shopping spree and bought herself a complete wardrobe and her first nylon stockings. With her sister and her brother-in-law, she watched a Portuguese bullfight, walked in the gardens of Cintra and in a car owned by the French Institute made a trip through the Algarve, smelling mimosas and watching an ocean calmed by the soft sky, whitewashed villages and baroque churches. But Lionel's Portuguese friends saw to it that she saw more than blue skies and pomegranate trees in bloom. Only one Portuguese in a hundred had enough to eat. Most went barefoot, railway stations were invaded by beggars, little girls in rags scavenged in trash cans. Lionel's friends were all opposed to the Salazar regime and felt France was the only hope. British business had considerable interests in Portugal and the Americans were negotiating bases in the Azores, meaning that Salazar could count on Anglo-American support, which was why it was so necessary to awaken public opinion in France. One ex-minister asked her to take back a letter to Georges Bidault. If de Gaulle would help him over-throw Salazar, the new Portuguese government would cede Angola to France. She delivered the message to Bidault realizing her act was futile.

Simone returned with a hundred pounds of goods—hams, sugar and eggs, real tea, coffee and chocolate—and triumphantly made the rounds of her friends. The girls got sweaters and shawls; Bost, Camus and Vitold got checkered fishermen's shirts from Nazaré. Vitold had bad news for her. He had quarreled with Badel, who no longer wanted to produce her play. But, Vitold assured her, he would find another theater. She wrote articles about Portugal in *Combat* under a pseudonym in order not to compromise her brother-in-law. *Combat* received encouraging mail from a number of Portuguese and a sharp rebuke from the Portuguese embassy.

Through Jeanine and Raymond Queneau, Beauvoir and Sartre met Michelle and Boris Vian and Alexandre Astruc. Twenty-four-year-old Vian was a black-humorist who had abandoned engineering to play jazz and to write. His lore and his activities were wide and included pornography, singing, acting, drinking, translating, inventing gadgets and writing an opera for France's foremost composer, Darius Milhaud. Under a pseudo-nym, he had just finished a scandalous novel called *J'irais cracher sur vos tombes* (*I'll Go and Spit on Your Graves*). Michelle, a tall girl with wil-lowy blond hair cascading over her shoulders, was as fanatical about jazz as was her husband. Astruc, who was blissfully drunk and asleep on the Vians' divan the first time Simone met him, was a twenty-two-year-old movie critic and would-be cinéaste.

Sartre wrote *Réflexions sur la question juive,* a 198-page disquisition on antisemitism and Jewishness that was to remain one of his more famous essays.[22] Jewish reaction would always be less than jubilant and often de-plore his lack of experience in the Jewish dimension while at the same time applauding his lancing portrayal of the antisemite. Sartre examined the Jewish question from a phenomenological point of view and developed portraits of what he called the "authentic" and the "inauthentic" Jew, the former being a Jew who had accepted his own Jewishness without neces-sarily opting for Jewish ethnicity or religion, and the latter a Jew trying to liberate himself by becoming *other* instead of seeking his own liberation *qua* Jew. Twenty years later, Sartre would say he should have probed his subject from the double viewpoint of history and economics but that his conclusions would not necessarily have been much different.[23]

22 Jean-Paul Sarte, *Réflexions sur la question juive,* Paris: Morihien, 1946; reedited Galli-mard, 1954; *Anti-Semite and Jew,* New York: Schocken, 1948.
23 In interview with *Al Hamishmar,* Tel Aviv, 1966; translated as "Sartre on Israel and Other Matters," in *New Outlook,* Vol. 9, No. 4, May 1966.

Boris Vian

Camus was about to leave for an American lecture tour and Little Bost was traveling in Italy with a group of journalists when Simone learned that Olga Kosakiewicz had been diagnosed as suffering from acute tuberculosis. Although specialists all contradicted each other, it was ascertained that both her lungs were affected. After a painful pneumothorax treatment she was sent to a sanatorium in the Alps for what promised to be a very lengthy convalescence. Her disease killed plans for a revival of *The Flies* as neither Charles Dullin nor Sartre could imagine another Electra.

For a few weeks alone, Sartre and Beaver went to Belgium, visiting Antwerp, Bruges and Ghent, after which he took his mother to the country and Simone went on a bicycling holiday. They met in Paris on August 6 as the atom bomb was dropped on Hiroshima. This meant the end of the war and heralded the possibility of perpetual peace and also the possibility of the end of the world. They argued about it endlessly.

Before the end of August, they finished the first issue of *Les Temps modernes*. France's scarce supply of newsprint was reserved for periodicals that had been in existence before the war and "authorized" Resistance newspapers, but Simone had seen de Gaulle's thirty-three-year-old information minister Jacques Soustelle and charmed him into allocating paper for a new 192-page monthly. Sartre wrote the introduction, saying *TM*—the initials were supposed to sound like the defunct *NRF*—would not be a political magazine. It would comment on political and social events, not politically, however, to serve any one party, but analytically so as to clarify the issue and take positions: "We don't want to miss anything of our time. There may have been better times, but this is our time; we only have this life to live, in the midst of *this* war and perhaps *this* revolution." The editorial board included Simone de Beauvoir, Michel Leiris, Maurice Merleau-Ponty, Albert Olivier and Jean Paulhan. Director Sartre, as a masthead announcement said, "received" on Tuesdays and Fridays between 5:30 and 7:30 P.M. at the editorial offices at Gallimard.

Sartre was assailed with contributions and also asked to contribute to magazines everywhere—for *Vogue* in America he wrote a long piece about new French literature in general and Camus in particular, summing up *La Peste* (*The Plague*), which Camus would only publish two years later.[24] He took part in a symposium and, in an answer to Catholic philosopher Gabriel Marcel, said, "I don't know what existentialism is." The protest was in vain. By October, existentialism was the new craze.

[24] "New Writing in France," *Vogue*, July 1945.

CHAPTER

NOVEMBER 1949

SIMONE WAS TAKEN ABACK by the insults. She had not expected critics to herald her book as the beginning of a new dawn for women, but the first volume had sold 22,000 copies in one week. Why did the second volume scandalize? Why did a woman journalist Claudine Chonez say, "You have been courageous and you're going to lose a lot of friends." Epigrams, epistles, admonitions and obscene invitations flowed into the offices of *Les Temps modernes,* where she had serialized three chapters of the second part of *Le Deuxième Sexe.*[1] She was called unsatisfied, frigid, priapic, nymphomaniac, lesbian, a woman who had had a hundred abortions and was an unwed mother. Some readers offered to cure her frigidity, others to titillate her clitoris. She was promised revelations in the coarsest terms in the name of enlightenment, beauty and poetry. She could understand anonymous maniacs sending in their lucubrations, but François Mauriac writing to one of *TM*'s contributors, "I now know everything about your boss's vagina!" and in *Le Figaro littéraire* undertaking an offensive against pornography in general and Simone de Beauvoir in particular!

The critics followed set formulas. They either said women had always been the equal of men or that women would always remain inferior. In either case what she said in *The Second Sex* was common knowledge or

[1] Simone de Beauvoir, *Le Deuxième Sexe.* I. Les faits et les mythes; II. L'Expérience vécue, Paris: Gallimard, 1949; *The Second Sex,* New York: Knopf, 1952.

there wasn't a word of truth in it. She was either a poor, neurotic woman, repressed and cheated by life, or she was a shrew, envious and embittered and full of inferiority complexes toward men and resentment toward other women. Hers was "a sad life" and her book was the result of personal humiliations. She was a misogynist who pretended to advance the feminist cause while in reality damning her sisters. "The theme of humiliation was taken up by a considerable number of critics who were so naïvely imbued with their own masculine superiority that they couldn't imagine that my femininity had never been a burden to me," she would write in *Force of Circumstance*. "The man I place above all others didn't consider me inferior to men." *The Second Sex* stirred animosity among friends. Camus accused her of making the French male look silly and said she should have presented the argument that a man, too, suffered from not being able to find a real companion in a woman.

The genesis of the book was *the Other*. It was Simone's realization that education divides the sexes from earliest childhood, that society is masculine and that its gender is constantly reaffirmed as such to the growing generation. What she had realized was that she had *not* had a boy's childhood, that she had not read the same books nor faced the same myths as boys, that woman is not man's brother but a being somewhat apart, usually *promised* equality but rarely granted the status of frank companion.

Together with Sartre and Lévi-Strauss she had been an admirer of *L'Age d'homme* (*Manhood*), the first volume of Leiris' autobiography and of his acknowledgment that a writer's subject is himself and that all writing is somehow fiction.[2] They admired *L'Age d'homme* because Leiris had chosen to examine his life as a synchronous phenomenon, analyzing it in one sweep in terms of the formation of his own language instead of hacking it up choronologically. Leiris was now working on a second volume, *Biffures,* where he planned to explore further the quirks of his childhood speech and with savant elisions try to fuse past and present, his book and his life.

In 1946, the idea of writing a similar "martyr-essay" had appealed to Simone. When she had talked about it to Sartre she had imagined she would easily dispose of what it had meant to her to be a woman. She had told him her femininity had almost never counted, to which he had answered, "All the same, you weren't brought up like a boy. This is something worth looking into further." She had indeed looked deeper into the subject and abandoned the idea of a personal confession à la Leiris in favor

2 Michel Leiris, *L'Age d'homme,* Paris: Gallimard, 1939; *Manhood,* New York: Grossman, 1963.

of a broad essay on the feminine condition. She had started at the Bibliothèque nationale with research on feminine myths and stumbled over one
surprise after another. Her visit to the United States and falling in love
with Nelson Algren had given the essay a new dimension.

It was Philippe Soupault who had managed to get her to America. The
former surrealist poet, who together with Breton had invented "automatic
writing," was with the cultural relations department of the Foreign Ministry when she and Sartre had met him at the Flore in the fall of 1946.
He had told her that if she was serious about going, his department could
organize a lecture tour. During his last visit, Sartre had addressed a Yale
University audience—telling his listeners the reason tradition-mired French
authors like Camus, Beauvoir and himself admired Faulkner, Hemingway,
Dos Passos, Steinbeck and Caldwell was these authors' innovative techniques.[3] Thanks to Soupault, she had been off in January 1947, with her
plane fare paid for by the cultural relations department. In New York,
she had met Dolores, who was about to leave for Paris, where she would
stay with Sartre until Simone's return. Graciously, Simone would write in
Force of Circumstance that Dolores "was as charming as Sartre had said
and has the prettiest smile in the world."

America had been four exhausting and exciting months. The opulence,
the shop windows, the streams of neon, the bars, drugstores, cars, hairdos,
overheated indoors and the sheer size of the country had made her dizzy.
To remember it all she kept a diary, part of which was serialized in successive issues in *TM* and published in volume as *L'Amérique au jour le jour.*
Her running *TM* commentary was harsher than Sartre's 1945 reportages
for *Combat* and *Le Figaro*. Her scrutiny was more decisive. America, she
wrote, was the homeland of capitalism, yes; but it had helped save Europe
from fascism. The atomic bomb assured it world leadership and freed it
from all fear, yet American intellectuals exhibited a chauvinism worthy of
her father's. They approved everything Harry Truman said; their anticommunism verged on neurosis and their attitude toward Europe and
France was one of arrogant condescension. "From Harvard to New Orleans,
from Washington to Los Angeles, I heard students, teachers and journalists
seriously wondering whether it wouldn't be better to drop their bomb on
Moscow before the U.S.S.R. was in a position to fight back. It was explained
to me that in order to defend freedom it was becoming necessary to suppress it." [4]

[3] Address published in *Atlantic Monthly,* August 1946.
[4] Simone de Beauvoir, *L'Amérique au jour le jour,* Paris: Gallimard, 1954; *America Day
by Day,* New York: Grove Press, 1953.

New York moved her. The first night she stood awestruck on the corner of Forty-second Street and Times Square and felt "cut off from both past and future." She admired the city's geometric layout, its Mediterranean-like damp winter—until it snowed—and tasted her first martini and lobster à l'Américaine with reverence. The question, she felt, was not whether to love America. "Those words have no meaning. America is a battlefield and there is no way of not being passionately concerned with its combat, a combat whose stakes challenge all limits."

She knew Stépha and Fernando Gerassi, and Sartre had given her some addresses, but she got tired of meeting émigré Europeans and was happy when she was invited to dinner by Ellen and Richard Wright. In Paris, Little Bost had introduced her to the author of *Native Son* and the Wrights were only in New York to pack as much of their Greenwich Village apartment as possible into trunks before heading back to Paris for an indefinite stay. To listen to "real jazz," Wright took her to the Savoy, where she was about the only white person present. A *Vogue* editor organized a cocktail party for her so she could meet the local literati. The booze was poured with liberality and the occasion turned into something of a verbal slugfest. Dwight Macdonald told her the way French people loved American literature was an insult, that America's true writers weren't Hemingway, Dos Passos, Caldwell or Steinbeck, but Thoreau, Whitman, Melville, Hawthorne and Henry James. Mary McCarthy, who was at the center of sophisticated opinion but had little love for her own kind, looked disconcerted as Philip Rahv wondered how Simone dared to have a philosophical opinion when she hadn't read Confucius and Jakob Böhme. When she met Macdonald and Rahv a few days later at *Partisan Review,* they both apologized and patiently explained to her that there was no such thing as one American literature. *Partisan Review* had published a piece by Sartre on committed literature [5] and Simone discussed the possibility of further exchanges with *Les Temps modernes.* Starting with the February issue, Sartre was beginning *Qu'est-ce que la littérature?* a major attempt at defining committed writing by asking the big questions—What is literature and for whom do authors write? [6] Someone took her to *The New York Times,* where an editor in a swivel chair ironically asked, "So France is having fun with existentialism?" finding it the utmost of self-conceit for an economically poor country to pretend it could think. Mary McCarthy offered to

5 "The Case for Responsible Literature," a translation of "Présentation" [of *Les Temps modernes*], *Partisan Review,* Vol. 12, No. 3, Summer 1945.
6 Jean-Paul Sartre, *Qu'est-ce que littérature?,* definitive edition, Gallimard, 1964; *What Is Literature?,* New York: Philosophical Library, 1949.

take Simone sightseeing, an experience that proved less than rewarding for either of them. Simone wanted to try a Horn & Hardart restaurant but if McCarthy and her friends went to an Automat it would give the impression they were slumming. In general, Simone had a way of being so furiously curious as a tourist that it taxed the patience, if not the goodwill, of any native.

Simone's first speaking engagement was at Vassar—"very feminine in a kind of cottoned and old-fashioned way"—where the French department was rehearsing a school production of Sartre's *The Flies*. She had missed by two weeks the Biltmore Theater run of *No Exit,* film director John Huston's first stage production, with expatriate French actor Claude Dauphin as Garcin (Alec Guinness played Garcin in the London version). She began to notice how consular and other official Frenchmen were stiff and unnatural when compared to "important" Americans, who seemed to know instinctively how to establish a human complicity. "I find this kindness both seductive and irritating. It expresses confidence, but it is ambiguous—generosity or hypocrisy?"

After three weeks in New York, her schedule took her by train and Greyhound bus to Washington and to Wesleyan College for Women in Macon, Georgia, where the main street looked like something out of Sinclair Lewis, back north through snowy landscapes to Rochester, Cleveland and Oberlin College in Ohio, the first integrated and coeducational university on her tour; Buffalo with a Picasso exhibition, Detroit, Pittsburgh and St. Louis. Thirty-six hours in Chicago were enough to see the museum, Michigan Avenue and to meet Nelson Algren, whose phone number they had given her at *Partisan Review*.

A year younger than Simone, Algren was the bard of Chicago's skid row who had not yet written *The Man with the Golden Arm* or *A Walk on the Wild Side*. Born in Detroit of Swedish-German-Jewish parents but reared in poverty in Chicago, Algren had behind him a University of Illinois journalism degree, wanderings at the bottom of the Depression, one unhappy marriage, jobs ranging from the Illinois Writers Project to venereal disease control worker for the Chicago Board of Health, three years with the Army Medical Corps and, most recently, two years of deliberate attempts at setting his life in order. He had written his first stories from experiences as migratory worker and jailbird in the Southwest, and in Chicago he had systematically collected material from the Polish neighborhoods of the Northwest Side, making friends with derelicts, hustlers and criminals, attending police lineups for scraps of dialogue and reading local papers for stories. Out of this had emerged *Somebody in Boots* (1935), an immature first novel deliberately Marxist and relentless in building up detail, and *Never Come Morning* (1942) about the Polish milieu and one Bruno Bicek whose dream is to be a heavyweight champion and who ends up a murderer. For the past two years, Algren had settled down in an austere but clean two-room apartment on Wabansia Avenue. Under the title *The Neon Wilderness,* he had collected twenty-four of his short stories, loosely constructed slice-of-life studies and nightmarish and grotesque yarns about police quizzing, army life, prostitution, gambling and life behind bars.

The phone communication had been difficult and when Algren picked her up at her hotel, all he knew was that she was a French author. She had had no difficulty understanding Dick Wright, but when she faced Algren in a little bar across from her hotel, she missed half of what he was saying. But she was in Chicago to *see* things and he obliged. During the next two days he showed her the electric chair, a psychiatric ward, neighborhood bars where he told her everyone was a sinister character and she answered, "I think you are the only sinister person around here." He took her to a midnight mission, claiming it was time to save her soul, to a cheap burlesque show on Maxwell Street, a police lineup and the zoo. He explained American literature and why he was the only serious writer in Chicago since Dick Wright had left.

Friends in New York had showed her the Bowery and Harlem. Algren showed her Chicago's West Madison. She felt misery couldn't be more horrible. Despite the language difficulties she asked questions. He had grown up here and explained how kids, like grownups, had formed gangs. He had reached adolescence with the Depression and had hopped on freight trains and worked as a hot dog vendor and a hundred other dumb jobs. He had stolen a typewriter in Alpine, Texas, and spent five months in a jail where he had met some of the characters who filled his stories—a one-armed man who bent tobacco cans with his calloused nub, an eccentric rodeo rider charged with two murders who devised a jailhouse game in which the participants whacked each other with a belt. During the war he had been in Germany and passed through Paris and New York but not stayed more than one day. He never left Chicago really. He knew no other writers; his friends were the people on West Madison and in the tenements on Division Street.

Simone was sorry to leave. Members of the French consular service took her to an elegant restaurant and before installing her in her sleeping compartment on the train to Los Angeles, limousined her through the Loop to show her Chicago's illuminated skyline. It was almost as beautiful as

New York's but she was glad she had peeked behind the facade and told herself she would be back. On the train, she read *Never Come Morning*.

California was sunshine, lectures at UCLA and Berkeley, Henriette Nizan, now remarried, and bars that closed at midnight sharp. It was Mexican barrios in East Los Angeles, Paramount studios and meetings with William Wyler and Darius Milhaud. It was a feeling of loneliness in L. A. despite Henriette's solicitude. It was breathtaking beauty in San Francisco and industrial blight in Oakland. In April, she was back in New York, after a month-long Greyhound bus trip through enchanting New Mexico, a gloomy Houston by night, a New Orleans where no one spoke French after all, and, after Charleston, FOR WHITES ONLY seating in the front of the bus.

New York felt tame and comfortable this time. She knew how to put a dime in the funny piggy bank next to the bus driver and how to cross streets against a red light. She spent a Spanish afternoon with Stépha and Fernando in the company of Miró, who had lived several uneasy years in Franco's Spain but whose paintings Peggy Guggenheim was selling like hot cakes. Painter-writer Carlo Levi, whom Sartre and she had met in Rome the year before, came to New York and it was her turn to show someone around. Levi's impressions dovetailed with hers; he was struck by New York's beauty, "inversely symmetric to Rome's." On April 9, she attended the premiere of *The Flies* at Erwin Piscator's 48th Street Theater. Mary McCarthy introduced her to twenty-two-year-old Gore Vidal, whose pederastic *Williwaw* was a succès de scandale. He looked like Fred Astaire, Simone thought, and invited them to dine on succulent T-bone steaks.

She spent three days at Smith and Wellesley colleges and felt more and more confused about American womanhood. In Greenwich Village she had been told by American men that they found their women tiring because of American women's constant need for respect and attention and that, anyway, these women were frigid. As someone had said, "All you have to see are the kisses they endure in Hollywood movies." Clothes and dates were the only interest of the girls at the two select Massachusetts colleges. Even the few who told her they wanted more than a husband in life tried to hide their ambitions. To be interested in important questions seemed gauche at these magnificent institutions. An older Frenchwoman who had taught at Wellesley for years explained to Simone what "necking" and "petting" meant and told her that sexual initiation didn't make girls grow up, that campus love was not so much youthful passion as a protraction of equivocal childhood games. When she reached Boston and some young men picked her up at the station for her speaking engagement at

Harvard, they pointed at Radcliffe girls and told her, "They come here to marry us."

Simone's college tour ended with Yale, Princeton and, in Philadelphia, Temple University—"situated in the heart of the city, without luxury; it's a state university." A Harvard student had said, "European students are intellectuls, we're not." She could think of lots of Sorbonne students who were not intellectuals, but she felt the Harvard student's remark was singularly true, that most American students avoided brilliant university careers, that to be too good was something to avoid.

In New York, she moved into the Brevoort on East Eleventh Street—"New Yorkers don't live on Times Square any more than Parisians live on the Champs Elysées"—and began to be more selective in her enthusiasm. On April 30, Algren came to town—to receive the American Academy of Arts and Letters award for *Never Come Morning*. The prize included a thousand dollars and Simone had fun seeing him discover New York. Then he was gone again.

She went to mundane parties and sat in Washington Square writing about American femininity. "I have met all kinds, some were good housewives absorbed by the worries of husband and children, others devoted teachers; B's husband was of delicate health, and it was she who, through courageous work, kept them alive; many had a living warmth, a feminine charm that many European women could envy them. And how to compare this young writer with her ugly and generous face, her poverty-stricken youth and penchant for alcohol with that beautiful and cold novelist who has already gone through three husbands and several lovers in the course of a cleverly laid-out career? That American women are not yet equal to their men is evident by their demands. They are scornful, and often rightfully so, of Frenchwomen's servility and readiness to smile at their males and to suffer their moods, but the tension with which they twitch on their pedestal conceals a similar weakness. The praying mantis is the antithesis of the submissive harem servant; both depend on the male. The Hegelian dialectic of master and slave is verified again—the woman who wants to be considered idol is really enslaved by those who worship her. Her life is spent trying to trap the male, to keep him subjugated. True liberty is positive; older women have told me that the preceding generation had more true freedom than this generation because feminism hadn't triumphed yet. Freedom comes when you exercise it. In the economic field there are still resistances to overcome, territories to be annexed, but the battle has been won. Instead of going a step further than their elders, women today are trying to enjoy standing still, which is wrong because an end is only valid if it is a point of a new departure." [7]

She was at the end of her long sojourn. Friends took her to see a futuristic ballet and the Wrights organized a farewell soirée and took her to dinner in Harlem when she got a letter from Sartre asking her to postpone her return because Dolores was staying another ten days in Paris. Simone felt silly. Algren had invited her to come to Chicago. She hesitated, then picked up the phone. Yes, he would be happy to see her.

He was at the airport when she landed. They spent a long, awkward day and evening of embarrassment, impatience, misunderstanding and fatigue in restaurants and bars. Late that night they became lovers.

Seven years later she would spread the three days with Algren over twenty moving pages of *Les Mandarins,* her most famous novel:

> He was naked, I was naked and I felt no uneasiness. His eyes could not hurt me; he didn't judge me. From the top of my head to my toes, his hands learned me by heart. Again I said, "I love your hands."
> "You love them?"
> "All evening I wondered whether I would feel them on my body."
> "You will feel them all night," he said.
> Suddenly he was neither awkward nor modest. His lust transfigured me; I who for so long had had no taste, no form, I again possessed breasts, a belly, a sex; flesh. I was nourishing like bread, I had smells like earth. It was so miraculous that I didn't think of measuring time or place. I only know that when we finally drifted off, one could hear the feeble trills of dawn.[8]

He called her "My little Gauloise" and on the last evening when they were on the banks of Lake Michigan and saw a shooting star, said, "Make a wish." She would be back. But it was out of the question to question the life she had built with Sartre for twenty years. She told him her life was permanently fixed in Paris; he believed her without really understanding what she meant.

Was it possible to reconcile fidelity and freedom? Fifteen years later, she would ask herself that question in *Force of Circumstance:* "Often preached, rarely practiced, complete fidelity is usually experienced by those who impose it on themselves as a mutilation; they console themselves by sublimations or by drink. Traditionally, marriage used to allow the man a few 'adventures on the side' without reciprocity; nowadays, many women have become aware of their rights and of the conditions necessary for their

---

[7] Beauvoir, *L'Amérique au jour le jour.*
[8] Simon de Beauvoir, *Les Mandarins,* Paris: Gallimard, 1954; *The Mandarins,* Cleveland and New York: World Publishing, 1956.

happiness—if there is nothing in their own lives to compensate for masculine fickleness, they will fall prey to jealousy and boredom. There are many couples who conclude more or less the same pact as Sartre and myself —to maintain throughout all deviations from the main path a 'certain fidelity.' *I have been faithful to thee, Cynara, in my fashion.* Such an undertaking has its risks. It is always possible that one of the partners may prefer a new attachment, in which case the other partner will consider himself or herself unjustly betrayed. In place of two free persons, a victim and a torturer confront each other." When *The Mandarins,* dedicated to Algren, made the affair famous and *Time* magazine tracked him down for *his* view, he shut up but in 1963 said that to publicize a relation existing between two people was to destroy it: "It shows the relationship could never have meant a great deal in the first place, if its ultimate use has so little to do with love. It becomes something else. See, the big thing about sexual love is it lets you become her and lets her become you, but when you share the relationship with everybody who can afford a book, you reduce it." [9]

When she reached Paris May 20, Dolores was still there and Sartre in a mess. Before leaving New York, Dolores had written that she would do everything to make him ask her to stay. He had not asked her and she now wanted to stay at least until July. She had been friendly to Simone in New York when they had been ships passing in the night. Now, the situation was becoming sticky.

Simone went to live in a little hotel near Port Royal in the Chevreuse Valley on the southern outskirts of Paris. Sartre practiced shuttle diplomacy. When he was with Beaver, they went for long walks along the paths Jean Racine had used two and a half centuries earlier. Certain nights he went into Paris to be with Dolores, but on nights when he stayed in Port Royal he received dramatic phone calls. Dolores could not accept that he would let her return to America and not see her for months on end. He felt guilty.

He had warned her that sharing his life with her was out of the question, but by saying he loved her, he gave lie to his own warning. "It was normal for M to think that things would change," Beaver would write in *Force of Circumstance.* "Her mistake was to take Sartre's profound convictions for mere verbal precautions. He had misled her insofar as he had not been able to make her understand his convictions and she, on the other hand, had not told him when she began the liaison that she might reject its limits. Perhaps he had been thoughtless in not having realized this. His excuse was that, while refusing to alter his relationship with me, he cared

[9] H. E. F. Donohue, *Conversations with Nelson Algren,* New York: Hill & Wang, 1963.

deeply for her and wanted to believe some sort of compromise was possible."

Their problems were not only amorous. Politically, friends both to the right and to the left turned on them, and their most recent works were greeted with hostility and, perhaps worse, indifference. Although it ran through fifty performances, *Les Bouches inutiles* had been less than a success. "This isn't theater at all," Jean Genet had told her during dress rehearsals, a verdict the critics had confirmed, and her novel, *Tous les hommes sont mortels* (*All Men Are Mortal*), also proved a critical and popular failure. If Blomart in *Blood of Others* had believed himself responsible for everything, her sixteenth-century hero in *All Men Are Mortal* was a pessimistic sketch of impotence and the waste of human life.[10] Renaming Mercurino Gattenara, Charles V's éminence grise, Fosca, she had created an Italian nobleman who drinks an immortality potion. Her point was to prove that immortality is meaningless because any individual would see his own projects ruined. The book is a grim portrait of the end of the Middle Ages, with its chaotic wars and economy, its useless rebellions and futile massacres—reflecting Beauvoir's own postwar view that the deaths of most if not all the Resistance fighters had been, if not in vain, at least of little importance and that she would have to accept that these lives must have had their justification, even if she and others could not hope always to remember. As a counterpoint to Fosca, she had created Régine, who wants to inhabit his immortal heart in order to become unique, but who crumbles. All her enterprises and her virtues conceal merely an absurd effort to exist, identical with the effort of everyone else. With terror Régine sees her life degraded into a farce before she sinks into madness. The critics talked about longueurs and called *All Men Are Mortal* an ingenious and often amusing book, which nevertheless remained a thesis novel.

The first three volumes of Sartre's *Les Chemins de la liberté* were judged a disappointment.[11] September 1938 and the "phony war" were long ago.

The ambitious work of fiction is the story of a group of people caught between individualism and collectivism. Mathieu goes in the direction of commitment, but his impulses toward individualism are as energetically

---

[10] Simone de Beauvoir, *Tous les hommes sont mortels,* Paris: Seuil, 1946.
[11] Jean-Paul Sartre, *Les Chemins de la liberté.* I. *L'Age de raison;* II. *Le Sursis,* Paris: Gallimard, 1945; III. *La Mort dans l'âme,* Gallimard, 1949; *The Roads to Freedom.* I. *The Age of Reason;* II. *The Reprieve;* III. *Troubled Sleep,* New York: Knopf, 1950 and 1951.

and sympathetically described as his appetite for political cohesion. In the 309-page *Age of Reason,* Sartre constructs a plot which takes successively the point of view of Mathieu, Boris and Daniel, caught in the problems of their personal lives. Unaware of the threatening war, they seek their choices in ways that are as many dead-end streets. In the 350-page *Reprieve,* the focus changes. We are now after Munich and sliding toward war. The number of characters increases and the Left Bank locus of *The Age of Reason* explodes. In a Dos Passos-like "simultaneity," characters scattered across the world are united in the same sentences, giving the effect of atomized individuality and labyrinthine consciences. With the third volume, the 293-page *Troubled Sleep,* the technique shifts again as Sartre tries to give a global view of the 1940 defeat.

The diversity of techniques and profusion of characters demanded a last volume that would be both moral conclusion and formal synthesis. But Sartre was now in the postwar era and—like Simone in *All Men Are Mortal*—disappointed by the thwarted expectations and broken promises of the Liberation. Logically, he could only engage Mathieu and the others in the Resistance, but seen in a 1947 perspective, the collaborator vs. Resistance fighter choice seemed oversimplistic.

In *TM* Sartre would publish *Drôle d'amitié,*[12] an excerpt of the fourth volume, which he planned to call *La Dernière chance.* He would never finish it, but in a 1959 interview would say the wartime choice was, in retrospect, painfully banal. "Today—and since 1945—the situation has become more complicated. You need less courage perhaps in order to make choices, but it is more difficult to choose. I cannot express the ambiguities of our time in a novel that takes place in 1943. This unfinished work bothers me, however. It's hard to begin another one when this one isn't finished." [13]

As an epic retelling of France's descent into the self-disgrace of defeat and Vichy and as a symbol of man's desperate need to imprison himself, *Les Chemins de la liberté* would grow in stature over the years. French anthologists would say that the huge unfinished work evoked a phase during which the individual was aware of his historical responsibility but no longer powerful enough to *make* history.[14] *Funk & Wagnalls Guide to Modern World Literature* would call it "one of the most outstanding

---

[12] *Les Temps modernes,* No. 49, November 1949.
[13] "Deux heures avec Sartre," interview with Robert Kantners, in *L'Express,* September 17, 1959; translated as "The Theater," in *Evergreen Review,* Vol. 4, No. 11, January–February 1960.
[14] *La Littérature en France depuis 1945;* Jacques Bersani, Michel Autrand, Jacques Lecarme, Bruno Vercier, eds., Paris: Bordas, 1970.

works of fiction of the century . . . and a demonstration of the fact that a masterpiece need not be innovative in form,[15] and the *Penguin Companion to European Literature* would say "the novels are brilliant in conveying the ambiguities of human choice, as they are at conjuring up the disquieting profusion of nature, the body's secret chemistry and the melancholy poetry of the urban scene." [16]

Dolores left—with Sartre accompanying her to Le Havre for her embarkation aboard a transatlantic liner—and instead of going to Cannes for the premiere of *Les Jeux sont faits* (*The Chips Are Down*), Jean Delannoy's film of the first script Sartre had written for Pathé in 1943, Sartre accepted an invitation to go to London for the British premiere of *The Victors* and *The Respectful Prostitute*. Simone came along. The director told them they would have a surprise. Indeed, he had cut out one whole act. On the night of the premiere, Rita Hayworth made a universally observed entrance.

Paris was sweltering and before Beaver returned to see Algren in Chicago, she and Sartre cooled off on a Scandinavian trip. In Copenhagen, Sartre was so quiet Simone feared a depression similar to the 1935 hallucinatory psychosis, but after Stockholm as they continued north to beyond the Polar Circle, his mood improved. By boat they reached a Lapp village surrounded by vast forests and lonely mountains. When they climbed one of the mountains and saw perpetual snow at 4,500 feet they were disturbed by the finitude of human life. "Even Sartre, less sensitive than I to the loneliness of things, was moved; that snow-capped landscape with its motley of stones where dusk melted into dawn would go on offering itself when our eyes had deserted it forever."

In mid-September, Simone flew to Chicago. The moment she looked Algren in the eyes, she felt she had been right in coming back.

On September 19, Sartre attended the Paris premiere of *Les Jeux sont faits*. Starring Micheline Presle and Marcello Pagliero (de Sica's *Bicycle Thief* hero) and featuring an imposing cast that included Dullin and Mouloudji, the picture was a critical and popular hit. The story has two people meet in a Sartrian limbo where they decide they are made for each other and are allowed to return to earth if, within twenty-four hours, they

[15] *Funk & Wagnalls Guide to Modern World Literature*, Martin Seymour-Smith, ed., New York: Funk & Wagnalls, 1970.
[16] *The Penguin Companion to European Literature*, Anthony Thorlby, ed., New York: McGraw-Hill, 1969.

In Stockholm in 1947
KEYSTONE

Screenwriter and leading lady, Micheline Presles,
at the shooting start of Les Jeux sont faits
RENÉ DAZY

have demonstrated that they are really in love. They die again when she
cannot forget her sister's plight and he abandons her to save his comrades
from the folly of a foredoomed uprising—thus affirming the existentialist
thesis that man is the sum of his acts and exists only insofar as he fulfills
himself.

During the fall of 1947 the existentialist craze reached high fashion.
For men the correct attire for a soirée of pub crawling in St.-Germain-des-
Prés included a black turtleneck; the feminine dress *de rigueur* was a
black fourreau, which Christian Dior called "le sack look." The Tabou in
the Rue Dauphine was the most famous existentialist boîte. Anne-Marie
Cazalis, who together with Boris Vian belonged to the St.-Germain-des-
Prés subculture, was the *patronne* at the Tabou. *Samedi Soir* had a financial
interest in the nightclub and gave it a torrid buildup, with unending
streams of stories about the habitués, the writers, starlets and VIPs who
pushed and shoved for room to listen to Vian at the piano or New Orleans-
style jazz records. Boris had just published *L'Automne à Pékin,* a poetic
fable charged with violence and fantasy, and *L'Ecume des jours,* a moving
love story that included portraits of Sartre and Beaver. The high priestess
of Le Club St.-Germain-des-Prés was young Juliette Greco, a raven-haired
singer with kohl eyes and a throaty voice, who belted out Vian's and
Mouloudji's *tristesse* with a magnetism that had men go weak in the knees
and women think they were la Greco. Sartre had only been in the Tabou
twice, but gossip columns called him the "grand priest" of nocturnal Left
Bank vice. Didn't he proclaim life to be absurd? Didn't his followers live
for nothing more than a good time? At a dinner, returnee publisher Pierre
Lazareff vowed that in taking over *France-Soir* he would not only make it
France's biggest evening paper, he would also have "existentialism's
scalp." But to demolish Sartre, Lazareff would have to talk about him,
so much so that the press was creating the publicity it was accusing Sartre
of seeking.

Sartre and Camus had had their differences, but they both believed existentialism could be a rational third choice between polarizing anticommunism and communism. After two months in office, Charles de Gaulle had
resigned in January 1946 as head of an all-party coalition, which had
included communists in the cabinet—and, as Secretary for Information,
André Malraux. De Gaulle had seen prewar party squabbling reappear
and his resignation, he hoped, would be a shock treatment. The country
would be frightened and he would be called back and then make his conditions—an American-style strong executive and a weakened legislative.
But the country had not fallen apart and it would be another twelve years

before France, on the brink of civil war over the disastrous Algerian adventure, would call back the tall general.

Instead, France had settled into the prewar pattern of waltzing governments, which ruled with razor-thin majorities and shaky coalitions and were overthrown by the confused and fickle National Assembly when they didn't resign themselves in order to reshuffle their ministers and maintain precarious parliamentary majorities for a few more weeks. The Stalinist coup in Czechoslovakia and the Berlin Blockade, which sent the Iron Curtain clanging down in the middle of Europe, polarized the country—and its intellectuals. To the right of the existentialists Malraux believed the continent was living its final Wagnerian twilight before monstrous empires would carve it up. On the communist left, Louis Aragon and his wife, Elsa Triolet, called Malraux a turncoat and false prophet who had betrayed his past and, by joining de Gaulle, become a fascist. In April 1947, de Gaulle had formed Le Rassemblement du peuple français (RPF), in the mind of its leader not so much political party as rallying point for national energies. The demographic breakdown of the RPF membership was 80 percent workers, small businessmen and civil servants, but the party cadres belonged to traditional right-of-center politics and even embarrassed Malraux, who considered himself de Gaulle's leftist flank. A month later, the communists had joined the opposition.

There was not much room for third choices, especially since the communists ruthlessly hammered home the point, "If you are not one of us, you are against us." If over the next years the RPF would eventually sustain a violent anticommunism and the French Communist Party call everyone else a fascist, Sartre and his "third choice" friends were not spared. The Communist Party called him a slimy viper, an agent of Uncle Sam, a scatological novelist and grand priest of a philosophy that puts man back on all fours. "You are preventing people from coming to us," Party ideologue Roger Garaudy told Sartre. And Elsa Triolet, "You are a philosopher and therefore an anticommunist." The most ludicrous attack had appeared in *Pravda* in January. "Existentialism, from the French: existence, teaches that all historical processes are absurd, all morality falsehoods," wrote D. Zaslavsky, calling existentialism "a nauseating and putrid concoction which bourgeois publicity tries to pass off as the newest and most original expression of philosophical fashion." [17]

Sartre took it all on the chin. Even if all dialogue seemed impossible, he could not imagine a left without the communists and wavered on whether to plunge in and actually create a political party or try to answer

[17] *Pravda,* January 24, 1947; translated and reproduced in *Les Temps modernes,* May 1947.

the communist attacks. In April, Arthur Koestler had tried to reconcile Sartre and Camus with Malraux. Sartre and Beaver had had an "undulating acquaintanceship" with Koestler since the Hungarian-born British author had hit Paris with *Darkness at Noon*. The French translation of this novel about an old-guard communist falling victim to Stalin's purges had become a postwar phenomenon in France and broken all French publishing records. Koestler—who would appear as Scriassine in *The Mandarins* —was the real anticommunist crusader, telling anyone who cared to listen that the world's most formidable war machine, the Red Army, was less than a hundred and seventy miles from France's border in its East German zone, but when he had asked Camus, Sartre and Beaver to come and meet Malraux, none of them had said No. Camus had begun the conversation and stumbled over the word "proletariat" and a nervous Malraux had cut him off, asking for a precise meaning of the term. Camus had become nervous and fluffed his definition. Sartre had gotten angry and Koestler's self-imposed peace mission had ended in failure.

Simone spent two weeks with Algren in Chicago and came back with stories of anticommunist hysteria sweeping the United States. A former Marxist like Algren was in danger himself, but he was keeping his head down and writing *The Man with the Golden Arm,* a novel about drug addiction. Simone read the first draft, typed on yellow paper and covered with deletions.

Algren asked her to stay with him for good and she explained it was not possible. They parted less sadly than in May, however, because they agreed she would return the following spring. Together they would make a trip that would last several months and include Mexico.

Unexpectedly, Sartre was given a chance to speak up on national radio. As France prepared to go to the polls in local elections—the first election in which de Gaulle's new RPF would test its voter strength—Lucien Bonafé, a former teacher colleague of Sartre active in the Socialist Party, got the state radio to offer Sartre a weekly broadcast, to be called "La Tribune des Temps modernes." Sartre accepted and, together with the *TM* team that included Simone, Bonafé, Merleau-Ponty and J. B. Pontalis, prepared six round-table discussions and a political sketch that were broadcast during October and November. During the election campaign, de Gaulle and his "delegate in charge of propaganda," Malraux, hammered home the need to defy communism and to rally to the defense of the republic. "Marxism is not to our left, it is to the East!" thundered Malraux. On election day, the RPF polled 37 percent of the popular vote (the highest percentage it would ever get).

Sartre and his team opened the first "Tribune des Temps modernes" broadcast with an appeal to listeners to reject the two-bloc Cold War dichotomy. On the air, Sartre said that to become part of either would aggravate the conflict between them. In their October 20 round table, Sartre, Beauvoir, Merleau-Ponty, Pontalis and Bonafé, with R. J. Chauffard playing a fictitious Gaullist, savaged the RPF. Sartre denounced the Gaullists for believing in the inevitability of World War III, Merleau-Ponty criticized the party platform, Simone wondered whether Malraux's "leftist flank" of the general could be said to be honest, which brought Bonafé to violently attack de Gaulle and to compare the general with Hitler. After an appeal for moderation by Sartre, Pontalis talked about de Gaulle's hauteur and scorn for the masses.

The broadcast provoked immediate anger. While a bemedaled group of former Gaullist Resistance fighters combed the Tabou and the Flore looking for Sartre to beat him up and former *TM* contributor and now RPF activist Albert Olivier called the members of the round table "virtual fascists," Malraux went straight to septuagenarian Gaston Gallimard with an ultimatum—either Gallimard dropped publishing *TM* or Malraux would quit, and with him would go Gide and most of the elder star authors of the house. The matter was settled in twenty-four hours. Sartre would remain a Gallimard author, but *TM* would go—eventually to the sponsorship of René Julliard, an up-and-coming publisher who would make his name and fortune by discovering Françoise Sagan.[18]

Two weeks after the de Gaulle broadcast, "La Tribune des Temps modernes" examined communism. The attack was moderate, but party member Pierre Hervé hit back savagely. Next, the *TM* team recorded a conversation with David Rousset, who had been a Trotskyite and had survived German deportation. Rousset, who sported a black eye patch and had gained back his prewar corpulence, was just back from a visit to Berlin and telling how the city was fissuring into "Western" and Soviet sectors. They prepared a broadcast on what conservatives called "the sordid materialism" of the masses, when on December 3, Christian Democrat Robert Schumann formed a coalition government and "La Tribune des Temps modernes" was canceled.

Sartre and Beaver spent Christmas and New Year's at Madame Morel's in Nantes. They suspected she had voted RPF, but for old times' sake

[18] See Axel Madsen, *Malraux,* New York: Morrow, 1976.

they attached no more importance to her political opinions than she to theirs. The atmosphere in the big country house was soothing and Sartre began writing *Les Mains sales* (*Red Gloves*), his first full-length play, while Simone returned to her essay on womanhood.

In February 1948, they were in Berlin, attending the German premiere of *The Flies*. "I felt uneasy getting on the train," Simone would write. "The idea of seeing Germans and talking to them was painful. But there it was! I had been taught, once, that to remember is to forget; time passed for everyone, for me as well. As soon as I set foot in Berlin I found my bitterness disarmed. Everything was in ruins; so many cripples and so much poverty. Alexanderplatz, Unter den Linden, everything was destroyed. Huge stone doorways without doors opened on to kitchen gardens, balconies dangled from facades of buildings that were nothing but facades."

The Flies was staged in an expressionist style; Apollo's temple looked like a bunker. Simone didn't find the play particularly well acted, but the audience applauded "because the play urged them to rid themselves of their guilt." When Sartre met director Jürgen Fehling and consented to an interview, he said that what *Les Mouches* had meant to occupied Paris in 1943 might also apply to occupied Berlin of 1948. "The question is not to find out why we are free, but what are the roads of freedom, and there we agree with Hegel when he says that no one can be free as long as all people aren't free. Our concrete, contemporary goal is threefold—to free man individually, which means realizing our total freedom and combatting everything that limits this freedom, to free man artistically, that is, to facilitate the communications of liberated men through works of art and, finally, the political and social liberation, the liberation of those who are oppressed, to liberate people from other people." [19]

Newspapers in the Soviet sector denounced *The Flies* for its alleged "antihumanism." When Sartre and Beaver were invited to lunch at a Soviet club, the Russian hosts thawed only slightly. Sartre was placed between a Russian officer's wife and a German lady who asked him to sign one of his books for her. He did so and turned to his Russian neighbor, saying, "I guess you find it silly, writing dedications in books." Not at all, she replied, tearing off a piece of the paper tablecloth for him to sign, but her husband gave her a meaningful look from across the table and she crumpled it up.

*   *   *

[19] "Jean-Paul Sartre à Berlin: Discussion autour des Mouches," in *Verger*, Baden-Baden and Paris, Vol. 1, No. 5, 1948.

Was there *any* choice except idealism and dialectic materialism? Rousset and several other socialist politicians had thought so and created Le Rassemblement démocratique révolutionnaire (RDR), a more middle-of-the-road party than its fiery name indicated. In February, they asked Sartre, Camus, Merleau-Ponty and André Breton to join in an appeal in favor of peace and a neutral and socialist Europe. On successive Saturdays they all met, and arguing every word and every comma, hammered out an appeal calling for a Europe united in peace. "It is not Europe that the Soviet Union fears but America's politics in Europe; it is not Europe that the United States fears, but the Kominform influence on European masses," they reasoned.[20] The group fell apart over capital punishment—with Camus and Breton demanding its abolition and the others feeling they could only back abolition as a political expediency—but Rousset asked Sartre to join the RDR executive committee. He accepted and for the next year devoted much time and energy to the party.

Sartre and Camus were drifting apart—Camus eventually to occupy a position midway between Malraux and Sartre in Cold War politics, while Sartre tried to stand still until he realized that the RDR corresponded to no viable political reality and, in 1952, tried to mend his fences with the communists. Both Sartre and Camus were horrified and fascinated by Stalin's Russia and both put great store in Yugoslavia's breakaway from Moscow. Both refused to subjugate their humanism to historical catastrophe, but Camus was seeking a humanism that would resist history and all forms of totalitarianism, while Sartre was trying to sketch a humanism that could espouse the forms of history and its more violent interludes. Their disagreement in the early 1950s would be central to modern literature insofar as modern literature is a literature of a divided left. From 1948 on, the pulsating life of existentialism, its internal problems and polemics, would increasingly be preoccupied with communism and the Soviet Union as Sartre in *Les Mains sales* (literally, The Dirty Hands) and Camus in *Les Justes* (*The Just Assassins*) questioned violence and the relationship between politics and morality, between revolt and revolution.

They still had things in common. They both hated Gaullism, they both refused the Légion d'Honneur which their friends in power wanted to bestow on them, but their discussions were losing spontaneity; points of dissension were left dangling. Camus had relinquished the editorship of *Combat* and in 1948 made a long sojourn in Algeria with Francine and

[20] "Appel du Comité pour le Rassemblement démocratique révolutionnaire," in *Combat,* February 27, 1948.

the twins before suffering his first smarting failure—*L'Etat de siège,* a theatrical replay of the theme of his bestselling novel *The Plague.* Yet *State of Siege* was his most dramatically effective play, in which he deliberately renounced realism in favor of the forms of Spanish Renaissance theater—lyricism, farce, monologue and choruses, singular confrontations and collective thrusts. For Diego, everything ends in failure. After the plague, law and order will again rule Cadiz and perpetuate evil, but the revolt and defiance of the young hero have shaken the grip that the scourge holds over a too submissive humanity.

Sartre finished *Les Mains sales* in March and could lean back and see what it meant to be a very hot author. In less than a month the play was premiered. Two months later it was published and eight months later it was running on Broadway. Directed by Pierre Valde and "amicably" supervised by Jean Cocteau, the Théâtre Antoine presentation had André Luguet in the role of Hoederer, the forceful communist leader, François Périer as Hugo, the young bourgeois convert assigned by the party to murder Hoederer because Hoederer no longer reflects the party line. Paula Dehelly and Wanda Kosakiewicz played the two militant women coming between Hoederer and Hugo.

Les Mains sales had its origins in a cease-fire incident during the Liberation of Paris and in the difficulties some of Sartre's students had had with the communists during the Resistance. The play had also been inspired by the assassination of Trotsky in Mexico City in 1940. At the *Partisan Review,* Simone had met one of Trotsky's former secretaries who had told her in detail how Stalin's agent had lived for a long time by his victim's side before killing him with an ice pick.

In an interview with *Combat,* Sartre said Hoederer represented revolutionary realism and Hugo revolutionary idealism and that he refused to take sides because a good play "should ask questions, not solve them." [21] The reviews were predictable, with the moderate and conservative press waiting for *L'Humanité*'s Guy Leclerc to call Sartre a "hermetic philosopher, a nauseating writer, a scandalous playwright and a third-class demagogue" before hailing *Les Mains sales* as an indictment of Stalin's methods and crimes. The play was a smash hit and ran uninterrupted at the Antoine from April 2 through September 20.

The Broadway version was a mess. As adapted by screenwriter Daniel Taradash and directed by Jed Harris (fresh off *The Heiress*), *Red Gloves* was completely changed to accommodate Charles Boyer as Hoederer (with John Dall playing Hugo). Three scenes disappeared altogether, prologue

[21] *Combat,* March 31, 1948.

and epilogue were cut by one third, apparently because Hoederer wasn't in them, and a whole speech was inserted about the assassination of Abraham Lincoln. When friends in New York notified Sartre, who in turn alerted his theatrical publisher, Nagel, producers Jean Dalrymple and Gabriel Pascal would not airmail a copy of the Taradash version. Instead, they wired back, "What are you worried about? You are making lots of money." [22] When Sartre publicly denounced the American production, which opened at the Mansfield Theater December 4, Dalrymple stabbed back. "If it is a vulgar common melodrama and an anticommunist tirade, then it is only so because that is the way Sartre wrote it," she told a news conference. "There is something endearingly absurd in Sartre's rather ungracious attitude toward his success in America. Is it modesty?"

Taking the brouhaha into account in reviewing the play, *New York Times'* Brooks Atkinson nevertheless called *Red Gloves* "a tiresome piece of work, redeemed only by the acting of Boyer and John Dall." [23] But *Theater Arts'* Roderick MacArthur flew to Paris to go over the original and the adaptation with the author.

"We sat down with the script and went through it line by line," MacArthur reported. "It looked as though it were still in a state of flux—some pages mimeographed, others typed by hand, large sections cut or changed with a fountain pen. 'There's nothing at all left of Joanna,' said Sartre. She had, incidentally, been named Olga in the original version. 'Now she says stupid things to Hugo, like: *You remember that night you stayed at my house after the others had gone?*' We went on to look at Party Boss Hoederer, the role played by Boyer. 'Here,' said Sartre, laughing, 'I can see what motivated their changes. Instead of a bomb wounding the liberal leader (called a Social Democrat by Taradash), it's Hoederer who gets it —so M. Boyer can wear a bandage in the next scene. In my play Hoederer is vulgar, brutal, human. He despises the upper classes. Upon their first meeting, Jessica says: *He's vulgar*. But in this'—Sartre held up the American script—'he is perfectly distinguished, good, tender, not tough, exquisitely polite, and calls a prince *Your Highness.*' "

Sartre showed MacArthur the missing scenes and how the key idea that no one can rule innocently had been turned around: "In Sartre's version Hugo is a pure revolutionary while Hoederer insists that *We must dirty our hands*. At one point in the Dalrymple version Hoederer says, *We have to keep ourselves so clean—we have to be so pure and fresh*. I said I was

[22] Quoted in "Author! Author?" by Roderick MacArthur, in *Theater Arts*, No. 22, March 1949.
[23] *The New York Times*, December 12, 1948.

confused. 'It confuses me too,' said the author. 'I suppose Hoederer just forgot himself there.' " [24]

In May, Sartre and Beaver welcomed the creation of Israel. In an article written shortly before the proclamation of Israel, he had demanded the creation of a Jewish state, armed by the United Nations "so as to be strong enough to be respected." [25]

After a short working vacation at a country inn in Cabris on the Riviera where convalescing Olga was living with Little Bost, they were to spend four months apart, Sartre with Dolores in Europe and Simone with Algren traveling through America. Reluctantly, Dolores had agreed to come to Europe for four months, but on the eve of Simone's departure, Dolores wrote to Sartre saying that under the circumstances she had decided not to see him again. This threw Simone into a quandary. "I wanted enormously to be back with Algren but after all I had only lived with him for three weeks; I didn't really know how much he meant to me," she would remember. "If circumstances had decided for me the question would have been academic, but suddenly I had a choice. I *could* stay with Sartre and was leaving myself open to regrets that might turn into a grudge against Algren or at least into resentment against myself." [26]

She opted for spending two months in America instead of four although she didn't write Algren about her changed plans. During her New York stopover, she spent a day with Stépha and Fernando Gerassi and attended the one hundredth performance of *The Respectful Prostitute* at the Bleecker Street New Stage. She went through the first twenty-four hours in Chicago with mixed emotions. Algren took her to see a gang of junkies he insisted she had to meet, but her anxiety was dissipated when she was alone with him. From Cincinnati, they sailed down the Mississippi aboard a steamboat that took a week to get to New Orleans. They stayed at a hotel where burlesque dancers and prostitutes wandered around the corridors in housecoats and the owner, a fat, half-mad Russian woman, obstinately decreed that Simone was also Russian.

From New Orleans they flew to Mexico and Guatemala, visiting Mayan ruins in Yucatan, Indian hovels in Guatemala City. During a long bus ride between Mexico City and Morelia, Simone announced she would have to be back in Paris on Bastille Day, and was astonished to hear Algren say he was getting tired of Indians, markets and of Mexico—in *Les Mandarins*

[24] Roderick MacArthur, "Author! Author?"
[25] "C'est pour nous tous que sonne le glas," in *Caliban*, No. 16, May 1948.
[26] Beauvoir, *Force of Circumstance*.

her fictitious Algren would send a letter to his editor behind her back asking for a wire saying he was urgently needed in New York.

They returned to New York sweltering in a heat wave and spent an uneasy week together before she flew to Paris on the Fourteenth of July, uncertain as to whether she would see him again. "If I had had the honesty and the intelligence to let Algren know the limits of my stay in advance, things would have worked out better. No doubt he would have received me with less ardor, but he would have had no reason to feel bitter toward me," she would write in *Force of Circumstance*. "Even if Sartre had not existed, I would never have settled in Chicago; or if I had tried, I probably wouldn't have been able to endure more than a couple of years an exile that would have ruined my reasons for writing. Although I had suggested it to him, Algren couldn't settle in Paris, be it even for six months of the year, to write. He needed to remain rooted in his country, in the city and the milieu he had created for himself. Our lives had been shaped and there could be no question of transplanting them elsewhere. Yet our feelings were, for both of us, much more than a diversion or an escape; each of us regretted bitterly that the other refused to come and live with him."

Sartre had spent the two months working on *Troubled Sleep* and on an essay on nineteenth-century poet Stéphane Mallarmé, when Dolores phoned from New York, saying she was coming to spend a month with him. Suddenly, Simone regretted having shortened her stay with Algren. She cabled him in Chicago to suggest that she return. He wired back, NO, TOO MUCH WORK, an answer that hurt her. Work was only an excuse, she felt. While Sartre traveled in southern France with Dolores, Simone stayed in Paris.

In September, Sartre and Beaver went to Algeria, refusing to feel happy as they traveled by taxi along the Mediterranean coast from Algiers to Djidjelli, and ended up having Little Bost join them. Simone wanted to see Ghardia in the Sahara, but they only got as far as Djelfa, halfway into the desert, because the heat was such that buses only ran at night.

Between August and October, Sartre saw himself attacked and condemned from both left and right. At a communist writers' convention in Wroclaw in Poland, Soviet author Alexander Fadeyev (who would himself be condemned at the 1956 Soviet Party Congress) called Sartre "a hyena in the form of a fountain pen." On October 30, the Vatican's Holy Office put all the works of Sartre on its Index Librorum Prohibitorium, the official list of books authoritatively forbidden to members of the Roman Catholic Church.

* * *

Fame was making café life difficult and often unpleasant, and when Lola and Mouloudji told Simone about a small furnished apartment becoming available in the Rue de la Bucherie, she snapped it up and, together with Sartre, began spending her evenings there. The tiny street near Notre Dame was fast becoming Arabic and offered an unending spectacle of Algerian street fights, junk merchants, bums of both sexes and hordes of cats. But Simone liked her apartment and decorated it with mementos of her travels. She also bought a record player; Sartre was discovering Arnold Schönberg and Alban Berg. Every week she received a long letter from Algren and every week she wrote back. After diplomatic postings in Vienna and Belgrade, her sister and brother-in-law returned to Paris to rent a pretty old house in Louvecienne. In their letters, Simone and Algren agreed that he would come to Paris the next summer.

Sartre's living with his mother had turned out to be tolerable only because he stayed away a lot. Anne-Marie had made the biggest room of the fourth-floor apartment at 42 Rue Bonaparte into Sartre's study, keeping the drawing room, together with a smaller bedroom, to herself. Eugénie, an elderly woman from Alsace who helped with the housework, lived in a backroom. During the afternoons, Cau was there and Sartre liked to receive visitors in the rather elegant, if book-cluttered, study overlooking the St.-Germain-des-Prés church, the Deux Magots and the fleeing perspective of the long Rue de Rennes and Montparnasse on the horizon. Anne-Marie had had different expectations. She had imagined her son's fame translating into a brilliant social life in which she would have been very close to the center. She would have liked to have courted honors for him and he constantly had to warn her about seeing journalists. She did not approve of Simone's and her son's life-style but was deeply devoted to both of them. She often accused them of "keeping things back" and questioned Cau and their friends. What she found most deplorable was Sartre's politics.

Simone was finishing the first volume of *The Second Sex*. It was decided to serialize it in *TM*, which Merleau-Ponty was now editing practically single-handedly although they all held a board meeting in Simone's apartment every other week. Sartre was also working intensely. When he wasn't torn from his writing by politics, he was finishing *Troubled Sleep*, starting the fourth volume of the now nearly one-thousand-page *Roads to Freedom* and elaborating a "Morale" promised since *Being and Nothingness*. Somehow, he managed to lose the several hundred pages he had written during the summer on Mallarmé and started all over again.

*Simone under her Picasso
in her Rue de la Bucherie apartment, 1949*
GISÈLE FREUND

Simone in her Rue de la Bucherie apartment, 1948
GISÈLE FREUND

Rousset and the RDR demanded an inordinate amount of his time. Since he had joined the executive committee, he had written two major appeals, given twenty major interviews and attended numerous meetings. In November and December he was called upon to share the podium with Rousset at two mass rallies. The "third" European solution seemed more urgent than ever. Marshal Josip Tito had defied Stalin, but the Berlin Blockade continued and the American presidential election was waged in an atmosphere of hysteria—with Thomas Dewey asking his fellow candidates what they would do when the Red Army occupied France. Successive French governments had dropped all pretense of living up to any of the promises of the Liberation and in Indochina and Africa were increasingly repressive. In early December, the RDR organized a rally in the Salle Pleyel, where Rousset worked himself into ecstasy while Sartre, Camus, Carlo Levi and Richard Wright listened politely. Rousset delivered himself of a much-applauded diatribe against the communists but the movement was beginning to fall apart. The grass root wanted to align itself with the socialist aims of the Communist Party while Rousset was sliding toward the right because the communists were hostile to the RDR.

In January 1949, Sartre got it from the communists again, this time from Lukacs, who came to Paris to launch the French translation of his book on existentialism and Marxism.[27] In a series of speaking engagements and interviews, the sixty-four-year-old Hungarian said the works of Sartre (and Samuel Beckett) reflected a society totally devoid of a future since existential man was without links to his fellowman. When *Combat* asked Sartre to answer, he said he didn't like to conduct philosophical debate in newspapers, but since Lukacs had thrown down the gauntlet, he could only reply that Lukacs was more preoccupied with social history than philosophy, that Marxist rigidity was scholasticism in new clothes. Lukacs answered back, denying Sartre the moral right to have opinions on Marxism and, inelegantly, calling him "a mediocre academic," whereas in his book he had labeled Sartre "an authentic and first-class thinker." This allowed Sartre to fire the last salvo and to wonder why, when Lukacs had been asked to recant his pre-Marxist ideas by Hungary's new masters, he hadn't had the courage to repeat after Galileo Galilei, "And yet it turns." Perhaps, mocked Sartre, "earth no longer turns for Lukacs." [28]

Stalinism—and anticommunism—reached a new pitch during the winter. Aragon was the communists' grand inquisitor, as quick now to discover plots and to denounce adversaries as he had been open-armed and a

[27] György Lukacs, *Existentialisme et Marxisme, op. cit.*
[28] In *Combat*, January 20 and February 3, 1949.

Sharing the podium with David Rousset
KEYSTONE

magnet of goodwill during the Popular Front days of a broad leftist brotherhood. Now he wrote *Les Communistes,* a two-thousand-page latter-day *War and Peace* to justify the French communists' 1939 embrace of Stalin's pact with Hitler. The French Communist Party was isolated—and aggressive, stigmatizing heretics and smoking out deviationists as the orthodox gloried in the virtues of authority and discipline. Sartre was now labeled "an intellectual cop" and Camus "a defrocked" leftist and "neofascist," while Garaudy bunched Sartre and Malraux together as authors of "a gravediggers' literature." [29]

At the opposite end of the political spectrum, the tone was often one of sacred duty. While Claude Mauriac founded *Liberté de l'esprit,* dedicated to defending "Western values," Malraux could call himself the true left and at RPF rallies deliver extraordinary pieces of verbal apocalypse about Stalin's camps and the "Tatar hordes" less than two Tour de France bicycle laps from France's eastern borders.

It was difficult to duck the issues. One day Roger Stéphane came to see Sartre with an English translation of "The Soviet Code of Corrective Labor" and asked *Les Temps modernes* to publish it. The Code appeared, under a signed protest by Sartre and Merleau-Ponty, in the May 1950 issue, a month before the outbreak of the Korean War. But *TM* remained silent on an odd American attempt at bankrolling the RDR. Rousset had come back from a visit to the United States saying he had found a way of procuring funds for their party—the Congress of Industrial Organizations (CIO) was willing to extend financial help. Sartre didn't approve. The RDR was a European movement; Americans were free, like Wright, to sympathize with it, but not to finance it. The money offer became even more suspicious when Wright told Sartre and Beaver that the U. S. embassy had pressed him to take part in a "Day of Resistance to Dictatorship and War," for which Rousset suddenly had money.

Sartre's defense of European culture took on the hues of Beaver's feminist rhetoric when he addressed a foreign affairs conference in April. Comparing economically dependent countries with women living in a masculine society for which they were not responsible but for which they created important works, he told the Centre d'Etudes de politique étrangère that French culture could only be saved in the bigger context of European culture. He mentioned that when it came to human nature and social organization, only Europeans and not Americans were pessimists. Writers, he maintained, could not stand aloof. "If we think it can all be saved by a kind of monkish withdrawal of writers to monasteries where

[29] Quoted in *Littérature en France depuis 1945, op. cit.*

we can discourse on birds while next door battles are in progress, our culture will truly be lost, and forever," he said, adding that culture was only one element in the historical process and that total problems could only be examined in a total context.[30]

The first volume of *The Second Sex*—at a brainstorming session where Sartre, Beaver and Little Bost had tried "The Other," "The Second" and "The Other Sex," Bost had come up with the definitive title—was published in June while *TM* serialized the "Sexual Initiation," "The Lesbian" and "The Mother" chapters from the second volume, which Gallimard brought out in November 1949. Simone had spent four years on her essay and was gratified to see it become a best seller. The triumph was lasting and worldwide.

Le Deuxième Sexe is, essentially, a dialectic-materialist view of womanhood, explaining woman not as essence—mysterious or otherwise—but in terms of her situation, particularly her economic situation. Woman's enslavement and liberation are consequences of economic dependence and economic emancipation, a view that is consistent throughout the nearly seven-hundred-page work. Beauvoir's most startling affirmation is perhaps her view that woman's enslavement was a historical necessity, that humankind's progress was gained *against* woman. Divided into 1) Facts and Myths and 2) Woman's Life Today, the first third of *The Second Sex* deals with the biological, social and historical facts of womanhood. Together with the introductory notion that only women, not men, can have self-doubts, the Facts and Myths are perhaps what appears least dated to modern readers. Much of Woman's Life Today seems academic, the tone somewhat sour, as points are driven home once too often, but Beauvoir's conclusion is valid some thirty years after it was written—that men and women need to recognize each other as peers. "To gain the supreme victory, it is necessary, for one thing, that by and through their natural differences, men and women unequivocally affirm their brotherhood."

Algren arrived, loaded with Scotch, chocolate, books, photographs and a flowered housecoat. To celebrate the arrival, Michelle and Boris Vian threw a party attended by everybody from Juliette Greco to René Guyonnet, who was translating Algren and having trouble with the Chicago slang. When Raymond Queneau said something funny, Algren made a forced smile until Michelle translated. Olga charmed him by listening to all his stories with wide-eyed wonder. Most important, Simone noticed,

[30] Published verbatim in *Politique étrangère*, June 1949.

Sartre and Algren liked each other. Sartre simply never experienced sexual jealousy.

On foot and in taxi—and once in a horse-drawn carriage—Simone showed Algren Paris and enjoyed his comments. He loved the streets, the crowds, the markets. He thought all the drivers were mad, loved the food and the Beaujolais and the ceremonial exchanges of conversation in neighborhood stores. In Chicago, he said, shopping was done in silence. One afternoon Sartre rented a car with chauffeur and, together with Bost and Michelle, took Algren and Beaver through the suburbs. They ended up at the pet cemetery in Clichy. Guyonnet invited Algren to go boxing with him and Jean Cau, Sartre's secretary, fast becoming a first-class journalist. Algren loved Mouloudji's singing at the Tabou, but loved even more Yves Montand's singing at the Club St. Germain. For the first time in her life, Simone drank champagne at the Lido.

Simone and Algren flew to Rome, going to dinner and bowling with Carlo Levi. But there were too many ruins and Rome was too quiet for Algren's taste and after a stop in Naples, they flew to Tunisia and toured Algeria and Morocco before being welcomed to Olga's and Bost's house at Cabris on the Riviera. One evening they rented a car and went to Monte-Carlo to lose a little money at the casino and, in Antibes, to listen to Greco singing *Si tu t'imagines*—the St.-Germain-des-Prés crowd was transplanting to nearby St. Tropez during the summer. Algren drank a lot and danced, first with Olga and then, gracefully, with a chair.

Back in Paris, the month of September was magnificent. "We had never got on better together," Simone would write in *Force of Circumstance.* "Next year I would go to Chicago; I was certain when I said good-bye to him that I would see Algren again."

During the refueling stop in Gander, Newfoundland, Algren discovered in a magazine that he had won the National Book Award for *The Man with the Golden Arm.*

CHAPTER

VI

OCTOBER 1954

SARTRE TOOK THE TRAIN from Milan. Beaver and Claude Lanzmann drove up, stopping in Genoa and Nice. When they checked into a hotel in Grenoble, a copy of *Paris-Presse* was lying on the reception desk. Simone opened it and saw a review of *Les Mandarins*. The piece was favorable. When she phoned Sartre in Paris, he told her *Les Lettres françaises* had also come up with a friendly notice. Both the bourgeois and the communist press liked her novel, as did the noncommunist left in whose name she had tried to speak in her book. To her surprise, she was greeted with approval from all sides and *Les Mandarins* sold forty thousand copies during the first month. She would earn a lot of money. "I had no pressing need for money since I had access to Sartre's," she would write in *Force of Circumstance,* "but I'd have liked to make my contributions to our common fund."

A purse, a world view and a quarter century of habits were what they had in common in the early 1950s, the period when they were the furthest apart. Simone lived with Lanzmann, a talented journalist, militant Zionist and ardent Marxist seventeen years younger than she. Sartre was the lover of Michelle Vian, now separated from Boris. Success, politics and fear of becoming irrelevant had changed their life-style and, indirectly, their intimacy, although it was hard for them to admit it. "Oh, why aren't you an obscure poet!" Beaver would say to Sartre when she

164

The Mandarin laureate
GISÈLE FREUND

saw him stagger around his workroom. She would see him work for
twenty-eight hours at a stretch, without sleep and almost without a break.
After a little sleep he would sometimes start work again, going around
the clock once more until he gave the impression of being deaf and blind.
"I missed his old insouciance and the good old days when we had so
much time—our walks, our strolls through Paris, our evenings at the
movies we never seemed to go to anymore," she would remember. "He
invited me to follow him along his path. 'You should read this!' he would
tell me, pointing to the books piled up on his desk. He would insist,
'It's fascinating.' I couldn't. I had to finish my novel. And then, although
I too wanted to know more about the world I was living in, it wasn't a
necessity for me as it was for him."

Success hadn't so much changed Sartre as created a distance between
them that she resented. His radicalization was both the result of the Cold
War and the need not to see his work trickle away into the sand. For
Simone the end of the affair with Algren had left a void that frightened
her. With Marcel Péju, Lanzmann had joined *Les Temps modernes* at the
beginning of the Korean War when Merleau-Ponty had wanted to de-
politicize the magazine and Sartre wanted it to become more militant.
Lanzmann was an exuberant twenty-seven-year-old who assailed their
world with extravagant behavior. The *TM* contributors met at Sartre's
every Sunday afternoon. Lanzmann and Péju helped Sartre give *TM* a
more political tone. Lanzmann would say the most extreme things in a
completely offhand tone. His mock-simple humor and extravagance of
speech and manner greatly enlivened the sessions. He was the kind of
man that many women found attractive; Simone too. In December 1952,
she was two weeks away from her forty-fourth birthday when they became
lovers during a trip to Holland, where they walked along frozen canals
and sat in taverns with drawn curtains sipping *advokats* and talking.
Algren, she would write, had belonged to another continent; Lanzmann
to another generation, but he restored to her a sense of purpose, joy,
astonishment, anxiety and laughter. "His youth doomed me to being only
a moment in his life; it also excused me, in my own eyes, for not being
able to give him the whole of mine." [1]

Lanzmann's Jewishness was a deep knot inside him that sometimes
made him see *all* gentiles as Hitler's accomplices. He had grown up happily in Clermont-Ferrand, the eldest son of a working family, and only
encountered antisemitism at thirteen. The experience had shaken his world
and he had only regained his pride when his father had been one of the

[1] Beauvoir, *Force of Circumstance.*

first members of the Resistance in Clermont-Ferrand. At nineteen, Claude had himself joined the maquis, an experience that had produced in him a precocious maturity and, after the war, made him into a super Jew, weeping with rage when evoking the holocaust and beaming with pride when he discovered someone famous was a Jew. He had visited Israel and discovered that there were not only a Jewish navy, Jewish towns, fields and trees, but also rich Jews and poor Jews. His astonishment had led him to ask certain questions about himself. When he talked about it, Sartre advised him to write a book combining an account of Israel with his own story. The book was not written, but in 1973 he wrote and directed *Pourquoi Israel? (Why Israel?)*, a documentary in the vein of *The Sorrow and the Pity*. It was an intense and provocative look at Israel. He had embraced Marxism, Simone would say, because it seemed to make human conflict intelligible, redeemed the future and somehow released him from his own subjectivity.

The meaning of history, Soviet concentration camps and the question of whether there was such a thing as "progressive" violence were at the core of the celebrated split between Camus and Sartre in 1952.

The darkest year of the Cold War—which saw the United States explode the first hydrogen bomb, the American people elect a general as their president and a dying Stalin start a pogrom because his Jewish doctors seemed incapable of saving him—was the year Sartre definitely abandoned the "third," neutralist stand and, despite violent communist attacks against the screen version of *Red Gloves*, moved closer to the communists again. In the deepening chill of the Cold War, the third stand became impossible and, in a crunch, he felt he could never be against the proletariat.

The occasion for the rapprochement was the arrest of Communist Party secretary Jacques Duclos during massive demonstrations against U. S. General Matthew Ridgway and the French government's refusal to liberate Indochina antiwar activist Henri Martin as long as the communists agitated for his release. Even more upsetting to Sartre than the Duclos arrest were the jeers from the hysterical anticommunist right. Sartre had been in Italy with Michelle and immediately returned when he learned of Duclos' arrest. "I had to write or I'd choke," he told Merleau-Ponty as he furiously began the first half of *Les Communistes et la paix*.[2] Communism, he said in the first installment published in *TM*, was

[2] Jean-Paul Sartre, *Les Communistes et la paix;* published in volume in *Situations VI*, Paris: Gallimard, 1964; *The Communists and Peace*, New York: Braziller, 1968.

a necessity. To dispel any ambiguity, he wrote: "The point of this article is to proclaim my agreement with the communists on a precise and limited number of questions and to use my reasoning, not theirs." [3] If he supported the communists, he said, it was for here-and-now political reasons, not because he favored Stalinist, or even Marxist, dogma. To be against the Party was simply to hurt "in the flesh the hopes of the despairing masses."

To be an honest progressive and to endorse communism, and with it, the Soviet Union, was not easy. The postwar era had revealed the existence of the Siberian death camps, where upward of seven million people had disappeared in ten years. The *gulags* and Stalin's police state were difficult to reason away—the communists never tried; they either denied them or defamed whoever criticized the U.S.S.R.—but Merleau-Ponty, and now Sartre, tried.

Their argument was ingenious. No one could deny that the 1936–38 purges had sent millions and millions to Siberia or that the present Soviet regime looked a lot like fascism. But should the Soviet Union—the only Marxist state—be judged with a bourgeois yardstick? When one took into account the conditions under which Soviet power had struggled—civil war, capitalist encirclement, Nazi menace and war—it was no wonder that its leaders had been obliged to resort to coercion. Also, communism was no overnight undertaking. To reach the ultimate just society meant taking detours and, as Sartre had said in *Red Gloves,* "to be ready to dirty one's hands." Perhaps a certain violent coercion was inevitable, but as long as this violence was progressive, as long as it was in the *right* direction, it was justifiable. And look at the other side. When liberals argue against Stalin's "terror," they do so by invoking a kind of Kantian humanism—man is an end; not a means—but where is the individual treated as an end? Wherever one looks one sees masters and slaves, hangmen and victims. Liberalism is not better than Stalinism because behind the pious Kantian rhetoric lurks nothing but man's inhumanity to man—colonialism, imperialism, and so on. *All* politics is coercion, and, in the best possible worlds, humanism is nothing more than a sweet dream. What is important is not what a social order *is* but what it *pretends* to be. What sets Marxists apart is their concept of the future. Whereas all bourgeois states seek to perpetuate themselves—and therefore their violence—the Marxist state foresees its own future disappearance. In this perspective the Soviet Union is "privileged" because Marxism pretends to put an end to

[3] "Les Communistes et la paix," in *Les Temps modernes,* No. 81, July 1952, and No. 84, October–November 1952.

masters and slaves. Fascist and liberal violence belong to the immediate history of mankind; communist violence is perhaps no more than the childhood disease of a new era, a detour that humanity has to make in order to reach true humanism.

The argument had been put forward by Merleau-Ponty in *Humanisme et terreur* and was now amplified by Sartre.[4] Objections were voiced. Raymond Aron wondered why we should believe Stalin when he calls himself a Marxist and why the collectivization of property should be a prerequisite for reaching true humanism, indeed why only the proletariat should be able to accomplish the essential change in human relations. The Catholic thinker Gaston Fessard said the master-slave dialectic was a dead-end street since nothing prevented new slaves from rising against new masters —the continued purges of Trotskyites and "fascists" inside the Soviet Union showed that—whereas the man-woman dialectic, for example, was based on an *immediate* recognition of reciprocal humaneness.

Then came Camus.

His book was *L'Homme révolté (The Rebel)*.[5] In it he argued that for some violence to be good one would indeed have to believe that history had both direction and meaning. To accept the idea that the rights and happiness of the present generation of Russians could be sacrificed for tomorrow's perfect society, one would have to accept that the Soviet Union was the creator, in the here and now, of an Absolute. But can man create *any* Absolute? Marxists should not "forget the present for the future, man's substance for the shadow of his power, inner-city misery for tomorrow's housing project, day-to-day justice for a vain promised land."

L'Homme révolté is not so much an indictment of Stalinism as of its justifications. The actual discussion of communism as society takes up only a few pages. What interests Camus is the way Marxists deify history, that what matters is not what they *do* but what they *want* to do, intentions above acts.

Camus asks whether intentions really mean anything. He rejects all messianism, Christianity included, and says Marxist theories on the future of mankind belong to the domain of utopia and mysticism. He attacks historical determinism and condemns the U.S.S.R. because of its death camps. No ends can justify unjust means, he says, and draws attention

[4] Maurice Merleau-Ponty, *Humanisme et terreur*, Paris: Gallimard, 1947; *Humanism and Terror*, Boston: Beacon Press, 1969.
[5] Albert Camus, *L'Homme révolté*, Paris: Gallimard, 1951; *The Rebel*, New York: Random House, 1960.

to the fascism that followed the French and Russian revolutions, the "Caesarism" that "Promethean" revolutionary action invariably seems to flounder into. Revolutionaries live in a never-never land of Absolutes— absolute justice making harmony and brotherhood reign while suppressing all contradictions, hence all freedom. In reality, men cannot be reduced to their "social, rational self," that is, to a "computable object" because their interests and values are diverse. It is contradictory to talk about absolute justice and freedom although justice and liberty are by no means incompatible. It is possible to reconcile *relative* justice and liberty.

In the final chapter Camus wonders whether revolutionary ideals aren't simply unattainable and whether they don't mask real metaphysical questions. What is wrong with revolutionaries, he feels, is that they believe mankind can be *consoled,* that it is possible to mathematically reduce the world's sufferings. "Injustice and suffering will remain and however much we limit them they will never cease to offend us." He cannot believe in salvation through religion, much less in redemption through history. Marxists deify history but they "dodge" (*esquiver*) the existence of metaphysical evil. Progress may indeed be possible in certain areas but, in their *essence,* things stay the same. Man's powers are finite.

L'Homme révolté appeared in November 1951. It was Camus' first work since renewed bouts with tuberculosis and marital disappointments and he wanted desperately that his new essays be recognized as a major statement on the postwar reorientation of political and ethical priorities. But *The Rebel* lacked the lancing concision of *The Myth of Sisyphus;* it was abstract, overlong and often pretentious in its judgments. What he demanded was fidelity—faithfulness to human nature, to a pagan ideal, a sunny Mediterranean contentment that renounces all Christian, Nietzschean and Marxian notions that man must transform the world, that convulsive efforts, struggles and excesses are progressive and transcendent.

At *TM* everyone was baffled. Because of his friendship for Camus, Sartre would prefer not to review *The Rebel* and for six months sought a volunteer who wouldn't totally demolish the essay. Francis Jeanson, who had joined the magazine the year before, agreed to do a circumspect piece. In April 1952, Sartre and Simone met Camus in a little café in the Place Saint Sulpice. Camus was unhappy with the reviews that had appeared so far and made sarcastic remarks about the criticisms, apparently taking for granted that *TM*'s critique would be favorable. A little later, Sartre met Camus alone and warned him that the *TM* review would be fairly cool. Camus seemed disagreeably surprised. It was the last time they saw each other.

Sartre persuaded Jeanson to tone down his review—there was no censorship at *TM*—then ran the piece, which reproached Camus for his "refusal of history" and his moralizing and ineffectual do-gooder's attitude, with an offer to publish whatever rebuttal the author might want to make.[6] Camus' reply was injudicious. He ignored Jeanson and addressed himself to Sartre. His tone was disdainful. Camus said he was tired of receiving "lessons in effectualness from those who never managed to put anything but their chairs in the direction of history." [7] Unerringly, he hit on a contradiction in Sartre's philosophy. In order to make the Soviet Union *the* exception, Camus charged, Sartre appealed to the humanist ideal of reconciliation, but in *Being and Nothingness* that very ideal was dismissed as a chimera.

Now Sartre answered.

"The question," he wrote, "is not whether history has direction and whether we should participate in it, but, since we are in it up to here, whether we should try to give history the direction we believe salutory and not refuse our assistance, however small it may be, when it comes to concrete actions to help shove it along." [8] His statement was amplified in the same issue by Jeanson: "We don't consider Stalinism to be revolutionary, but it is the only movement that pretends to be so and to appear to be able to rally a proletarian majority. We are therefore both for and against it—against insofar as we criticize its methods; for insofar as we don't know whether revolutionary attempts are in fact obliged to make detours before resulting in a better social order and whether in the end these perverted twists aren't preferable to the total doom of revolutionary enterprise." [9]

Sartre's *Réponse* was excellent insofar as it attacked Camus' tactics. Sartre pointed out that anticommunists rejoiced when the communists inflicted sufferings rather than deploring any inhumanity. He was careful to describe himself as "not a Marxist" and point out that *TM* had not ignored the question of the Siberian labor camps. He was effective in drawing attention to a certain arrogance and egocentricity of Camus' arguments, but he was uneasy on the central question.

How could it be otherwise? How deeply could Sartre believe that history had the direction and meaning that Marx assigned to it? In 1952, his most recent philosophical work was *Being and Nothingness* in which

---

[6] "Albert Camus ou l'âme révolté," in *Les Temps modernes*, No. 79, May 1952.
[7] "Lettre au directeur des Temps modernes," *ibid.*, No. 82, August 1952.
[8] "Réponse à Albert Camus," *ibid.*, reprinted in volume in *Situations IV*, Paris: Gallimard, 1964.
[9] "Pour tout vous dire . . ." *Les Temps modernes*, No. 82, August 1952.

he intimated that man's willingness to kill his own kind was, like death, unsurpassable (*indépassable*). Such a view was incompatible with the "scientific" Marxist optimism of ultimate social justice, as were his notion of authenticity—readiness for perpetual self-examination—and his denunciation as "bad faith" of any attempt at dodging the existence of human misery. Sartre paid a magnificent—some would say subconscious—compliment to Camus when he told the author of *The Rebel* that his position left him nowhere to go but to the Galapagos. Did Sartre remember that among those who had gone to the remote islands to be stimulated to extraordinary activity was Charles Darwin?

As philosophical debate, the Camus-Sartre disagreement is central to modern thinking because it comes to grips with "historicity," which has largely superseded metaphysical and religious explanations of man's temporal dimension and direction. Prophetic Marxism continues to refuse to consider man's future as an infinite process and instead invests a party, a nation, or an individual, with the task of resolving the innate contradictions of human fate. How can one imagine an end to history and how can the end-all be reduced to a finite doctrine related to the ownership of means of production? What do our individual lives have in common with the history of our species? [10] In *The Rebel*, Camus said that even if a Marxist future would glow, this would not deliver us from the anxieties of the cosmic absurdity, and in his "Lettre au directeur des *Temps modernes*" he wondered whether history can have any direction at all. "To legitimize the position he [Jeanson] takes on my book, he would have to show that history has a necessary direction and end, that the atrocious and contorted face it shows us is not a delusion but that, on the contrary, history progresses *inevitably,* although with ups and downs, toward the moment of reconciliation when we can jump into infinite liberty." Sartre answered that to ask whether history had a direction was meaningless. "The problem is not to *know* its end, but to give it one."

Camus and Sartre still had many things in common—as Aron would say, "a common desire for truthfulness, a common refusal of illusions and false pretenses, a common way of confronting the world, a kind of stoicism" [11]—but politically they were drifting in opposite directions. For Camus, politics was a waste of time; for Sartre literature was becoming a waste of time. Camus was anxious to free literature from its subordination to immediate political "revelancy" and himself from "issues." Sartre, on

[10] Cf. Eric Werner, *De la violence au totalitarisme: Essai sur la pensée de Camus et de Sartre,* Paris: Calmann-Levy, 1972.
[11] Raymond Aron, *L'Opium des intellectuels,* Paris: Calmann-Levy, 1955.

the other hand, was entering his most politicized period, culminating in *The Words*, which he said was his "good-bye to literature."

For Camus, the quarrel over *The Rebel* resulted in a profound inner crisis and, publicly, in a fall from his pedestal as guiding light for a postwar generation. He had always resented being treated as a rival of Sartre's; now, he seemed to many to be irrelevant, a solitary and somewhat cranky supernumerary. Hurt, he wrote *La Chute (The Fall)* and had his hero say, "My relations with others have become difficult, as if both subtly and suddenly out of tune with the sentiments of my contemporaries." The main character was both self-portrait and caricature of Sartre, a black picture of the intellectual as con man, enjoying both his guilt and his fame.

For a while, Camus returned to journalism at the new weekly *L'Express,* but he could neither dissociate himself from his *pieds-noir* compatriots' rearguard action to keep Algeria French nor endorse a colonial policy he profoundly abhorred. Many felt disturbed and appalled by the silence he felt compelled to observe on the Algerian tragedy. He found literary creation too solitary and returned to the theater, as adapter and director of stage versions of Dino Buzzati's *Un caso clinico,* Faulkner's *Requiem for a Nun* and Dostoevsky's *The Possessed.* The new departures he planned after *L'Exil et le royaume (The Exile and the Kingdom)*—six short stories published in 1957, the year he received the Nobel Prize— were cut short on January 4, 1960, when he was killed in a car accident.

If Sartre was ready to relegate literature to a peripheral place in his concerns, he was still fascinated by literary figures—books on Mallarmé and Genet were in the works, and his *opus magnum* on Flaubert was still to be written—and, when the split with Camus occurred, he had just behind him yet another theatrical triumph.

The play was *Le Diable et le bon Dieu (Lucifer and the Lord),* an extravagant, heroic-comical transposition to Reformation Germany of a conflict between morality and action, means and ends. *Lucifer and the Lord* is about Goetz, a blaspheming, treacherous, cruel freebooter and soldier of fortune who with his private army burns and loots, dedicating himself to evil in order to affirm, against God, his own nature. At the moment he is about to massacre the townfolk of an invaded city, he converts—at a roll of dice—to goodness, giving his lands to peasants, creating a City of Happiness and devoting himself to saintliness. His actions provoke the peasants to a real and disastrous revolt. But Goetz is also buffoon, Don Juan, Buffalo Bill and "one for all" D'Artagnan of the kind for whom the twelve-year-old Sartre loved to invent complicated and mysterious adventures.

Starring a very truculent Pierre Brasseur as Goetz, Jean Vilar as a servile priest, Maria Casarès as the shrew, Hilda, who is Goetz's match, Henri Nassier as the baker, Nasty, who is ready to sacrifice generations for future justice and peace, and Wanda Kosakiewicz as Catherine, *Lucifer and the Lord* was the theatrical event of the 1951–52 season. It ran uninterrupted for a hundred and twenty performances at the Antoine and was continued during the following season, when Parisians were treated to the screen version of *La Putain respectueuse,* directed by Marcel Pagliero and Charles Brabant, and with Barbara Laage as Lizzie McKay and Walter Bryant as the black fugitive.

Under Louis Jouvet's direction, *Le Diable et le bon Dieu* started rehearsing before Sartre was through with the third act and the premiere was highlighted with gossip column reports of a Sartre-Jouvet battle over cuts in the text (it was to be Jouvet's last stage direction, as the celebrated actor-director died two months later). Catholics called the play "a war machine against God" and Catholic author-reviewer Henri Daniel-Rops managed to get himself smuggled into the Antoine during a run-through and to warn his readers that Sartre's new work was a piece of "absurd blasphemy." [12] On the communist side, Elsa Triolet condemned the play because the militant Nasty provokes Goetz's own peasants to start an uprising when they are not yet "ripe" for revolution.[13] Sartre gave interviews right and left, telling *Samedi Soir* that if his play was permeated with Christianity it was because the sixteenth-century subject he was dealing with was religious civil war [14] and *Le Figaro littéraire* that he wasn't trying to prove anything, least of all the nonexistence of God.[15] To *Paris-Presse,* he said that all love was in a sense directed against God. "When two people are in love, they are in love against God. All love is against the Absolute insofar as it is its own absolute." Regarding his supposedly pernicious influence on youth, he answered that various periods had witnessed a convergence of youth and certain literary forms. "We are accused of corrupting, Simone de Beauvoir, Camus and I, because we propose a morality; people who simply show a self-indulgent image of a period's vices and pleasures are never attacked." [16]

Although Sartre would never completely rewrite the nearly five hun-

---

[12] In *L'Aurore,* June 9–10, 1951.
[13] In *Les Lettres françaises,* June 14, 1951.
[14] *Samedi-Soir,* June 2–8, 1951.
[15] *Le Figaro littéraire,* June 30, 1951.
[16] *Paris-Presse,* June 7, 1951.

dred pages on Stéphane Mallarmé he had lost in 1948, he didn't give up writing a book on the nineteenth-century poet. Like Baudelaire, who first influenced him, Mallarmé turned from reality toward an ideal world of the intellect and over the span of a banal life as English teacher and woman's magazine editor lived a totally interiorized adventure expressed in extremely dense and compressed poetry. Sartre considered Mallarmé the greatest poet of the French language, felt Mallarmé's life was very different from his biography and saw in his allusive, elliptical "non-Euclidean" syntax and oracular language a "polite terrorism" with a near-revolutionary scope. The projected book was not written but Sartre published an essay that became the preface to a Gallimard reedition of Mallarmé's *Poésie*.

Saint Genet, Comédien et martyr was a foreword that got out of hand. Considered something of a monster at its publication, the 578-page *Saint Genet* was philosophical essay, literary criticism, moral treatise and psychoanalytical biography, inquiry into a man's conscious choice of his own awareness and thesis on a writer's liberation through the assimilation of his private obsessions.[17] Sartre's intention, as he wrote in a brief introduction, was to show "the limits of both psychoanalytical interpretation and Marxist explanation . . . to show that genius is not a gift but a way out for certain desperate individuals." Sartre finds in Jean Genet's life and conduct the perfect instance of Existential Man—the individual who consciously chooses his own being and then enacts the consequences of this choice. To find Genet's "kindred souls," Sartre goes back to François Villon and the Marquis de Sade, writers who also seemed vicious and perverse to their contemporaries, who also suffered persecution and imprisonment and whose residual meaning still haunts our moral consciousness. Genet, by his own confession, is the ideal illustration of the fact that perception and the perceived cannot coincide—that I can never know myself save in terms of what I am not. To Sartre, Genet is an authentic contemporary, someone who despite adverse conditions has managed to become something else than what his environment made him out to be.

Sartre had been working on *Saint Genet* during his and Simone's traditional retreat to Madame Morel's home near Næntes when they learned that Dullin had died of cancer. Camille had not made his last years any easier since she was drinking excessively. For a "Tribute to Charles Dullin,"

[17] Jean-Paul Sartre, *Saint Genet, Comédien et martyr*, Paris: Gallimard, 1952; *Saint Genet, Actor and Martyr*, New York: Braziller, 1963.

which friends organized in February 1950, Sartre and Beaver carried Camille, drunk, in tears and with her hair and clothes in disorder, from a taxi to a box at the Atelier Theater where she stayed hidden during the ceremony. Dullin died a few months after Sartre had returned from *his* Central American tour with Dolores. They had visited Mexico and Guatemala, Cuba, Panama, Haiti and Curaçao, but nothing was solved in their relationship although Dolores decided to move to Paris, even if Sartre wasn't exactly enthusiastic about the idea.

Because of Algren's long visit the previous summer and Sartre's Central American tour with Dolores, Sartre and Beaver hadn't traveled together since their brief Scandinavian tour. In 1950, they made up for it, before Simone was to go to Chicago for another two-months' stay with Algren. At Michel Leiris' suggestion, they visited Africa, from Algeria to French Equatorial Africa. As usual, Simone was in charge of the itinerary and when she learned it was possible to rent seats next to the drivers of trans-Sahara trucks, she made reservations from Ghardaïa, in southern Algeria, to Timbuktu, in what would become the Republic of Mali in 1960. The fifteen-hundred-mile truck ride took three weeks, with a week-long layover in Tamanrasset, an oasis town where the wives of French army engineers wore hats, spied on each other and gossiped. Sartre and Beaver continued from Timbuktu to Goa, on the Niger, where the temperature was 110°F. and Sartre came down with tropical fever. A doctor prescribed quinine and Sartre was stretched out, unconscious, under a mosquito netting for two days. As soon as he could stand up, they flew to Bobo-Dioulasso in Upper Volta. Sartre's fever persisted until Bamako, where the heat in their room was so suffocating they slept on the balcony. In the morning they saw everybody else had done the same thing; the balcony was piled with half-naked bodies. They escaped the heat in Dakar and, since Simone's sister and brother-in-law were living in Casablanca, returned home via Morocco.

Just as Simone was about to fly to Chicago, the Korean War broke out. The North Korean attack across the 38th Parallel, the U. N. Security Council call on member nations to furnish armed assistance to South Korea and President Truman's ordering U. S. air and sea forces into battle caused war jitters in Paris. If the new People's Republic of China attacked Taiwan, the United States would intervene and the Soviet Union would be obliged to back up China. Everyone was talking about the Red Army occupying Paris. Despite her desire to see Algren, Simone hesitated. Sartre told her to go. He really didn't think World War III was about to break out and, he said, she could always get back. She left.

For a whole year Algren had written funny and tender letters; now he told her he didn't love her anymore but that they would have a nice summer together anyway. She was disconcerted. The apartment on Wabansia Avenue and Algren's awkward presence felt suffocating, but with the $15,000 he had earned from the movie rights to *The Man with the Golden Arm* he had bought a house on Lake Michigan in Miller, Indiana, and once they were there their existence settled into a tolerable routine. The property sloped down to a lagoon where Algren had a boat. At night the steel mills of Gary lit up the sky. Simone read a lot. Algren went to Chicago by himself for several days. Neither of them was a good swimmer and his clumsy but dramatic rescue of her from drowning brought them closer again. The movie sale had taken Algren to Hollywood where he had met his former wife and at the end of Simone's stay he announced he was thinking of remarrying her. "So be it," she would write in *Force of Circumstance*. "By this time my despair had drained me of all feelings, and I could no longer react to anything. It was Indian summer by then; I walked around the lagoon, blinded by the beauty of the foliage, red-gold, green-gold, yellow-gold, copper and flame, my heart numbed, believing neither in what was past nor in whatever lay ahead." In *Les Mandarins,* she would say that what he had wanted was a woman who was all his, and reproach herself for thinking his life poetic when it was austere and lonesome. "For a moment he had thought he could escape loneliness, he had dared to wish for something else. He had been disappointed; he had suffered and gotten hold of himself again."

When Simone returned to Paris, Sartre had broken up with Dolores and the Korean War psychosis was at such a pitch that Camus had told Sartre to emigrate before the Russians occupied France. Dolores' decision to come and live in Paris had not brought them closer. On the contrary, they had quarreled and separated. The only memento Sartre had of Dolores was a tape recorder, a novelty in 1950, that she left him. He had a lot of fun surreptitiously recording conversations of friends and playing them back to them.

In September, General Douglas MacArthur's forces shattered North Korea's advances and in October swept north across the 38th Parallel. The new threat was that communist Chinese "volunteers" would be thrown into the war. The conflict provoked disagreements between Merleau-Ponty, who was practically in charge of *Les Temps modernes,* and Sartre, as Merleau-Ponty wanted *TM* to sit out the war and Sartre wanted their magazine to speak up on the issue. In exchange for American military aid in its now four-year-old guerrilla war in French Indochina, the Antoine Piney administration endorsed the American idea of rearming Germany and consented to the establishment of American bases in France. To most leftists, it meant the United States was secretly occupying France. When *The Nation* asked Sartre to contribute an article to its eighty-fifth anniversary issue, he wrote a long piece that showed his bewilderment and pessimism but also a prescience of wars to come. "Your morality is generous and puritanical and you carry out a policy that contradicts your morality, with a bad conscience and a feeling of a curse hanging over you," he wrote to his American readers. "So there you are, dragged into the infernal round that leads you to war in Korea, to fight the North Koreans in the midst of a population whose feelings for their defenders are, to say the least, doubtful simply because you didn't manage to free the South Koreans from their poverty through agrarian reform when you could still do it, and, later, because you didn't come to grips honestly with the problems of Korean unity for fear that the communists in the North would win in the whole country." [18] He wished that the best in American spirit would win out and that Washington would have the courage to try a real policy of "calculated risk"—a policy of risking not war but peace.

Sartre and Beaver spent Christmas Eve with Olga, Wanda, Little Bost, Michelle Vian and the mime Scipion. In January 1951, Simone managed to talk Sartre into coming to the Auron ski resort in the southern French Alps so he could have peace and quiet to write *Le Diable et le bon Dieu*. Little Bost came along, too, but Sartre never left the hotel. "When I went into his room at five o'clock, light-headed from the air and the mountain smell, he would be writing away, rolled up in a cocoon of smoke," Simone would remember. "It was with great difficulty that he would tear himself away even for dinner in the vast dining room." Michelle Vian had a house in Saint Tropez and Sartre and Beaver asked her to find them an apartment nearby. It turned out to be ice-cold and to overlook a narrow street, and they moved to Cannes, Sartre still buried in sixteenth-century Germany. With his pianist wife, Pierre Brasseur came down to talk over his role, regaling them with hilarious imitations and risqué stories about famous people he had met. Veteran film director Fernand Rivers also came down to confer on the screen adaptation of *Les Mains sales*, in which Brasseur would play Hoederer and Daniel Gélin Hugo.

Simone's correspondence with Algren continued. Like Camus, Algren thought Sartre should leave France before the Red Army occupied Paris and offered the beach house in Miller to Sartre and Beaver. Algren himself was in trouble. Anticommunist hysteria was sweeping Hollywood and

18 "The Chance of Peace," in *The Nation*, December 30, 1950.

it was out of the question that "pinko" John Garfield star in *The Man with the Golden Arm;* indeed out of the question, it seemed, that the picture be made at all. Algren had not remarried his former wife but to Simone it made little difference. He wrote her in Saint Tropez suggesting that she spend October with him in Miller. "He was offering, in all honesty, the friendship that is always so easy to maintain when two people have parted without bitterness and live in the same city. I consulted Sartre. 'Why not?' he said. I accepted." [19]

For a summer holiday, she and Sartre in the meantime went to Norway, Iceland and England. On a cruise ship they sailed over the arctic "top" of Norway and in Kirkenes took a bus to the Russian border where they stood staring across the no-man's-land and the barbed wire toward the Russian sentries and the country that emotionally meant too much to them. During the cruise Simone showed Sartre the first draft of *The Mandarins.* He told her it was going to be her best work but suggested that the plot be better constructed, the episodes linked better and that she introduce some suspense.

Sartre was becoming intimate with Michelle Vian. He had always found her attractive with her cascading blond hair, her vivacious gestures and sphinxlike reserve. Discreet and yet very much there, she fitted into the little family that too-famous Sartre and Beaver increasingly preferred to spend their leisure time with—Olga, Wanda, Little Bost and soon-to-join Lanzmann. Unlike her sister, Wanda, Olga was going downhill emotionally and professionally and now was definitely a financial charge of Sartre's. Since her divorce from Marc Barbezat, she had lived off and on with Bost. Too eager to resume her acting career after her bout with TB, she fluffed her comeback badly and, hurt, abandoned her acting altogether. As a journalist, Bost was a faithful *TM* collaborator but he was also following his famous brother's footsteps into movie writing—he was now adapting *Les Main sales* with Fernand Rivers and was also working with Alexandre Astruc on *Le Rideau cramoisi,* which in 1952 would be both Astruc's and Anouk Aimée's breakthrough (with Jean Aurenche, Pierre Bost was France's most famous screenwriter and "dialogiste").

Simone spent October in Miller. Algren was going to remarry his ex-wife. The stay was peaceful in the Indian summer splendor and at the end they agreed that to keep the good-bye to a minimum he should only

[19] Beauvoir, *Force of Circumstance.*

take her to the train station in Gary and not come to the airport. When she said thanks for everything, and added that they at least felt real friendship for one another, he burst out, "I can never offer you less than love." His words, after the four peaceful weeks, upset everything. "All the past flooded back into my heart, all my work was undone, life was unbearable," she would write in *Force of Circumstance*. "In the taxi, in the train, in the plane, in a cinema in New York that evening watching a Walt Disney film in which animals endlessly devoured each other, I wept without stopping. In my room in the Lincoln Hotel, my eyes brimming with tears, I wrote Algren a short letter asking if everything was all over or not."

She received his answer in Paris. "One can still have the same feelings for someone and still not allow them to rule and disturb one's life," she would quote him as writing. "To love a woman who does not belong to you, who puts other things and other people before you, without there ever being any question of you taking first place, is something that just isn't acceptable."

It could not be otherwise. Whomever Sartre and Beaver would fall in love with, these people could never take the first place. Their life was what it had always been, but it took on a new transparency that never ceased to amaze acquaintances and friends. In his intimate life, Sartre needed to breathe scrupulously clean air. He had always preferred the company of women to that of men, but it was unthinkable that he would lie, least of all to Beaver.

He seldom indulged in reminiscences, envy or regrets. His pride was increasingly in what he planned to do, a kind of detached vanity that tried to be free of circumstances and sometimes succeeded. Sometimes this vanity brought him into conflict with facts that could not be pushed aside, but he was indifferent to failures and eagerly plunged forward into new undertakings.

When Simone and Claude returned from Amsterdam and decided to live together, she didn't see any less of Sartre than before, but their habits changed. She was unwilling to give up the long travels she and Sartre made together several times a year, but she was afraid of not seeing Lanzmann for months on end and all three agreed that sometime in the middle of these holidays Lanzmann would join them for a couple of weeks. The attempt to work out a ménage à trois with Olga had not been successful largely because of Simone's jealousy. This time it was more successful. Jealousy was unknown to Sartre.

Lanzmann's presence freed Simone from the pangs of middle age and she reached out greedily. The burying of Algren had been painful as she had realized that her age and the circumstances of her life made the likelihood of a new love less than probable. But now, three years later, Claude's spontaneity and natural freedom in expressing his feelings, which Simone found irresistible, infused her with a new vitality. His youth stopped her age-anxiety attacks: "Two or three times he saw me going through one and he was so scared that a command was established in every bone and nerve of my body never to yield to them. I already found revolting the idea of dragging him into the horrors of declining age," she would write in *Force of Circumstance*. Their life together developed its own pattern. He earned a living as an Agence France-Presse wire service rewrite man and had time to spare for both *TM* and personal writing. In the mornings, they worked side by side in her little apartment in the Rue de la Bucherie, he on his book on Israel; she on *Les Mandarins*. Despite the piles of books, the apartment was big enough for two, but it was very old and the ceiling leaked.

Sartre lived many places—at his mother's in the Rue Bonaparte principally, in random Left Bank hotel rooms when he didn't want anybody to find him, and at Michelle's. A mother of two, Michelle was wealthy independently of Boris, whose fame would remain largely underground until after his premature death at thirty-nine from a painful heart disease, when the French flower generation would make him a patron saint of cheerful anarchism.[20] Both Sartre and Beaver were happiest in the tiny circle she often assembled in her apartment—Olga, Bost, Wanda, Michelle and Claude. They understood each other at the twist of a smile and took to eating together as often as possible in La Palette, a new bistro they found on the Boulevard Montparnasse.

But Sartre and Beaver now spent no more than half the year in Paris. Their travels became increasingly frequent, and from 1953 on they began to live in Rome during the summer.

For their writing they needed each other. As Sartre would say in a rare personal interview in 1965, "It's hard to tell what you owe someone. In a way I owe her everything. On the other hand, I would obviously have written even if she hadn't existed, since I wanted to write. But why is it that my complete confidence in her has always given me complete security, a security which I wouldn't have had if I'd been alone, unless I

---

[20] His 1950 "paramilitary vaudeville" *Equarrissage pour tous* would only be translated into English in 1968, as *The Knackers' ABC*.

were puffed with pride, as many writers are and which I am not, though I may be in other areas. When I show her a manuscript, as I always do, and when she criticizes it, I get angry at first and call her all kinds of names. Then I accept her comments, always. Not as a matter of discipline, but because I see that they're always pertinent. They're not made from the outside but with an absolute understanding of what I want to do and, at the same time, with an objectivity that I can't quite have." [21]

In the spring of 1953, Simone had the satisfaction of seeing *The Second Sex* published in the United States unsoiled by salacious comment. But *Les Mandarins* wasn't coming easily. Since Sartre had read the first draft during their Norwegian cruise, she had rewritten it completely. He told her to keep working. "Irked by the conventions of the novel, I had accepted them but not done so wholeheartedly; it was too short, too long, scattered; the conversations didn't ring true; I wanted to show particular individuals with their doubts and certainties, challenged both by others and by themselves, wavering between clear-sightedness and excessive simplicity, between prejudice and sincerity and now, suddenly, instead of creating people I seemed to be expounding ideals." [22]

Her characters are herself as Anne and Sartre as Dubreuilh, with Camus, Aron, Algren, Koestler, David Rousset and others appearing under various disguises. Anne and Dubreuilh are married and in the beginning the parents of a scrawny, pain-in-the-neck teenage daughter barely over her love for a Jewish boyfriend who, like Bourla, has died in the Nazi camps. Nadine sleeps around a lot—to still the pain and to bug her indulgent and professional parents—Anne is a psychiatrist and Dubreuilh a political journalist. Among Nadine's conquests is Henri, her father's near-contemporary, editor of a former Resistance newspaper that cannot find its line in postwar politics and is losing its circulation. Henri is trying to terminate a long, now painful affair with Paule, an increasingly neurotic woman (whose real-life "double" no one could put their finger on but a character in whom several of Simone's friends recognized themselves). The background is the postwar era, from the euphoria of the Liberation and the lingering hatred of resurfacing collaborators to the gradual disillusion of noncommunist leftists, their difficult relations with the Communist Party and their contradictory feelings for the United States and the Soviet Union.

When Lanzmann read the manuscript, he persuaded her to explain more

[21] "Sartre Talks of Beauvoir," interview with Madeleine Gobeil, translated by Bernard Frechtman, in *Vogue,* July 1965.
[22] Beauvoir, *Force of Circumstance.*

fully the reasons for the distance both Dubreuilh and Henri try to keep between themselves and the communists. Until then, she had felt no need to explain. Claude was, like Sartre, a fellow traveler, explaining his non-membership in the party by his subjectivity, even though he rejoiced at each step Sartre took toward the communists. Simone was the one who hesitated the most, fearing that the communists would hurt Sartre and take him too far from his own truth. But Stalin died in the spring of 1953 and with him, it seemed, a barbarian age. Three months later, a standoff armistice was reached in Korea. The new word in East-West relations was a "thaw."

In February 1954, Elsa Triolet invited Sartre to join an East-West writers' dialogue in the Belgian seaside resort of Knocke-le-Zoute, and Michelle, Beaver and Claude drove him up there in Simone's new Aronde car—Sartre would never learn to drive. The communists and fellow travelers Triolet had gathered included Carlo Levi, the elderly Konsantin Fedin who had survived all the purges but written nothing important since *The Brothers* in 1928, and the new "East Germans," Anna Seghers and Bertolt Brecht. The author of *The Threepenny Opera* threw the windup conference into an uproar when he asked in an innocent tone whether the final text couldn't include a protest against American nuclear tests. Fedin and Sartre bypassed Brecht's suggestion and Sartre found himself invited to Moscow by the Russian delegation.

He was overworked when he left and Simone was worried. He had overexerted himself for more than a year and was suffering from high blood pressure. His doctor had prescribed a long rest in the country; all he did was take more drugs. He had barely slept for several nights before leaving because he had to finish his preface to Henri Cartier-Bresson's photo reportage book on China, *D'une Chine à l'autre* and an introduction to a Giacometti exhibition. From Moscow's National Hotel, he assured her by telephone that he was recovering from his overexertion and that he could see the Red Square from his window. He visited the university and went sightseeing. Konstantin Simonov, who hadn't written *anything* since 1942, invited Sartre to his dacha, which finally did him in. A four-hour banquet accompanied by flows of Georgian wine and twenty toasts in vodka, followed by similar receptions in Leningrad and Moscow made him stagger home to Paris more dead than alive.

In October, Simone received the prestigious Goncourt prize for *Les Mandarins,* which in hindsight French literary anthologies would call the most representative novel of the postwar era, "marking the end of existentialism by comparing its writers—respected and disarmed—to Chinese mandarins.'' [23] To celebrate, they had a ''family'' lunch at Michelle's, where Sartre presented Simone with an appropriate gift—a biography of the Goncourt brothers.

A month later began what would become the Algerian war.

[23] *La Littérature en France depuis 1945, op. cit.*

CHAPTER

NEW YEAR'S 1961

"YOU SHOULD VISIT CUBA," Sartre told Aragon across the table.

"We're too old for that," Aragon answered. Elsa Triolet was sitting next to him.

"Come on," smiled Sartre, "you're not much older than I am."

"How old are you?"

"Fifty-five."

"It's at fifty-five that it begins." [1]

Elsa gave the table a graceful account of how she was now forced to put false tears in her eyes and, in her knees, "parallel hearts." They were at a dinner at the Soviet embassy in the Rue de Grenelle in honor of Galina Nikolayeva, the author of a book that dealt interestingly and even romantically with a subject that Beaver found badly treated in the West—work. Simone was seated next to François Mauriac, who had attacked so fiercely *The Second Sex*. It was the first time she had met the Nobel laureate. Sartre had told her Mauriac could be mordant but she decided either old age or Gaullism had extinguished Mauriac's waggish gifts.

"To the new decade," a bilingual cultural attaché proposed.

They all lifted their vodka tumblers. A little later, Simone invited Nikolayeva and her husband to visit with her and Sartre at her apartment. The author of *The Engineer Bakhirev* suffered a serious heart disease and

[1] Beauvoir, *Force of Circumstance.*

on the appointed day had an attack. Her husband came, however, with an interpreter and during the conversation behaved as if he had an entire Soviet delegation standing behind him. He told Sartre and Beaver that the writers of the Soviet Union would be very happy to see them in Moscow. Sartre answered that Simone and he would be very happy to go.

So many things were new. Nikita Khrushchev was the ruler of Russia. He had de-Stalinized the country, inaugurated peaceful coexistence and a Soviet rocket had taken photos of the "far side" of the moon. In Cuba, Fidel Castro celebrated his first heady year in power as international folk hero and American blacks were protesting lunch-counter segregation in southern states. The only place where nothing seemed to budge was in France.

It was over two years now since de Gaulle had been brought back to power. In May 1958, a demoralized and near-seditious army had threatened to let events in Algeria run away with themselves. The sixty-eight-year-old general had been the towering strongman the army wanted and the million *pieds-noir* integrationists saw as their only hope for keeping Algeria French after the Indochina debacle. By a take-it-or-leave-it constitutional referendum, de Gaulle had created his own Fifth Republic and offered independence to seventeen African and Caribbean territories, but the war continued, with its clandestine torture of suspected Moslem terrorists by French soldiers, the indiscriminate terrorist bombings both by paramilitary Arab groups and by French "ultras." From the beginning the French army had been the million *pieds-noir* settlers' most powerful ally. French officers had left Indochina deeply impressed with the political techniques of Mao Tsetung as transmitted onward by Ho Chi Minh. Whole classes of Saint Cyr graduates had disappeared in Vietnam and officers and career soldiers had felt betrayed by a weak civilian government. Animated by a "never again" resolve and a contempt for democratic compromises, they also had a morbid respect for the merciless efficacy of National Liberation fronts, whether Vietcong or Algerian "fellaghas." Like their Portuguese counterparts in Angola a decade later, they had been conquered by the enemy, not just in the sense of losing battles but in the sense of accepting his ideas. They had read Lenin and Mao, rejecting the theory but adopting the "peoples' war" action tactics. As soldiers and, increasingly, as occupying force of the nine-tenths Moslem majority of Algeria, they had felt forced to resort to mass punishment, indiscriminate terrorizing of civilian populations and, in the day-to-day combat with an enemy that all too easily melted into an anonymous Arab crowd, to torture in order to obtain information.

Torture was a taboo subject. That French soldiers brutalized Fédération de libération nationale (FLN) militants had been a known fact during the Fourth Republic, even if the majority of Frenchmen refused to believe it, but the practice was incompatible with de Gaulle's concept of France's civilizing mission, and his Cultural Affairs minister André Malraux had told his first news conference that "as far as I and *you* know, no acts of torture have occurred since de Gaulle went to Algiers." Malraux had invited France's three Nobel Prize winners, Mauriac, Camus and Roger Martin du Gard to go to Algiers to investigate the allegations of continued torture. Martin du Gard was dying, Mauriac too skeptical and *pieds-noir* Camus not too anxious to associate himself with an open anti-*Algérie française* initiative. Torture had not gone away but spread, to the embarrassment of Malraux, against the "left flank" of the regime.

From the beginning, Sartre and Beaver had been against the war.

Twice *Les Temps modernes* had been seized for printing seditious material, its officers subjected to police searches and Francis Jeanson jailed for sympathizing too actively with the FLN. From draftees, *TM* collected eyewitness accounts of incidents of torture, looting and dead-of-night massacres and for every testimony published ten others were mailed in. Now the Interior Department had banned *La Gangrène,* a book written by Bachir Mouzama and three other tortured FLN students. When Sartre organized a protest, Simone was threatened by a police commissioner. "We didn't know everything, but we knew a lot, too much," she would write in *Force of Circumstance* about the Algerian war. "My own situation with regard to my country, to the world, to myself, was completely altered by it all."

Sartre was the unrelenting antiwar activist. Before anyone else, he saw the total dimension of the colonial question and spoke up about it. His peace-rally speeches and numerous writings for *Les Temps modernes, L'Express* and veritable underground newssheets were filled with trenchant, verifiable and often ironic facts and figures. When communists and socialists were still looking for reforms and seeing light at the end of their own tunnels, he was already for the enemy. "There is no such thing as a good white settler and others who are villians; there are white settlers, period; and the sooner we understand that, the sooner we can understand why the Algerians are right and why their liberation and that of France can only come with the shattering of colonialism," he told a rally in January 1956, when communist votes helped Pierre Mendès-France's ruling social-radical coalition to pass a Special Powers act and authorize the sending of draftees to North Africa for what the government called "the last quarter hour" of the war. "What is important, is to fight on the side of the Algerian people so as to deliver *both* them and us from colonial tyranny." [2]

The "last quarter hour" translated into an all-out war effort in which all Arabs became suspect. Implacably, Sartre wrote that torture was a hopeless escape from fear. "We want to tear from *one* throat in the midst of cries, vomit and blood, *everyone*'s secret. Useless violence. Whether the victim speaks or dies in the process, the multiple truth is elsewhere, always elsewhere, out of reach. The torturer becomes Sisyphus. If he applies the screws he must always start over again." When he wrote this in *L'Express* in February 1958, the news magazine was seized.[3] Three years later a first bomb would explode in the hallway at 42 Rue Bonaparte. If die-hard *Algérie française* terrorists couldn't find a way to "hit" Sartre they could always try and kill his seventy-nine-year-old mother.

The Algerian quagmire had oozed over from Indochina. The jungle war against Ho Chi Minh's nationalists had remained distant and, to most Frenchmen, vague and unreal until it was too late and, on May 7, 1954, twelve thousand men surrendered to Vo Nguyen Giap's guerrillas at Dien Bien Phu—the first time a western army was defeated by a Third World Liberation front. Two months later, Mendès-France had met the North Vietnamese delegation in Geneva to give Vietnam the independence de Gaulle had promised Ho Chi Minh in 1945, but successive communist-socialist coalitions had reneged on it in the name of a million Catholics in Indochina. The Geneva Agreement had divided Vietnam at the 17th Parallel and promised national elections within two years to reunify the country. Mendès-France was the rallying point of everything that was progressive in professional politics. During his seven months in office in 1954–55, he managed to offer solutions to some suffocating problems. He gave Tunisia home rule, and national politics a new forward thrust by announcing future government actions in advance and explaining them on national airwaves.

While Mauriac, Camus, Malraux and *L'Express* editor Jean-Jacques Servan-Schreiber rallied to Mendès-France's support and talked optimistically about a New Left, Sartre continued his tortuous fellow traveling,

[2] Speech before a rally of the Comité d'action des intellectuels contre la poursuite de la guerre en Afrique du Nord, reprinted in *Les Temps modernes*, No. 123, March–April 1956, and in volume in *Situations V*, Paris: Gallimard, 1964.
[3] "Une Victoire," in *L'Express*, February 17, 1958, reprinted in *Situations V, op. cit.* When *L'Express* was seized, excerpts of Sartre's article were reprinted in foreign newspapers, notably *The Observer*, London, March 9, 1968.

published the third installment of *Les Communistes et la paix* and, with the political farce *Nekrassov* suffered his first theatrical fiasco.

Nekrassov was a satire about anticommunism and journalism, "in the vein of Aristophanes." The hero was the swindler Georges de Valera masquerading as the fake Russian poet Nekrassov. Sartre had difficulties finishing the play because he didn't want to make Valera an out-and-out bastard or a last-curtain convert, and, as had been the case with *Le Diable et le bon Dieu,* rehearsals started at the Antoine too soon. Michel Vitold played Valera—and Wanda Kosakiewicz was Veronique—under Jean Mayer's direction. The opening-night audience was hostile and the members of the press didn't like to see their profession lampooned although they laughed their heads off. The reviews were devastating. When Sartre agreed to see a reporter, his interviewer was more interested in asking whether he recognized himself in Dubreuilh in *Les Mandarins* ("In a sense, Dubreuilh has nothing to do with me. He takes up a political position and assumes political responsibilities that mean he has gone much further than I'') than hearing what had gone wrong with the play.[4] *Nekrassov* lasted sixty performances.

Sartre was more lucky on the screen. "Typhus," that first script he had turned in when he had been on the Pathé studios payroll in 1943, had, as *Les Orgueilleux* (*The Proud and the Beautiful*), become a smash hit, the 1953 Venice film festival winner and, somewhat incongruously, made him an Academy Award screenwriting nominee for the 1956 Oscars. As screenplayed by the Aurenche-Bost duo and directed by Yves Allégret, *Les Orgueilleux* had Michelle Morgan as the wife of a typhus victim in a squalid, diseased and desperate Mexico and Gérard Philippe as a drunken derelict wreck of a doctor. "An existentialist soap opera," sniffed *Time*[5] when the film reached America, where the Sartrian origins were heavily publicized.

Jacqueline Audry directed the screen version of *Huis Clos*. Colette's sister, who had taken Sartre and Beaver to visit a movie studio when they had been provincial schoolteachers and she a script girl, had directed five features, including a *Gigi* with Danielle Delorme, when she asked him for permission to adapt the play. He offered to redo the text, but she declined his offer. It was *No Exit* she wanted to bring to the screen. Her adaptation, approved by Sartre, "opened up" by having the trio in hell watch scenes from their former lives through a window screen that, at the end, they

---

[4] *Le Monde,* June 1, 1956.
[5] *Time,* June 18, 1956.

discover had been walled up. The critics considered Arletty miscast as Inez—in a 1965 television adaptation Lanzmann's actress sister, Evelyn Rey, would play the lesbian—but the picture was a success. At the moment existentialism lost its significance, popular sentiments caught up its themes, climate and abstractions.

Books were written about Sartre. The first was Francis Jeanson's *Le Problème morale et la pensée de Sartre,* which Sartre himself considered the best outline of his ethics.[6] Emmanuel Mournier, the founder of *L'Esprit* magazine, which expressed a low-key, interiorized Catholicism, explored Sartrian existentialism from a Christian viewpoint and found him marked by Protestantism.[7] In England, Iris Murdoch wrote a balanced appreciation of Sartre as philosopher and man of letters, comparing *Les Chemins de la liberté* with L. H. Myer's philosophical novels.[8] With *The Tragic Finale,*[9] Wilfred Desan wrote one of the first American university press books on Sartre, a careful exposition of the central themes of the Sartrian ontology, and followed up with *The Marxism of Jean-Paul Sartre.*[10]

A book that hurt was Merleau-Ponty's *Les Aventures de la dialectique,* which appeared in May 1955.[11] To Merleau-Ponty, ethics was still associated with political action and Marxism still appealed to him because of its relentless realism when it came to moral relations between man and industrial society, but he could not accept communists' neglect, or sometimes outright denial, of moral individuality. In his new book he revealed a continued sympathy for Marxism, but also a strong contempt for the degenerating of Marxist theory within the communist movement. He made it clear he now thought history to be plural and contingent and seemed disposed to believe that no single revolutionary movement against *any* particular class of the social structure could claim to be the unique agency of historical process. As for Sartre's attempts at revising Marxism, he called that nothing less than "ultrabolshevism."

"To say, like Sartre, that communism will become the truth means to bet on our forgetfulness, on the vertigo that liberty and the future produce in us while at the same time to cover the Party with a veil of reason, but people already told Pascal that an eternity of imaginary happiness cannot

6 Francis Jeanson, *Le Problème morale et la pensée de Sartre,* Paris: Myrte, 1947; reissued as *Un quidam nommé Sartre,* Paris: Seuil, 1965.
7 Emmanuel Mournier, *Malraux, Camus, Sartre, Bernanos,* Paris: Seuil, 1953.
8 Iris Murdoch, *Sartre, Romantic Rationalist,* New Haven, Yale University Press, 1953.
9 Wilfred Desan, *The Tragic Finale,* Cambridge: Harvard University Press, 1954.
10 Wilfred Desan, *The Marxism of Jean-Paul Sartre,* New York: Doubleday, 1965.
11 Maurice Merleau-Ponty, *Les Aventures de la dialectique,* Paris: Gallimard, 1955.

make up for an instant of life," Merleau-Ponty wrote. What was wrong with Sartre's thinking, he reasoned, was his being-for-itself and being-in-itself dualism, the "folly" of his prereflective cogito and his notion that we are responsible for all our predicaments, ideas and feelings even when we refuse such responsibility.

Sartre didn't answer Merleau-Ponty; Simone did. She found Sartre's ideas already sufficiently distorted and misunderstood and rather contentiously tried to set the record straight on Sartrian dialectics.[12] Unlike the quarrel with Camus, the difference with Merleau-Ponty did not lead to a lasting split. The following March they met at a conference in Vienna and onstage bantered about Nikita Khrushchev's call for East-West co-existence.

After a decade of fighting political windmills, history suddenly seemed to be on the side of Sartre and Beaver and to carry them effortlessly forward. At the Twentieth Party Congress, Khrushchev denounced the personal rule and cult of Stalin and seemed ready to inaugurate greater cultural liberalism in the Soviet Union. In America, Senator Joseph McCarthy and his witch-hunt was also yesterday and President Eisenhower's "atoms for peace" led to the first Geneva summit conference. At the first Afro-Asian conference in Bandung, India's Jawaharlal Nehru and Yugoslavia's Josip Tito launched the idea of a nonaligned "Third World." Simone went with Delegate Sartre to the Helsinki Congress of the Peace Movement and heard Ilya Ehrenburg tell her it was perhaps not yet the opportune moment for a Russian translation of *Les Mandarins* although everybody who read French in Moscow had read it, and American students were predicting a great success for the U. S. edition. Next, Sartre told her they had been invited to China.

From September to November 1955, they traveled through the Soviet Union and the People's Republic. China was still three years away from the Great Leap Forward. To pull the country together, Mao Tse-tung was following Russian models, even if the Chinese were already uncomfortable with the idea of planning superstructures and wanted to get back to the experimental tradition they had so successfully developed during the Yenan period in the mid-1940s. What struck Sartre and Beaver was the difference between China and the U.S.S.R. The Russian Revolution in 1917 was the aftermath of defeat; the 1949 Chinese Revolution followed victory. The paradoxical result was that the Chinese Revolution had managed

---

[12] "Merleau-Ponty et le pseudo-sartrisme," in *Les Temps modernes*, No. 114–115, June–July 1955; reprinted in *Privilèges*, Paris: Gallimard, 1955.

to ban inflation, misery, wobbly insecurity, anarchy and local despotism that usually accompanied revolution. "The cause of all revolutionary terror has been the weakness of the central government," Sartre told journalists on their return. "If terror is unknown in China, if the Mao Tse-tung government has shown an admirable moderation, it's because his victorious army has been able to take root in the people and thereby give the central government what no revolutionary government had ever had at the outset —the serenity of total power." [13] In a singular way, China made Sartre think of death. Everything was "tomorrow," from people's complicity that excluded foreigners to the sense that the country's most tangible reality was a future that only the next generation would see. "A brand-new hospital, white-walled and modern but still awaiting part of its equipment and all of its patients, a factory as big as a city but still empty, all those ruins of the future make you think about death much more than the Coliseum." In Peking, Sartre was interviewed by *The People's Daily* and, together with Simone, received by Marshal Ch'en Yi, Mao's foreign secretary. Simone put down her impressions in *La longue marche,* written in a pedantic tone and peppered with statistical data and, she would admit in 1963, somehow her most laden book.[14]

Upon their return, Simone went traveling in Spain with Lanzmann and Sartre began writing the screenplay for *The Crucible,* Arthur Miller's play about the 1690 witch-hunt and trial in Salem, Massachusetts. Sartre had not liked the ambiguous ending of Marcel Aymé's stage adaptation at the Théâtre Sarah Bernhardt with Yves Montand as Miller's hero. John Proctor refuses to sell his name to the witch-hunters who expect him to embrace the communal guilt sweeping Salem. Sartre felt that Miller's play had been emasculated. In the screen adaptation, written during the winter of 1955–56, Sartre coarsened Miller's text while remaining faithful to its spirit, increased the importance of deputy-governor Danforth and eliminated a sympathetic clergyman. Entitled *Les Sorcières de Salem,* the film was directed by Raymond Rouleau who also played Danforth, and starred Montand and Simone Signoret. When it was released in April 1957, critical and public reception was polite, with Sartre blamed for too long-winded speeches and Rouleau for too static direction.

[13] "La Chine que j'ai vue," in *France-Observateur,* December 1, and 8, 1955, and "Sartre Views China," in *New Statesman,* December 3, 1955.
[14] Simone de Beauvoir, *La longue marche,* Paris: Gallimard, 1957; *The Long March,* Cleveland and New York: World Publishing, 1958.

Like *Nekrassov, Les Sorcières de Salem* was something Sartre felt he had to do. The theme was the question, Is life worth losing for beliefs that end with life? Also, McCarthyism had offended him personally. American students had attended the Helsinki Peace Conference as surreptitiously as Algerian delegates and the State Department had taken Algren's passport away from him. Off and on, Algren was corresponding with Simone and looking forward to the day he could travel again. In the meantime he was involved in a losing fight with Otto Preminger, who was the producer-director of *The Man with the Golden Arm,* starring Frank Sinatra and Kim Novak. With the Writers Guild of America and the Authors' League of America backing him, he was suing Preminger over money and credits on the screen version of his novel, the first movie to break the taboo against drug addiction.

Algren claimed he was less than happy when the American edition of *Les Mandarins* appeared in 1956. Dedicated to him and containing graphic descriptions of their thinly fictionalized love life, *The Mandarins* resulted not only in coy journalistic attention but in flattering invitations from literary ladies: "And I quote, 'Why don't you spread your favors around?' 'When you get to New York, call me at the Hotel So-and-So,' signed, 'P.S. And it'll be good.' To these letters I didn't make any answer. Except there was one I answered. I said, 'You'll have to remember that this relationship of which you just read involved a man who was thirty-one and I'm now sixty-six, so there's not much point any more, is there, dear?' " [15] In the Rue de la Bucherie apartment Lanzmann answered the phone one evening and told Simone the operator was giving advance notice of a person-to-person call from America. But Algren canceled the call. Simone dropped him a line and the correspondence resumed. It would not be until 1959 that he was able to get a passport.

It was not easy to be a leftist in France in 1956. In March, new socialist-radical Premier Guy Mollet granted Tunisia and Morocco independence, and called the Algerian war "cruel and lunatic." A month later, he capitulated to the army and the million *pieds-noir,* intensified the war and started a home front propaganda that tried to paint Algeria's Moslem majority as friends of France and the rebellion as the result of an "Islamic conspiracy" promoted by the Arab League and Egypt's Gamal Nasser. After *L'Humanité* published accounts of French army atrocities, the government tried to muzzle the leftist and extreme-leftist press. Several journa-

[15] H. E. F. Donohue, *Conversations with Nelson Algren, op. cit.*

lists were indicted and others called traitors. Hanging on to Algeria became a matter of honor, dignity and grandeur. There were 190,000 French soldiers in Algeria in March; by June there were 380,000.

Protest did exist. Meetings, demonstrations, strikes and obstructions at the departure of troop trains were organized. In January, Sartre spoke at a Paris antiwar rally and at the Vienna meeting in March of the Peace Movement tried to have the war condemned, but the French Communist Party was afraid of appearing less than nationalistic and the Soviet Union feared a French defeat would turn Algeria into an American zone of influence.

In June, Sartre met Arlette Elkaim, a seventeen-year-old student preparing for the Ecole Normale in suburban Sèvres. The daughter of a Jewish merchant in Constantine in eastern Algeria, she had written to Sartre after her philosophy teacher had expressed displeasure at her choice of Sartrian ethics for her term paper. A girl of frail beauty and nervous intellect, Arlette soon became his mistress and when, two years later, it was rumored that she was pregnant and Sartre was ready to marry her, she nearly caused an unthinkable rift between Sartre and Beaver. Eight years later when the Algerian war was a fading nightmare but Algerian nationals living in France could easily be deported, Sartre asked a court to allow him to adopt Arlette.

In October, Sartre broke noisily and eloquently with the communists. Michelle, Sartre, Simone and Lanzmann had traveled through Greece and Yugoslavia and Sartre and Beaver were alone together in Rome on October 24 when the Soviet army invaded Hungary. They were sitting at Chez Georges on the Via Veneto with movie designer Renato Guttuso and his wife repeating to each other what French and Italian newspapers said about Russian tanks. The invasion gave a lie to the promises of the Twentieth Party Congress of not violating the principle of nonintervention.

Lanzmann flew down and drove back with Simone in her car. On his return from Italy, Sartre was repelled by the French Communist Party newspaper treatment of the Hungarian tragedy in general and *L'Humanité* editor André Stil in particular for calling the workers of Budapest "the dregs of the fallen classes." Without going back on everything he had tried to accomplish since his rapprochement with the communists in 1952, Sartre condemned the armed Soviet intervention in an interview with *L'Express* that was a sensation in France and much quoted abroad. "I condemn entirely and without reservations the Soviet aggression," he said. "Without laying the responsibility at the feet of the Russian people, I say again that its present government has committed a crime and that factional struggle among its leaders has given the power to a group (military "hard-liners," former Stalinists?) that after having denounced Stalin behave like Stalinists. All history's crimes are forgotten; we have forgotten ours and other countries will forget them little by little. It is possible that there will be a day when the Soviet Union's crime will be forgotten, if its government changes and if new men try to really apply the principle of equality among social nations. For the time being, one can only condemn. I break regretfully but totally with my friends the Soviet writers who do not denounce (or cannot denounce) the massacre in Hungary. It is impossible to be friends with the dominating faction of Soviet bureaucracy: What dominates is horror." [16]

He was hardest on the French Communist Party, saying that after years of anxiety, spite and bitterness it might perhaps be possible to forgive the Soviet Union, especially if Russia had a radical change of politics. "But I must say that it will always be impossible to reestablish relations with the people now running the French Communist Party. Every one of their sentences and their gestures is the end result of thirty years of lies and sclerosis."

The break was shattering for Sartre and painful for Beaver and the friends who followed them. It meant that the Soviet Union was not "privileged" since its politics didn't contain an implicit moral evaluation of itself. It meant Camus and Merleau-Ponty had been right, that Sartre's *Les Communistes et la paix* was a fraud and that his formula, "Without the Communist Party no socialist solution is possible in France," was no longer valid. Irritatingly, it also meant the right had not been totally wrong even if it was sickening to listen to reactionaries committed to keeping Algeria French at any cost talk about the Hungarian people's right to self-determination.

The Hungarian uprising had coincided with the British-French military intervention in Egypt over Nasser's nationalization of the Suez Canal and the two countries' pullback the next day under joint American-Soviet pressure. The caving-in to the pressures of the U. N., the Eisenhower administration, the Khrushchev regime and the British Labor Party was resented as a "national humiliation" in France. Suez muddled the Hungarian issue and conservatives reacted to Sartre's break with the communists by congratulating him on his adroitness.

Together with other noncommunist members of the Peace Movement Sartre forced a resolution through the national council demanding the

[16] *L'Express,* November 9, 1956.

evacuation of Soviet troops from Hungary. He resigned from the France-U.S.S.R. Association, wrote a foreword to a Hungarian exile's book [17] and answered a collective letter from Soviet authors deploring his attitude, saying that to him the crime was not only to attack Budapest with tanks but that it had been made necessary by twelve years of Soviet terror and stupidity.[18] In January 1957, *Les Temps modernes* came out with a "triple" issue devoted exclusively to the Hungarian revolt. In a twenty-page editorial outlining the magazine's new goals, he wrote that an alliance with the communists would compromise the last chances of a united French left and that the only way to help the Communist Party was to help it de-Stalinize itself.[19] The idea of overcoming the Hungarian crisis by changing the Party from within through what Simone called "living Marxism" was taken up by a number of party members and advocated by an even larger number of fellow travelers.

Something like living Marxism was being tried, cautiously, in Poland. The return of Wladyslaw Gomulka had meant an end to forced collectivization, a lifting of censorship of printed matter and theatrical performances and, in the arts, the abandonment of the "social realism" doctrine. Sartre and Beaver were invited to a Polish embassy dinner where Jerzy Lisowski, the editor of the Cracow magazine *Tworczosc,* told him intellectuals in Poland thought his words were directed especially at them and the ambassador invited him to come to Warsaw for the Polish premiere of *Les Mouches.* It was cold in Warsaw in January but the welcome was ardent. Discussions were held in overheated coffeehouses and at the home of Jerzy Andrzejewski, the author of *Ashes and Diamonds,* who played an important role in the Gomulka thaw (and would soon resign his Party membership in protest against creeping new censorship). At Lisowski's suggestion, Sartre wrote fifty dense pages on his newest thinking on Marxism and existentialism. The *Tworczosc* piece became the core of *La Critique de la raison dialectique,* Sartre's last major philosophical work.[20]

The question he asked in the essay for the Polish magazine [21] and amplified in a *TM* piece seven months later,[22] was, Do we have the means

---

[17] François Fetjö, *La Tragédie hongroise,* Paris: Flore, 1956.

[18] Published in *Literaturnaya Gazeta,* November 21, 1956. Sartre's answer appeared in *France-Observateur,* November 29, 1956.

[19] "Le Fantôme de Staline," in *Les Temps modernes,* Nos. 129–130–131, November–December 1956–January 1957.

[20] Jean-Paul Sartre, *La Critique de la raison dialectique,* Paris: Gallimard, 1960; *The Problem of Method,* London: Methuen, 1964.

[21] "Marksizm i Egzystencjalizm," translated by Jerzy Lisowski, in *Tworczosc,* Vol. 13, No. 4, 1957.

[22] "Questions de méthode," in *Les Temps modernes,* No. 139, September 1957.

today of establishing a structural and historical science of the origins, developments and beliefs of man? The question would torture him for the next three years, chain him to his desk for ten hours a day and make him swallow amphetamines—up to twenty a day. "The amphetamines gave me a speed of thought and writing that was at least three times my normal rhythm and I wanted to go fast," he would say twenty years later. "*La Critique* was written against the communists but from a Marxist point of view because I felt the communists had completely twisted Marxism around."

Sartre felt the break with the communists in the flesh like an exile and a "waiting-room void." The only thing to do, he felt, was to try to think through to the end the ideas the communists refused to think. It was also an attempt at solving his own contradictions. In 1952, he had defended the Soviet Union against charges of coercion; now, after Budapest, he condemned it for the same reason.

His answer in the nearly eight hundred-page *Critique* is not that he had been wrong but that Marxism is no longer a living organism but a frozen dogma, a mausoleum full of mummified concepts and a state religion no longer tolerating unfettered analysis of real situations. To regain its vigor, Marxism will have to stop trying to suppress what is singular and specific and drop its "lazy" clichés, edifying formulas and knee-jerk reactions to current events. Marxists cannot both dismiss Valéry as a petit bourgeois poet and at the same time dodge the logical follow-up question, Then why aren't all petit bourgeois Valérys? To dissolve all people into their classes is to diminish them, it is to make them passive, not active agents of the class struggle. If one regards the French revolutionary wars as nothing more than schemes invented by the merchant class, then all real people of the Revolution fade away and, logically, all events are nothing more than chance happenings. Human life ends up being a random occurrence.

The only way to overcome this lazy, stunted Marxism is to allow dialectic reasoning to turn on itself and to examine its own historical determinism and its own knowledge. How do we know history, how much can be known, what part of the human being is subject to materialistic dialectics? To answer this we must go from broad historical sweeps to the "dated, real struggle," to the singular, the existential dimension of history. The role of the individual must be recognized. People make their own history and they don't always do it the same way. In the end, we are responsible for what circumstances make of us.

Declaring that existentialism can only be an "ideology" inside Marxism, Sartre tries to show that the Party, in relation to the masses, is a necessary reality because masses do not, by themselves, possess *spontaneity*. But conversely, as soon as the Party becomes an institution, it also becomes reactionary in relation to what it has itself brought into being, namely the *fused group*. Also, he says, to understand the individual, to understand history and itself, dialectic Marxism must incorporate the contributions of American sociology and Freudian psychoanalysis.

It was Simone who was reading David Riesman's *The Lonely Crowd,* C. Wright Mills' *The Power Elite,* William Whyte's *The Organization Man* and Auguste Spectorsky's *The Exurbanites* while Sartre furiously wrote *La Critique* and ransacked the French Revolution for heuristic examples of "concrete determinants." She was beginning to write her autobiography. It was an old project, dating back to her attempts at writing about Zaza. But to resurrect her childhood was not as easy as she had thought. Dates and events had to be researched in libraries and, she felt, writing her biography made as many demands on her powers of imagination as fiction. Sartre's diversion from *La Critique* was to write an essay on Tintoretto for Gallimard's lavish coffee-table series on Renaissance painters.

The Algerian war was the depressing background and unwelcome distraction. Sartre appeared as a character witness for an Algerian youth accused of murdering a pro *Algérie française* Moslem, and Simone for one of her former students in Rouen who had married an Algerian and stood accused of having conspired in a terrorist's bombing. Simone was revolted when Camus went to Stockholm to receive his Nobel Prize and, in front of an enormous audience, declared, "I love justice, but I will fight for my mother before justice," a sentence that amounted to saying he was on the side of the *pieds-noir.* "This hypocrisy, this indifference, this country, my own self, were no longer bearable to me," she would write in *Force of Circumstance.* "All these people in the streets, in open agreement or battered into a stupid submission—they were all murderers, all guilty. Me, too. 'I'm French.' The words scalded my throat like an admission of hideous deformity. For millions of men and women, old people and children, I was just one of the people who were torturing them, burning them, machine-gunning them, slashing their throats, I deserved their hatred because I could still sleep, write, enjoy a walk or a book."

Underhanded censorship was everywhere. Twelve years after Robert Brasillach's execution for his Hitlerian politics, his play *La Reine de Césarée* was finally being staged, only to be picketed to death by Resistance veterans. And the government managed to harass the theater that put on *Le Balcon,*

Jean Genet's ambitious vision of the world as a whorehouse of illusions where false bishops, judges and generals play out their fantasies while in the real world outside a revolution is in progress. Sartre couldn't help seeing the parallel and writing a searing little essay on the political constraints on Parisian theater.[23]

To escape having to listen to French people and having to see paratroopers on Place St. Germain, Simone and Lanzmann went to Italy. They toured the south, went to Sicily and drove back up to Rome. There, she stayed a month with Sartre and together they went to Capri to spend another month by the sea. They lived at an uninviting hotel in the center of town where few tourists ventured, climbed as far as the palace of Tiberius, walked along the sea and inspected the lurid red villa that the recently deceased Curzio Malaparte had willed to the writers of the Chinese People's Republic. Sartre was interviewed by *Welt am Sonntag* and talked to Simone about Tintoretto. After midnight, when the last tourists had gone, the view of the stone staircase leading down from the Salotto, with a few couples or groups melting away in the darkness, reminded him of Tintoretto's ability to bring the spectator right into the action of a painting by his choice of unusual viewpoints or a tilted angle of vision. Seen from the top, the people at the bottom seemed remote and noble like actors in a mysterious play. To study Tintoretto more closely, Sartre went to Venice while Simone joined Lanzmann in Milan.

When they returned, the war was still there, interminable. Poupette and her husband were living in Paris, but family get-togethers were painful. Lionel defended the government's antiterrorist search-and-destroy missions in the Algerian countryside and pacification program in Algiers. "After all, we've put a stop to the terrorism in Algiers," he would say, making Simone fly into a rage.

In February 1958, Sartre got the idea of writing a play about a family's reaction to a son's return from a war in which he has taken part in inhuman acts; a family's reaction to an unjust war and defeat. Some of the most frightening accounts they had published in *TM* were eyewitness reports from draftees who had taken part in torture or transcripts of their depositions at trials. Besides working on *La Critique* and the Tintoretto essay, Sartre began writing the new play. A meeting with Arthur Adamov, whose absurdist play *Paolo Paoli* was turned down by several theaters as politically too risky, convinced Sartre he could never make his family

[23] "Quand la police frappe les trois coups . . ." in *France-Observateur*, December 5, 1957; in volume in *Situations VII*, Paris: Gallimard, 1965.

French. If he made his soldier and family German, however, he could say even more devastating things. His hero would be a survivor of Hitler's war and his family consenting victims of a war over which they had no hold but for which they, too, were responsible. The play was easy to write. It was an illustration of *La Critique;* illustration of the "serial otherness" of individuals making history even if it is not the history they set out to make, and dealing with the responsibility of the soldier who went too far.

He had to put everything aside to write *Une Victoire,* conceived as a foreword to Henri Alleg's book about his torture at the hands of the 10th D. P. paratroop regiment in July 1957, but published separately in *L'Express,* which was immediately seized, and in book form in Switzerland.[24] A member of the Communist Party, Alleg had been the editor of *Alger républicain* from 1950 until the newspaper's suppression by military authorities five years later. He had gone "underground" with the FLN and had been arrested in June 1957, kept in solitary and been subjected to "the question" at the El-Biar paratroopers' camp. In April, Sartre signed, together with Martin du Gard, Malraux and Mauriac, a "solemn" address to President René Coty, calling on the government to condemn publicly and unequivocally the use of torture.

Sartre was broke.

The realization was sudden and came in the form of a tax assessment of twelve million francs ($266,000). He had always spent money freely, but earned a lot too. Claude Faux, Sartre's secretary since Jean Cau had graduated to full-time journalism, administered the current accounts. Gallimard and Julliard paid $1,600 a month in book royalties and for the *TM* editorship. From Gisèle Halimi, Sartre's and Simone's lawyer, came another $2,000, the monthly income from theatrical and film royalties plus, most important, foreign rights. How he managed to go through nearly four thousand dollars a month was something of a mystery to Sartre himself, if not to Faux and Halimi. Besides his mother, a lot of people lived off him. He gave money away all the time and the constant traveling was expensive. He liked to carry a lot of cash on him, often as much as a million francs ($20,000). Simone told him it was ridiculous. He agreed but continued, saying that together with his glasses, cigarettes and lighter, money "defined" him and gave him a silly feeling of superiority. He tipped excessively, reasoning that since waiters lived exclusively from tips it was his duty to see to it that they lived well.

Anne-Marie and John Huston came to his rescue. Somehow his mother

24 Henri Alleg, *La Question,* Lausanne: La Cité, 1958.

had managed to syphon off vast sums from his fifteen years of high-power liberality. Quietly, the tax bill was paid, but now he was really destitute.

As he wondered how to tide himself and the "family" over, someone told him the director of *The Treasure of the Sierra Madre* and *The African Queen* wanted to see him. Sartre told Faux to make an appointment. Huston showed up one morning and proposed that Sartre write the screenplay about Sigmund Freud. Twenty-five million francs ($550,000). Sartre said Yes.

The project was complicated and passably Hollywoodish. Screenwriter Charles Kaufman had been interested in doing a picture on Freud since he and Huston had written and directed a searing war documentary on psychological combat shock, *Let There Be Light*. In 1947, Kaufman had approached Twentieth Century-Fox, but Freud's daughter, Anna, had warned she would not allow a film biography to be made about her father. Freud's son, Ernst, still opposed the idea, but, as Huston explained to Sartre, they had all decided to ignore such threats. "Freud belongs to the ages and we have found that his life can be dramatized without permission of his heirs as long as we portray no living characters and don't malign the subject." What intrigued Huston—and made Sartre sit up and listen—was Huston's idea of showing Freud before he was famous, at the time, around thirty, when he was completely wrong, when his ideas had led him into hopeless error.

Sartre told Huston it was ironic that he, Sartre, who had always denied the existence of the unconscious, should be asked to write the story about the grand master of the unconscious. "Precisely," said Huston. "I don't want you to talk about the unconscious." The more they talked, the more interesting the project appeared. It wouldn't be easy of course. For one, it would be hard to show how Freud arrived at the right ideas without showing where he had gone wrong. Also, like most scientists, Freud had been a good husband and father. He seemed never to have been unfaithful to his wife, and indeed to have been a virgin until their wedding night. "One hears rumors of previous escapades, but I ascribe them to the devotion of his admirers; psychoanalysts don't want us to think that this man who knew so much about sexuality, came to marriage utterly unfledged," Sartre would tell Kenneth Tynan nine years later.[25] Huston, who had just finished *Moby Dick* and was living in Ireland, brought Twentieth Century-Fox's Darryl Zanuck along one day. It was agreed Sartre's screenplay should end with Freud discovering the Oedipus complex.

La Critique, Tintoretto, the play and now Freud. Théâtre Antoine-

[25] Kenneth Tynan, *Tynan Right and Left,* New York: Atheneum, 1967.

owner Simone Berrieu, who had produced *The Respectful Prostitute, Red Gloves, Lucifer and the Lord* and *Nekrassov,* had a self-styled first-rejection right. When she read the first outline of the new play, she said she would open the fall season with it. Rehearsals, of course, would have to start in late August or early September at the very latest.

Sartre popped amphetamines and chained himself to his desk. "It was not a case of writing as he ordinarily did, pausing to think and make corrections, tearing up a page, starting again," Simone would remember. "For hours at a stretch he raced across sheet after sheet without rereading them, as though absorbed by ideas that his pen, even at that speed, couldn't keep up with. To maintain this pace I could hear him crunching Corydran capsules, of which he managed to get through a bottle a day. At the end of the afternoon he would be exhausted; all his power of concentration would suddenly relax, his gestures would become vague, and quite often he would get his words mixed up. We spent our evenings in my apartment; as soon as he drank a glass of whiskey the alcohol would go straight to his head. 'That's enough,' I'd say to him; but for him it was not enough; against my will I would hand him a second glass; then he'd ask for a third. Two years before he had never needed a great deal more, but now he lost control of his movements and his speech very quickly and I would say, 'That's enough.' Two or three times I flew into violent tempers, I smashed a glass on the tiled floor of the kitchen. But I found it too exhausting to quarrel with him and I knew he needed something to help him relax." [26]

Civil war seemed imminent as the government was incapable of either waging war or making peace. Sartre protected himself by furious work. For Simone it was more difficult to escape into work. In June, Lanzmann left her.

It was normal—Claude was thirty-three; she was fifty. She had expected it from the beginning, but it was hard to stop being indispensable. A friendship would persist, she was sure, but she had regarded the relationship as being beyond time somehow. "The dangerous age" with its symbols and organic disturbances, the mistress-benefactress often attempting to buy a mirage of affection, of admiration, of respect from a younger lover; she had described it all in *The Second Sex.* Now she was there.

Sartre's preoccupation with his work and his drug stupor didn't help. They had dinner with Zette and Michel Leiris who since the last time they had met had swallowed an almost fatal dose of barbiturates and had been saved only by a difficult operation and a lengthy, painful convalescence.

[26] Beauvoir, *Force of Circumstance.*

Simone listened as Sartre and Leiris talked about uppers and downers and, the latest, antidepressants that Leiris was taking. When she asked what antidepressants did for him, Michel said, "They de-depress you." When she asked him to be more precise, he said, "It means you know everything's just as awful as it was before; only you're not depressed."

In June 1958, the events in Algeria swept away the Fourth Republic. The sixty-eight-year-old General de Gaulle went through the motions of having himself elected by the parliament he was about to abolish. His "restoration" had become possible because in him merged the hopes of those who believed—or pretended to believe—that only he could keep Algeria French, and of the minority who felt only his immense prestige could make France accept the inevitable emancipation of Algeria.

Sartre could think of nothing more depressing than Gaullism and, with Beaver, left for Italy in mid-June and stayed there until the end of the year. They stayed in Venice and in Spoleto—Simone correcting the proofs of her *Mémoires d'une jeune fille rangée*—before settling in Rome. Sartre called his play *Les Séquestrés d'Altona* because his soldier hero, Frantz, has imprisoned himself since World War II in a windowless room of the family mansion in Altona, a suburb of Hamburg, and because the whole Krupp-like family is sequestered in contradictions, failure and solitude.

Simone Berrieu had seen Sartre stumble into her office in his amphetamine haze and, when offered a Scotch, put it down where there was no table. Immediately, she told him to go and see a physician and canceled the fall premiere of the new play. He had only listened to her after he had scared the wits out of Beaver by doodling sentences that made no sense. The doctor had told him he was only inches away from a cardiac arrest. Sartre had promised Beaver that the Italian sojourn would also be a vacation. "I was never scared myself, though I realized I was pretty damaged," he would say eighteen years later. "I stopped—during two months I don't think I did anything; then I began to work again, but *Les Séquestrés d'Altona* was off for another year."

Through Italian papers, they followed de Gaulle's trip to Algeria to answer the delirious European crowds with his Machiavellian "I have understood you!" and his call for a September 28 constitutional referendum which, if passed, would create the Fifth Republic. *L'Express* editor Servan-Schreiber flew to Rome and got Sartre to write three articles against a yes vote. Sartre was still not well but wrote the pieces—and Simone edited them.[27]

[27] In *L'Express*, September 11, 18 and 25, 1958.

They stayed at the Albergo Nazionale on the Piazza Montecitorio off Via del Corso because of the air conditioning. Sartre screwed the temperature down to near freezing and it was in his room that Simone huddled in a blanket and first read *Les Séquestrés d'Altona,* which in English would become *The Condemned of Altona.* Carlo Levi introduced them to Alberto Moravia, who told them about his innumerable and improbable car accidents, and they met Merleau-Ponty and his wife who were on their way to Naples.

De Gaulle won his referendum by an unprecedented 80 percent yes vote. Sartre kept on working, popping Optalidon, Belladenal and Corydran to whip himself into working shape and to still recurring dizzy spells and splitting headaches. He had a hard time walking and began to stutter. By mid-October, Simone forced him to seek treatment. The diagnosis was a fatigued left ventricle of his heart. The cure—rest. Sartre kept on working.

Simone didn't feel well herself. When *Memoirs of a Dutiful Daughter* was coming out, she was on sedatives to allow her to sleep without nightmares. The success of her autobiography was the best medicine and, once Sartre was out of danger, affected her more intimately than the reception of any of her other books. She was flooded with letters. "Ghosts rose out of the past, some annoyed, some kindly," she would write in *Force of Circumstance.* School friends I'd treated rather sharply smiled at the awkwardness of their youth; friends I'd written about sympathetically got angry. Some former students of the Cours Désir approved of the picture I had painted of our education; others protested. One lady threatened to sue. The Mabille family were grateful to me for having made Zaza live again."

Sartre improved slowly and 1959 began with a happy event. Fidel Castro, who was described as a sort of Cuban Robin Hood, came down from the mountains with his guerrilla revolutionaries. On New Year's Day dictator Fulgencio Batista fled the country and a week later the bearded Fidel and his men entered a delirious Havana.

De Gaulle named Michel Debré his prime minister and Malraux his secretary for cultural affairs, but the war continued. Francis Jeanson had been totally radicalized and had joined the FLN as editor of an underground sheet called *Vérité pour. . . .* At the beginning, the clandestine paper had analyzed the economic and political causes of the war; now it preached open desertion. Sartre felt he had to grant *Vérité pour . . .* an interview that could appear under his own name so as to provoke the army to seek an indictment against him for aiding and abetting the enemy. This was not to be the last time Sartre would try to bait the de Gaulle government.

In Britain, Bertrand Russell had made a life-long career of needling governments into making fools of themselves in courts. Now the leader of the nuclear disarmament movement—and soon to interject himself in the Cuban missile crisis—Russell had cheerfully introduced the concept of civil disobedience to Anglo-Saxon jurisprudence. Approaching ninety, he was still protesting, crusading and periodically throwing the Foreign Office into bouts of apoplexy and despair, even if the British government no longer threw him into jail as it had done when he had agitated against the draft in the middle of World War I.

The white-maned, pin-sharp Russell was still writing philosophic history and in *Wisdom of the West* had just taken Sartre to task for ignoring necessity. "What is at bottom opposed by Sartre is the rationalist conception of necessity, as found in Leibniz and Spinoza and inherited by the Idealist philosopher," Russell wrote in his new illustrated history of philosophy.[28] Centering his review of existentialism on *Being and Nothingness,* he said that Sartre's view of man continuously choosing his destiny implies a rejection of freedom as being attuned to the workings of necessity. "In its criticism of the rationalist view of necessity, existentialism is drawing attention to an important point. However, it does not make a philosophic criticism so much as an emotional protest on psychological grounds. It is from a mood of feeling oppressed that existentialism stages its rebellion against rationalism. This leads into a somewhat strange and personal attitude toward the world of fact which constitutes an obstacle to freedom. The rationalist sees his freedom in a knowledge of how nature works; the existentialist finds it in an indulgence of his moods." Of *Being and Nothingness,* Russell said it was eccentric and "for poetic vagueness and linguistic extravagance" in the "best of the German traditions."

Sartre and Beaver spent a month in Rome, he finishing *Les Séquestrés d'Altona,* she beginning *The Prime of Life,* the second volume of her autobiography, which would deal with her coming of age and meeting Sartre. As always they criticized each other pitilessly. When she read a new ending to the play in which the family sits in judgment of Frantz, she told Sartre how disappointing this scene was compared to a previous draft. He went back to the earlier version saying he wasn't sure why he had changed it.

[28] Bertrand Russell, *Wisdom of the West, A Historical Survey of Western Philosophy in Its Social and Political Setting,* London: Rathbone, 1959.

When she read this reworked scene, she felt it was the best he had ever written.

It was a trying time for them. Sartre was deeply involved with Arlette Elkaim and if the pregnancy alarm proved false, Sartre's willingness to marry the now twenty-year-old Arlette was more than Simone could take. "He cannot do that to me," Simone told friends at the height of the crisis, but the friends didn't altogether agree. Before the war, when Sartre had proposed to *her*, Simone had said No and was now in no position to cry foul.

In the face of Simone's fury, however, Sartre relented, and instead of making Arlette his wife would eventually make her his daughter.

On September 16, de Gaulle offered Algeria "self-determination" with three choices—total "Francization" (the very ugliness of the term was, in the mouth of this political esthete, proof that he rejected it himself), outright independence (which he called "secession") and "association," which he obviously favored. The FLN's reaction was far from negative, but the *Algérie française* diehards answered him with barricades in Algiers, a wave of violence in Algeria and in Paris and a succession of plots on his life.

Les Séquestrés d'Altona premiered a week after de Gaulle's self-determination offer. Starring Serge Reggiani as Frantz, Fernard Ledoux as the father, old von Gerlach, Lanzmann's sister, Evelyn Rey, as Johanna, Frantz's sister, Robert Moncade as Werner, Gerlach's youngest son and Wanda Kosakiewicz as Werner's wife, Leni, the play was greeted with enthusiasm. The critics called it one of Sartre's most important plays, if not his best, and the popular success was such that its run at the Antoine lasted ten months and was followed by an even longer run in 1965 at the Athénée Theater. Massive and ambitious, lumpy and outsized, *The Condemned of Altona* is a burning dramatization of the question, How can modern man assume responsibility for a history that disfigures him?

As the curtain goes up, old shipbuilding tycoon von Gerlach learns from his doctor that he has only a short time to live. Making plans to put his house in order, he summons his idealistic son Werner and the latter's wife. An older brother was presumably killed years ago after being mentioned as a war criminal at the Nuremberg Trials. Then the terrible secret of the house in Altona comes out—Frantz is alive. For fifteen years he has locked himself up in his room, cared for by his sister.

Frantz is Sartre's Everyman, a man obsessed by the torture he committed on the Russian front, haunted by the Nuremberg judgment, which held a collective Germany responsible for the crimes of Nazism. Frantz decides

Arlette Elkaim and Sartre at
The Condemned of Altona *rehearsals*
ROGER-VIOLLET

to assume his own and his country's destiny in the face of history's judgment, but to retain an ounce of innocence he must appear not only as a defeated person but as a victim. Which is why, fifteen years after the war, he has invented a martyred Germany still in ruins. He assumes all guilt, but within a planned folly in which he flees into ever deeper lucidity and mythomania. Hell, here, is not other people, but a century crushed by its crimes, our century with its partly guilty, partly innocent heroes, half accomplices, half victims. As in *Huis Clos,* survivors are fascinated by their past and square off and destroy themselves. As in "La Chambre," one of the short stories of *Le Mur,* Frantz's madness slowly infests those who come in contact with him. As in Sartre's hallucinatory psychosis of 1935, monstrous crabs hang from the ceiling of Frantz's room. To this court of crabs, he addresses tape-recorded pleas of innocence to future centuries.

Les Séquestrés is Sartre's richest, most difficult play, an attempt at judging the century from the outside, through future consciences to whom this century is nothing more than a dead object. The play is devoid of all bourgeois moralizing. It is also his most rigorously constructed piece of dramaturgy. In *No Exit,* the characters talked about the past; here the past ends up modifying the present. If Frantz commits suicide in the end it is not because of guilt but because he realizes his own uselessness. In interviews, Sartre said he wanted to show people *after* their crimes. His subject, he said, was the draftee returning from Algeria where he may have taken part in inhuman acts, "someone we cannot despise or laugh away," and that if he had chosen a Krupp-like family it was because such a family gave him the inner contradictions between Germany's industrialist who despised the Nazis but collaborated with them, people who thought *against* but acted *for.* "In this way I could show the problem of *collusion* which is essential to understanding man." [29] When asked if he were Frantz himself, he said only insofar as the character "represents the negative of one of my fondest dreams—to be in a cell, to be able to write in peace." [30] The crabs are inside Frantz's own head. "Since Frantz is guilty, he makes his judges as frightful as possible. I believe that the tribunal of history always judges men according to standards and values which they themselves could never imagine. We can never know what the future will say of us. It may be that history will consider Hitler a great man—though that would astonish me enormously—and in any case, there is always Stalin! The point is that we know we shall be judged, and not by the rules we use to judge ourselves.

29 In *Théâtre populaire,* No. 36, August 1959.
30 "Entretien avec Sartre," by Madeleine Chapsal, in *L'Express,* September 10, 1959; in volume, Madeleine Chapsal, *Les Ecrivains en personne,* Paris: Seuil, 1960; in *Between Existentialism and Marxism,* New York: Morrow, 1976.

And in that thought there is something horrific. Moreover, it has been said that progress is made laterally, in a sideways motion, like the movement of crabs. That was also part of my idea." [31]

Sartre flew to Ireland to talk *Freud* with Huston. The script Sartre had come up with would make a seven-hour movie. Huston and his producer, Wolfgang Reinhardt, ordered cuts and Sartre deleted some of the scenes, bringing the length down to six and a half hours. Huston had just finished shooting *The Misfits* with Clark Gable, Marilyn Monroe and Montgomery Clift and told Sartre he was so taken with Clift that he had decided "Monty" should play Freud. While Huston went horseback riding over the moors, Sartre kept trimming, paring the script down page by page, but there were problems. Huston didn't understand the unconscious, and Sartre didn't understand the exigencies of commercial filmmaking. But Sartre was paid his contractual half million dollars and the break was halfway amiable. Huston retained Sartre's idea of fusing several of Freud's patients into one Anna O., and together with Reinhardt, returned to the ten-year-old version written by Kaufman. Sartre returned to Paris realizing he had a new command on Freudian thought and psychoanalytic theory. The principal shortcoming of psychoanalysis, he felt, was its lack of dialectics, its inability to make phenomena derive from each other in such a way as to make each forward step conditioned on the previous one while at the same time containing and superseding it. In dialectic thinking, each step may contain the previous step but it can never be *reduced* to its predecessor. Psychoanalytic theory was syncretic, that is, it compared opposites; it wasn't a way of being.

Freud led him to a renewed interest in Flaubert. Sartre had been writing on Flaubert on and off since 1954. In 1957, *TM* had announced the coming publication of a Sartrian essay on Flaubert, but the promised piece had become a chapter of *La Critique,* showing the inadequacy of both Marxist and Freudian methods in studying a person's life. Psychoanalysis shows the development of the individual; Marxism the development of the social environment, but neither of them shows the *encounter* of person and history. But why Flaubert? people asked Sartre. Because Flaubert was one of the rare historical or literary personages to have left literally tons of information about himself. He often wrote letters to several persons the same day, with slight variations between them, adding up to thirteen volumes of correspondence, each of six hundred pages. With Flaubert it was possible to study the man through his acts and the acts through the

[31] Kenneth Tynan, *Tynan Right and Left.*

man. Indeed, it might be possible to reconstitute how Flaubert came to be the author of *Madame Bovary* and not of some other book.

Simone was also dabbling in screenwriting. André Cayatte had come to filmmaking from the legal profession. A trained lawyer, he had directed three films about the injustices of France's legal system. In the popular *Nous sommes tous des assassins,* starring Mouloudji, he had combined an attack on capital punishment with the question of individual vs. mass killing in time of war. In *Justice est faite,* he had examined jury service and in *Avant le déluge* he had taken on juvenile delinquency, presenting impressive material although the overall effect was ruined by too much preaching. Cayatte's screenwriter on *Nous sommes tous des assassins* (*We Are All Murderers*) had been none other than Belgium's Paul-Henri Spaak, two-time prime minister, NATO Secretary-General and Council of Europe founder. To Simone, Cayatte now suggested that she work with him on a film about divorce. She wasn't particularly interested in "the problem of the couple," but Cayatte had a novel idea. He would make two films of the same couple, one film giving the woman's, the other the man's version of the conflict that divides them. She objected that the life of any couple is a story with two faces, not two distinct stories. Cayatte insisted, but when he read her script admitted that the divided form was ruining it.

She realized Cayatte had approached her because she was thought of as having a taste for "problem" novels. People increasingly turned to her, especially younger women feeling trapped in situations—husband, child, work—which they had helped to create although sometimes despite themselves. In her screenplay, Simone was at pains not to prove anything and to leave scenes and sentiments ambiguous. Cayatte found it confusing and stuck to his *his-her* gimmick. "I would have preferred to capture the audience by less obvious methods," she would remember. "But I had no complaints; Cayatte knew what he wanted and it wasn't what I was giving him. I understood perfectly why he decided not to go with it."

Simone was alone in Sartre's apartment January 4, 1960 when Lanzmann called to say that Camus had been killed in a car accident. Instead of taking the train, Camus had decided to take editor Michel Gallimard up on his offer to drive back to Paris with him, his wife and their teenage daughter. Michel Gallimard had been at the wheel, Camus next to him and Madame Gallimard and the daughter in the back seat when the Facel-Vega had swerved out of control and hit a tree on Nationale 7 at Sens, eighty miles south of Paris. Camus was killed instantly; the others all survived. On Camus' body police had found the unused railway ticket. When Simone put down the receiver she told herself she wouldn't cry because Camus had not meant anything for a long time. When Sartre got home, he was also disturbed and they spent the evening with Little Bost talking about Camus. Before going to bed, Simone swallowed her first atropine pills since Sartre had begun to recover. Instead of going to sleep, she remained wide awake and finally took a long walk through drizzly Left Bank Paris, ending up at the Avenue d'Orléans where derelicts were sleeping in doorways. "Everything tore at my heart; this poverty, this unhappiness, this city, the world and life, and death," she would write in *Force of Circumstance*. "When I woke up, I thought: He can't see this morning. It wasn't the first time I had said that to myself, but every time is the first time."

Sartre and Beaver were more together again, spending long evenings listening to records—Webern was their latest discovery—and often on Sundays taking long walks along the Seine, behind the Panthéon where Sartre had spent his childhood or in the working-class Ménilmontant district. On such walks they would lament the way age seemed to have blunted their curiosity. Sartre would tell her he thought their lack of enthusiasm for new travels was more the result of physical exhaustion than moral fatigue and as she didn't want him to overexert himself again, she readily agreed. Not that they lacked invitations. Carlos Franqui, the fiery black-mustached editor-in-chief of Havana's *Revolución,* was in Paris on a blitz tour through Europe and when he met them told them it was their duty to come to Cuba and see a revolution actually in progress. Although they felt great sympathy for Castro, Franqui's offer left them almost indifferent. And when Jorge Amado and other Brazilian leftists invited them to their country their reaction was just as half-hearted.

But in mid-February they flew off to Cuba, Sartre with a contract with mass circulation *France-Soir* to write a series of articles on the new Cuba. Their arrival was bewildering—ears still blocked, the sun beating down, flowers were thrust into Simone's arms, compliments, press conferences ("What do you think of the Cuban revolution?" one journalist asked Sartre. "That's what I've come to find out," he answered). From the beginning, the sojourn took on the aspect, pace and repercussion of an official visit. Sartre met privately with Che Guevara, crisscrossed the island with Castro, held numerous talks and even spoke on Cuban TV. Simone, Sartre and Castro went speed boating and attended the funeral of the first victims of anti-Castro sabotage bombings.

The United States' hostility to Castro was beginning; the U. S. ambassador to Havana had left, but, as far as Sartre could see, the revolution was still in its honeymoon—a mass of seething and slightly confused hopes

Speedboating with Fidel Castro, November 1960
GÉRARD ALCAN

devoid of machinery and bureaucracy. For the first time Sartre and Beaver were witnessing rebels triumphant, a people and its liberator-soldiers still radiant with victory and purpose. It was like a carnival replay of all the things he had been writing in *La Critique,* the moment of "fusion" when revolutionary spontaneity could move mountains. And it was the opposite of the Algerian quagmire (a letter from Lanzmann announced the arrest of members of Francis Jeanson's group). When Sartre was interviewed on TV, he said that what moved him above everything else in the Cuban revolution was the idea of every literate Cuban teaching five illiterates to read and write, and the absence of preconceived ideology which made the Cuban experience free of dogma and so different from traditional communist revolutions.[32]

Sartre had visited Havana with Dolores in 1949 and in his sixteen *France-Soir* articles, edited by Lanzmann, compared pre-Castro Cuba with what he saw in early 1960.[33] A conversation he and Simone had with Castro on people's needs and expectations was reprinted verbatim because Castro's ideas echoed Sartre's: " 'We must demand everything possible of everybody,' Castro said abruptly. 'But I'll never sacrifice this generation for those to come.' "

From Havana, Sartre and Beaver flew to New York. They had never been in the United States together and firmly told a Cuban U. N. attaché to rearrange his press party for them at another time so that by car and on foot they could plunge into the city. After the multicolored tumult of Havana, New York on a cold March Sunday seemed bleak and almost poverty stricken. People in the streets looked shabby and seemed rather bored.

Algren had managed to get himself a passport and was already in Paris after a boozy visit with Brendan Behan in Dublin, when Sartre and Simone returned. Algren had grown older, wore contact lenses and was happy to have been able to leave the United States. "Once I used to live in America," he said. "Now I live on American-occupied territory." What he could not forgive in America was the arrogance of the respectable classes. They were more intolerable than ever, he said. Society was always right and its victims treated as criminals. He stayed in Simone's apartment and she introduced him to old friends and new—Sartre, Michelle, Bost and Olga, but also Lanzmann and Monique Lange, a Gallimard editor accustomed to shepherding foreign authors around Paris.

---

[32] Televised press conference, reprinted in *Revolución,* March 11, 1960.
[33] "Ouragan sur le sucre," series of sixteen articles, *France-Soir,* June 28–July 15, 1960; in volume, *Sartre on Cuba,* New York: Ballantine, 1961.

At the Sorbonne, Sartre gave a conference on the theater. He spoke for over two hours and, wrote John Weightman in *Encounter*,[34] seemed to have been able to continue all night. Sartre criticized both Beckett's and Ionesco's theater as bourgeois and Brecht's epic theater for turning audiences into ethnographers discovering savages and saying, "Hey, they're like us!" The only valid theater, he summed up, was a dramatic theater.

The Algerian war wasn't going away. Algeria's *pieds-noir* had answered de Gaulle's self-determination project with barricades in the streets of Algiers. One morning, Simone got a call from their lawyer Gisèle Halimi asking to see her immediately. Halimi was just back from Algiers where she had made preliminary court motions in the defense of Djamila Boupacha, an Algerian girl who had been hideously tortured although she had freely admitted to being a terrorist. When Halimi had seen her client, the girl was pale and emaciated, visibly in a state of shock. She still had skin burns and said she could cite witnesses. Halimi had told her to make an official deposition and to further delay her trial had requested an inquiry. Would Simone write a newspaper account of the affair?

From the girl's deposition, Simone fashioned an article and sent it to *Le Monde*. The big afternoon daily published it after toning down "thrusting a Coke bottle into her vagina" to "thrusting a Coke bottle into her womb," and saw its overseas edition suppressed in Algiers—losing four hundred thousand francs, as Simone was pointedly told. Halimi and Simone organized a Djamila Boupacha Defense Committee. Françoise Sagan supported the campaign in *L'Express* and two women deportees who had suffered torture in Nazi camps joined the committee. In Algiers, the prosecutor offered a deal. If Djamila would let herself be declared insane, her inquiry into her torture would become invalid but she would be set free. Halimi refused and by midsummer Djamila was transferred to a French prison and a judge from Caen put in charge of the investigation.

A first attempt at a negotiated peace collapsed and Sartre told *Vérité-Liberté*,[35] a new war protesters' newspaper, that a victory for the FLN was a victory for everything that was sane. The interview was alleged to "provoke servicemen into disobedience." This charge led to the confiscation of the issue in which Sartre's interview appeared and to the surveillance of the paper's editorial staff. More important, Sartre's idea that the French left would have to declare itself to be on the FLN's side contained the kernel of the Manifesto of the 121. An imposing group of intellectuals, teachers

[34] *Encounter*, June 1961.
[35] *Vérité-Liberté*, July–August 1960.

and artists—one hundred and twenty-one originally—signed and publicized this antiwar protest whose most devastating paragraph invited France's drafted youth to disobey. This invitation to open rebellion within the armed forces was so radical that *L'Express* and *L'Humanité* disapproved, and when the August issue of *Les Temps modernes* published the text, the magazine was immediately confiscated. Sartre and Beaver were not the instigators of the Manifesto but were among the first to sign it and on September 8, *Paris-Presse* carried a front-page headline, JEAN-PAUL SARTRE, SIMONE DE BEAUVOIR, SIMONE SIGNORET AND 100 OTHERS RISK FIVE YEARS IN JAIL. On September 8, Sartre and Beaver were in Rio de Janeiro, but the French embassy immediately let it be known that Sartre would be arrested the moment he put his foot on French soil.

Their visit to Havana had made them curious about the huge under-developed and semicolonized Brazil where revolutionary forces had not been unleashed. Amado had persuaded them that Malraux's Brazilian high-profile visit as de Gaulle's Cultural Affairs minister needed to be countered (Malraux's twenty-seven-year-old daughter, Florence, had been one of the one hundred and twenty-one) and in mid-August they had landed in Recife. Bahia, Rio, São Paulo, Belo Horizonte, Brasilia, the visit turned into a three-month crisscross of press conferences, TV appearances, meet-ings, book signings, dazzling excursions through coffee plantations, passion flower groves and for Simone alone, Manaus in the Amazon interior, which gave her typhoid fever that had her hospitalized in Recife. News from home was scattered, but a letter from Lanzmann in October told them the *TM* offices had been searched, that many more had signed the Mani-festo of the 121, that the original signatories had all been declared non-persons in subsidized theater and on national radio and TV. French legion veterans had marched five thousand strong on the Champs Elysées shouting "Shoot Sartre!" and *Paris-Match* had headlined an editorial, SARTRE, CIVIL WARMONGER.

The French embassy in Rio was maintaining the rumors that Sartre would be arrested as soon as he got back and the French colony in Recife said Simone's illness was diplomatic and that they were afraid of returning to France. A recent letter from Lanzmann said the general feeling among their friends was that they should get no closer to France than Barcelona. In November, they flew to Spain via Cuba—Sartre realizing how the regime had hardened and that the honeymoon was over. Jean Pouillon and Little Bost met them in Barcelona and told them what had happened. Communist and socialist youth groups, and trade unions had taken various forms of action against the war, university teachers had launched an appeal

Visiting with the Caraja Indians in central Brazil
KEYSTONE

At a Brazilian beach, October 1965
A.F.P.

for a negotiated peace, a student protest had been an enormous success despite truncheon charges by police. The measures taken against the hundred and twenty-one had backfired for the government; the TV actors guild had gone on strike when Evelyn Rey had been suspended from a program. On the other hand, Marshal Alphonse Juin had launched a countermanifesto against "the professors of treason," the National Union of reserve officers was demanding that action be taken against the hundred and twenty-one and their names had been posted in all mess halls.

From Paris, Lanzmann told them on the phone not to take the plane home because the airport welcome might be stormy and result in reporters' questions that they might answer in such a way that police would arrest them. They crossed into France in Bost's car. The French border inspector told them apologetically that he had orders to advise Paris when they crossed, then had them sign in the visitors' book.

Once in Paris, they got themselves a lawyer and undertook all the necessary arrangements to get themselves arrested. The police commissioner who came around to see them at Simone's apartment helped them phrase their statements and to vary them a little. On the eve of their court hearing, the examining magistrate reported sick. A new date was set; then that was postponed *sine die,* supposedly because their files were still at the prosecutors' office. Next they learned the charges had been dropped.

The government was not eager to prosecute—there were rumors that President de Gaulle himself had intervened with a decidedly Gaullian phrase, "One doesn't arrest Voltaire." Sartre tried to counter with a press conference in Simone's apartment where he told thirty French and foreign journalists how the government refused to prosecute. The press printed a summary of his statement but the incident remained closed.

The Prime of Life came out and sold forty thousand copies in one month, making Simone wonder if she was becoming a best-seller manufacturer. Many critics assured her she had just written her best book and she found there was something disquieting about this verdict.

On New Year's, there was a dinner at the Soviet embassy and Sartre and Beaver agreed to attend. It was the first time they went out at night since their return.

CHAPTER

VIII

MAY 1968

IN THE MAY EVENTS, those lyrical riots that led to de Gaulle's downfall and were to reverberate through the French national conscience for years, Sartre discovered that one could be to the *left* of the Communist Party. The "events," which echoed Mao's cultural revolution, the Berkeley riots, Che Guevara's guerrillas, and the "spring of Prague," totally radicalized Sartre and Beaver—militant feminism was just around the corner—as youth openly displayed its beguiling strength. Now both in their sixties, they saw their grandchildren's generation trade on a visionary and amplified "now" and *do* the things they had written about for decades. The youth not only showed Gaullist France to have remained a "blocked" nation, a country not yet decolonized at home, it "occupied" universities and factories, criticized the very notion of the Communist Party as a political structure and declared intellectuals to be obsolete.

Sartre and Simone were not on the St.-Germain-des-Prés barricades sniffing riot squad tear gas or occupying the Sorbonne to turn it into a Maoist "université critique." Too long habits of political impotence, age, worries about his mother's declining health and the intractable Flaubert kept Sartre on the sidelines until May 11, when he told a radio audience that the students were right in smashing up the Sorbonne. Simone was deep into her book about old age, but she signed a manifesto on May 9 and, together with Sartre, expressed her solidarity with the *contestataires*.

Not that anyone else had seen the events coming. Everything had

seemed calm, even serene, during the spring of the year Gaullism celebrated its tenth year in power. The headlines of May 1 were concentrated
on Czech Premier Alexander Dubcek's May Day appeal for "socialism with
a smile" and on Hanoi's refusal to meet American peace terms and not on
the disciplinary expulsion of one Daniel Cohn-Bendit, leader of student
activists at Nanterre University on the western outskirts of Paris. Cohn-
Bendit, a German national of varied origin, was accused of masterminding
sit-ins, distributing tracts on campus and disrupting lectures and exams.
When the Nanterre administration closed the university to bring the "hot
heads" to heel, Sorbonne students took up the cause and decided to hold
disruptive study sessions of their own. Rector Jean Roche demanded police
action to clear out the "rebels" and for the first time in a century, police
invaded the hallowed halls of learning. Three days later, a student march
clashed with police on Boulevard St. Germain resulting in a number of
wounded students.

De Gaulle was on the eve of leaving for a Romanian state visit and his
premier, Georges Pompidou, was scheduled to fly off on a tour of Iran
and Afghanistan. "Kids' stuff," the general huffed when Pompidou made
a worried remark before leaving for the airport. During the following
three days, the government, and *L'Humanité,* condemned "splinter fac-
tions" fomenting trouble while tens of thousands of students demonstrated in Paris with a three-pronged demand—the immediate reopening
of the Sorbonne, the pullback of police and the freeing of arrested students. On May 9, Education Minister Alain Peyrefitte almost managed to
defuse the situation by promising the reopening of the Sorbonne. When
Nanterre students occupied their university, however, he refused to have
police evacuate the Sorbonne. As teachers' and students' unions issued
orders for an unlimited strike, students began building street barricades
in the Latin Quarter. In the evening, Roche tried to reopen negotiations
but refused to free arrested students. At 2 A.M. on the 11th, Paris police
chief Maurice Grimaud announced on a bullhorn that he had received
orders to bring down the barricades. When the smoke cleared two hours
later, the streets were littered with three hundred wounded and the wrecks
of gasoline-bombed cars. Riot squad police instituted a tactic of hot pursuit and chased demonstrators into apartment buildings to club them,
making public opinion turn against the government and denounce excessive police brutality. Five hundred demonstrators were arrested.

No one dared to wake up de Gaulle. The next day, Pompidou returned
from Kabul and immediately took energetic measures. He denounced
police brutality, had twenty-five of the original twenty-eight arrested stu-

dents set free and announced that the Sorbonne would reopen the following morning. But student leaders had already escalated the confrontation
by persuading organized labor to call a one-day general strike. On May
13, eight hundred thousand people marched behind student leaders, liberal faculty members, union chiefs and leftist political figures, shouting,
"We want a people's government!" and "Ten years are enough!" The
march was not all harmony. Union leaders had tried to have Cohn-Bendit
excluded and with bullhorns and loudspeaker vans did their best to limit
the contact between workers and students.

Ignoring the recommendations of his advisers, de Gaulle refused to
postpone his visit to Romania. The day after his departure, young workers occupied the Sud-Aviation aircraft plant; the following day, the giant
Renault car plant was disrupted by militants. By May 17, the movement
had spread to hundreds of businesses. What really frightened the government was that the events were not controlled by big labor or the Communist Party. On the 17th, de Gaulle cut short his visit to Bucharest and
in a public reassessment of the situation managed to insult the whole of
France's youth. Had he lost touch? A May 24 appeal in which he offered
to hold another referendum in June was mediocre, hesitant and revealed
the government's confusion.

Sartre spoke to the militants occupying the Sorbonne on the 20th. The
news that he was in agreement with the rebels spread through the Latin
Quarter and when he mounted the big amphitheater podium the hall
was dangerously overflowing and Simone and Marguerite Duras never
made it inside. There were fears that the crowd could turn ugly. Sartre
endorsed the students' action and said big labor was afraid of their "wild-
cat democracy." For an hour he answered questions. Simone and several
friends waited for him at the Balzar café and she was relieved to see him
appear, followed by a horde of students, journalists and photographers.
Next, Sartre became a *Nouvel Observateur* reporter interviewing Cohn-
Bendit.

On May 24, Pompidou tried to buy peace with major wage concessions,
including a 10 to 30 percent boost in minimum wages. When the union
leaders presented the package to Renault workers, they were jeered. The
country seemed to slide toward anarchy. De Gaulle's offer of a referendum
was booed and the leftist organizations, including the Communist Party,
seemed out of touch with their rank and file.

De Gaulle appeared dejected and was heard muttering that the people
no longer wanted him, but this master strategist knew his people and how

Addressing the overflowing
amphitheater crowd at the Sorbonne, May 20, 1968
KEYSTONE

to give every gesture a dramatic significance. To become legend and myth again, he disappeared. Cabinet members were told he had left by helicoper for his Colombey-les-deux-Eglises retreat in eastern France, but no helicopter landed there. Instead, it was rumored that he had flown to Germany, to the French armed forces headquarters in Baden-Baden. The rumors were true. Much later, he would say he had actually expected a communist coup d'état.

As it was, the few hours spent with Supreme Commander Massu—another near-mythical figure, a former paratroop commander of Algiers who deviously had backed legitimacy during a 1961 generals' putsch against de Gaulle—were enough to provoke a reaction. Instead of pitying and booing the aging head of state, public opinion divided sharply. Did Massu tell de Gaulle that the army was behind him, that not all youths were at the barricades, that despite the strikes that paralyzed public transportation, soldiers on leave were returning to their units? De Gaulle never said what Massu told him, but at noon on May 30 he resurfaced dramatically in Paris. He energetically called his cabinet together and had air time cleared for a major address to the nation. Pompidou agreed that backlash support was swelling but counseled elections instead of a referendum. An election lost, Pompidou told de Gaulle, was not the end of the world; a referendum lost would bring down the regime. After the 4:30 P.M. address in which de Gaulle announced a June 30 general election and a future referendum, the tide was turning. For years, the revolutionary forces would argue why they had hesitated at the brink.

The Sorbonne held out another ten days. Simone visited there June 10 when the situation was turning sour. At night, the university was filled with hippies, drug traffickers were peddling in the corridors and at a hastily organized infirmary students stole morphine capsules. The perimeters were defended by "Katangans," helmeted students armed with iron bars and led by mercenaries wholly devoid of political convictions. A doctor urged her to write an article on the "decay" at the Sorbonne, but she refused. Two days later, the revolt collapsed. In an interview with Germany's *Der Spiegel*, Sartre said the communists had been afraid of the events, that the "revolution" had gone as far as it could but that it had invalidated Herbert Marcuse's "pessimsism" and resulted in the total politization of France's youth.[1] To *Le Nouvel Observateur*, he said the "uncontrolled" student violence wasn't so much the expression of anarchy as of hope for a different society.[2]

[1] *Der Spiegel*, July 15, 1968.
[2] *Le Nouvel Observateur*, June 19–25, 1968.

In August, the Soviet Union invaded Czechoslovakia to choke off the Dubcek government's socialism with a smile, and from the Venice Film Festival, where Sartre was backing Maoist filmmakers' demand for doing away with all "star system" prizes and competition, he denounced the invasion and in an interview with the communist daily *Paese Sera* called the Soviets "war criminals." Three months later, Simone and he were in Prague, ostensibly for the Czech premieres of *Les Mouches* and *Les Mains sales,* in reality in a defiant gesture against the Soviet tanks on Wenceslas Square. "I don't know a single progressive who hasn't condemned the arrival of foreign troops in Czechoslovakia," he told *Svobodne Slovo.* "More and more people are realizing that despite all your trials and tribulations, you have proved that there can be other roads to socialism." [3] They were guests of the Czech Writers Union, as they had been in 1963, and met Antonin Liehm and Milan Kundera, now debarred from publication and banned from public libraries. After the last curtain of *The Flies,* Sartre was called to the stage. Liehm had told him he could speak openly and as the audience urged him to give his views he said he looked upon the Soviet aggression as a war crime, that he had written *The Flies* to encourage the French to resist and that he was glad his play was now being performed in occupied Czechoslovakia.

The worst danger to his personal safety was not to speak out in Prague. It had been during the summer of 1961 and the following winter when members of the Organisation de l'Armée secrète (OAS) had tried to assassinate him. The first bombing by this Keep-Algeria-French-at-any-cost terror organization had come July 19. A charge of explosives went off in the hallway at 42 Rue Bonaparte. No one was hurt, but Sartre decided to move his mother to a hotel on Boulevard Raspail. The seventy-nine-year-old Anne-Marie didn't mind the change. Although she had help, the housework tired her. The hotel freed her of these obligations, she had her own furniture, her heirlooms and her favorite books and record player. The Schweitzers were a musical family and Anne-Marie's taste was discriminate. She was not afraid of avant-garde music—it was in her company that Simone first heard Alban Berg's *Wozzeck.* During these years, Simone and she had become close. Joseph Mancy had never wanted to meet his stepson's mistress and until his death in 1945, Anne-Marie had met Sartre and Simone without telling her husband. "Madame Mancy had a submissive devoted nature; she was full of gratitude because her hus-

[3] *Svobodne Slovo,* November 30, 1968; reprinted in *Le Monde,* December 1–2, 1968.

band had assumed the care both of her and her child; she always thought he was right," [4] Simone would write in *All Said and Done,* the last volume of her autobiography. "She didn't say so, but she disapproved of my way of life. It was less her preconceived notions that troubled me than her apparent spinelessness. She spoke in short, interrupted sentences, making an excessive use of the word 'little' in order to weaken her meaning. For example, in a tearoom she would ask the waitress, 'Where is the little powder-room?' Her tone of voice was usually plaintive. She said she suffered from a great many little aches and pains, and she never admitted to having any pleasure. As she saw it, life was a collection of wearisome duties. She never presumed to give a personal opinion on any subject—her absent husband still governed her thoughts."

Her naïveté was something of a burden for Sartre and Beaver. Once, she gave photographs of Sartre as a child to a stranger who told her his student sister in America and her whole class profoundly revered the French philosopher. When the picture appeared in *Samedi-Soir* as illustration to a venomous article, Anne-Marie received her son and Simone in tears. Sartre begged her to avoid contact with the press, but she was incurable. She talked too much and, aware that she had been careless, resented the reproaches Sartre never formulated. She was completely devoted to her son and liked to believe she was necessary to him. "Like many women whose existence is 'relative,' she lived in a constant state of worry," Simone would write. "It distressed her profoundly if Sartre were attacked in the papers. She quite lost her head when we gave a lecture or had a play put on. The rehearsals were often stormy; she heard rumors, and she was consumed with anxiety. She was afraid that Sartre might offend the theater management, the producer, the audience. On first nights she was in torment if she overheard a criticism or if she thought the applause lukewarm." Most deplorable to her were her son's political attitudes, even if in time she often adopted some of his opinions and in her eighties felt entirely liberated. "It is only now when I'm eighty-four that I have really broken free from my mother," she told them.

Sartre and Beaver were packing to leave for the summer in Rome when the OAS bomb blasted a hole in the hallway at 42 Rue Bonaparte. Simone had hoped he would work less if away from home, but Merleau-Ponty's death and Frantz Fanon's coming to Rome kept him busy. Merleau-Ponty was Simone's age, fifty-three, and Sartre decided to devote an issue of *TM*

[4] Simone de Beauvoir, *Tout compte fait,* Paris: Gallimard, 1972; *All Said and Done,* New York: G. P. Putnam's, 1974.

to his old friend and fellow existentialist. Popping Corydran until in the evening he was quite deaf, he retraced his friendship with Merleau-Ponty, and through it, the history of *Les Temps modernes.*

Fanon was a dying man. This black revolutionary and member of the underground provisional government of the Algerian Republic was a Martinique-born psychiatrist who had turned unorthodox Marxist and Third World ideologue out of hatred for the suffering and oppression he had seen in Algerian hospitals in the 1950s. He had found himself treating both torturer and tortured and had developed the theory that the mental disturbances he was witnessing were the byproduct of colonialism. Hunted by French police and dying of leukemia, Fanon had asked Sartre, through Lanzmann, to preface his book, *Les Damnés de la terre,* an incendiary manifesto proclaiming that the oppressed could only attain human dignity through violence.[5] On his way to cobalt treatment in northern Italy in the company of his French wife, Josie, Fanon met Sartre and Simone for lunch in Rome. He was feverish and predicted a French invasion of Tunisia within the next forty-eight hours. When Simone broke off the conversation at 2 A.M. the following morning, politely insisting that Sartre needed rest, Fanon was outraged. No one in the provisional government slept more than a few hours, himself included. "I'd give twenty thousand francs a day to be able to talk to Sartre from morning to night for two weeks," Fanon later told Lanzmann. For three more days, they carried on their marathon talks and when Fanon came back through Rome after his cobalt treatment they talked another day. Fanon had a razor-sharp mind and was endowed with a grim sense of humor. He explained things, made jokes, questioned Sartre and Beaver and told stories. Sartre's foreword to *Les Damnés de la terre* was the most violent text he had ever written, declaring his complete solidarity with the Algerian terrorists and, by extension, with the struggle of all colonial people. Ironically, Josie Fanon had Sartre's preface deleted from the 1968 edition because she objected to his stand on the 1967 Israeli-Arab war.

The Italian capital was becoming a second home. Sartre and Beaver spent four months in Rome and were back again in December. They usually stayed in a double suite at the Albergo Nazionale in Piazza Montecitoria, sleeping late, spending the mornings working, the afternoons strolling and stretching the evenings far into the night. They had drinks in the Piazza Sant' Eustachio until noise and vendors made them prefer the Pi-

[5] Frantz Fanon, *Les Damnés de la terre,* Paris: Maspero, 1961; *The Damned,* Paris: Présence africaine, 1963.

azza Santa Maria in Trastevere where they would sit absorbed in the foun-
tains and the faded gold of the mosaics, or the Piazza Navona they had
first fallen in love with forty years earlier. When these piazzas were invaded by cars, tourist buses and red-balloon sellers, the square by the
Panthéon became the new hangout. People would often ask for their
autographs—gracefully, Simone thought—and young men, particularly
revolutionaries from Latin America, would sometimes ask Sartre for appointments. They often lunched at Carlo Levi's and Sartre met several times
with Communist Party chief Palmiro Togliatti, a Marxist Sartre liked for
the degree of independence from Moscow he maintained.

Rome lulled Simone into a sense of security, but once back in Paris, the
Algerian conflict closed in on them again. The OAS had answered de
Gaulle's "disengagement" plan for Algeria with attempts on his life. On
December 19, Sartre and Beaver took part in an illegal anti-OAS demon-
stration with Lanzmann and a journalist whose apartment had just been
bombed. Shortly before Christmas, Sartre and Beaver found it prudent to
move into a tenth-floor studio in an as-yet-unfinished highrise at 222
Boulevard Raspail, rented in Claude Faux's name. It was none too soon.
On January 7, 1962, a blast ripped through the upper floors of 42 Rue
Bonaparte. The bomb had been left on the floor above Sartre's, blowing
up two apartments on the fifth floor as well as the bedroom on the floor
below. Sartre's apartment came through rather unscathed, but the staircase
was hanging out over a void. No one was hurt.

Together with "certain well-known persons," Sartre was offered police
protection and during the day two uniformed policemen paraded outside
222 Boulevard Raspail. Sartre thought that more than anything else the
police protection advertised where he lived and when a *pied-noir* who had
refused to collect funds for OAS had his shop bombed on the corner,
Simone had a housing agent find them an apartment at 156 Quai Louis
Blériot with huge picture windows overlooking the Seine and west-end
Paris.

With the publication of *Djamila Boupacha,* it was Simone's turn to be
a terrorist target. Originally, she had written a foreword to Gisèle Halimi's
book on the tortured girl, but she accepted coauthorship in order to share
legal responsibility.[6] According to eminent confreres of Halimi, the justice
department and the army could probably be accused of obstruction of
justice in the Djamila Boupacha case and that even if specific indictments
could not be served, the exposure could only damage the remaining resolve
of prosecutors of other similar cases. When Simone went to 222 Boulevard

[6] Simone de Beauvoir, Gisèle Halimi, *Djamila Boupacha,* Paris: Gallimard, 1962.

*Police inspector surveying damages
to 42 Rue Bonaparte after second assassination attempt*
KEYSTONE

Raspail to pick up the mail, the superintendent told her he had received an anonymous phone call: "Watch out! Simone de Beauvoir is getting blown up tonight." The threat never materialized.

And then, suddenly, it was all over. On March 18, 1962, representatives of France and the provisional government of the Algerian Republic signed the Evian Agreement resulting in an immediate ceasefire and provisions for a referendum in Algeria to decide the country's future. The OAS answered with a new wave of terrorism that in Algeria included indiscriminate murder and systematic sabotage. But even the "ultras" were defeated when the French population of Algeria ignored OAS orders to stay put and began a mass exodus to France.

In April, Sartre received a letter from his mother's cousin. "Each time I see your name among those fighting against atomic war, I feel how close I am to you," wrote the eighty-seven-year-old Albert Schweitzer from his leprosy hospital in Gabon, where he had read about the bombing at 42 Rue Bonaparte. Sartre wrote back. It was the first time he had heard from his great uncle's son since Charles Schweitzer had taken him to the ancestral home in Alsace.

Sartre and Beaver heard, from Lena Zonina, their Soviet translator and travel companion, the news of the people of Algeria voting 5,975,581 to 16,534 for independence. They had arrived in Moscow June 1 as the guests of the Union of Soviet Writers, and were entertained more graciously than during Sartre's solo trip in 1954. Receptions were not drinking bouts and banquets were not propaganda harangues. They met old friends like Konstantin Simonov and Konstantin Fedin and younger authors like Evgeny Yevtushenko and Andrei Voznesensky. People invited them to their homes and the Writers Union put a chauffeured car at their disposal. They visited Rostov, Kiev and Leningrad. At a disarmament and peace conference in Moscow, Sartre spoke of the need to "demilitarize" culture.

They returned via Poland and spent the rest of 1962 in Rome, Sartre finishing *Les Mots* and Beaver *Force of Circumstance*. The only disagreeable moments in this first year of peace—the Algerian war cost 14,500 French combatants and an estimated 150,000 Moslem lives—was *Freud* and Vittorio de Sica's screen version of *Les Séquestrés d'Altona*. Huston had shot *Freud* in Vienna and Munich during the fall of 1961 with Montgomery Clift as Freud and Susannah York as the composite patient character Sartre had invented. Persistent press flak reported Sartre's and Anna Freud's objections and even if the final screenplay was credited to Charles Kaufman and Wolfgang Reinhardt, reviewers still referred to the Sartrian origins.[7] *The Condemned of Altona* was downright painful. After suc-

[7] See *Variety*, November 1, 1961.

cessively rejecting adaptations by Jules Dassin (approved by Sartre) and
Cesare Zavattini, producer Carlo Ponti had *Judgment at Nuremberg*
scripter Abby Mann rework *Les Séquestrés* into a pat, anti-German muddle
of a movie. De Sica's directing was reduced to aiming the camera, as *Time*
said, "at a famous face and hop[ing] for the best." [8] The famous faces
included Maximilian Schell as Frantz, Fredric March as old Gerlach,
Françoise Prévost as sister Leni, Robert Wagner as brother Werner and
Sophia Loren as Werner's wife (a love interest of sorts was written in
between Frantz and his sister-in-law). Sartre asked that the credit crawl
read "freely inspired by" his play, but wasn't even successful in getting
his name off the film. He never saw the picture.

Les Mots was many things to Sartre—deceptive account of the origins of
the self, truculent memoir of a childhood and the sardonic realization that
behind the love of words was perhaps nothing more than puerile neurosis.
The Words was a dialogue between the mature Sartre and his childhood,
both the mirror of a remote era and the transcription of his coming to
terms with his past. Sartre had written the first draft in 1954 when he had
plunged into politics alongside the communists and been forced to question
his own profession. "Thrown into the atmosphere of political action, I
suddenly looked into the kind of neurosis that had dominated my entire
work up to then," he would say at the publication of *Les Mots* in 1962.
"Simone de Beauvoir had guessed all this before me. It's of course in the
nature of all neurosis to think of itself as normal. I had simply taken it
for granted that I was made to write, and it took me thirty years to get rid
of that idea." [9] *The Words* was a logical consequence of the essays on
Beaudelaire, Mallarmé, Genet and Flaubert, which all examined why a child
or an adolescent would want to be a writer. With Freud, Sartre believed
everything in an individual's existence meant something and that nothing
in a life was really accidental. With Marx, he believed the individual *was*
his environment, but on his own he also thought that childhood—usually
neglected by Marxists—fashioned prejudices and aberrations not accounted
for by the individual's milieu yet made this environment appear as a "singular event."

Les Mots was unique in Sartre's work and was immediately recognized
as such. Dedicated to "Madame Z" (Lena Zonina—a Russian edition appeared less than a year after the Gallimard original), the slim, one hundred seventy-page volume was exceptionally well received. Sartre put
literature on trial while effortlessly using its effects and resources, critics

[8] *Time,* September 27, 1963.
[9] In interview with *Le Monde,* April 18, 1964.

agreed. They saw it as his return to literature, a glorious book written by a Sartre at the peak of his terse and pungent style. As an autobiography, *The Words* was considered an instant classic, and it was understood that the book had been one of the determining factors in the Swedish Academy's decision to give Sartre the 1964 Nobel Prize for literature. The priceless comment on *Les Mots* came from Anne-Marie. Said Sartre's eighty-one-year-old mother: "Poulou hasn't understood anything of his childhood."

Simone wrote beautiful things in the epilogue of *Force of Circumstance:* "There has been one undoubted success in my life—my relations with Sartre. In more than thirty years, we have only once gone to sleep at night disunited."

The night had been at the height of the drama over Olga Kosakiewicz in 1936 when Simone had not yet learned to dominate her jealousy and what she called "my spontaneous possessiveness." Except when traveling they had been in the habit of sleeping apart. Their teaching careers in opposite ends of France had facilitated the habit. The acquired practice had been reinforced during the busy middle years when Sartre, always a night owl, popped amphetamines to write nights on end. Ironically, sleeping together would finally become a way of life in old age when Sartre's blindness would make it unsafe for him to trot back to Boulevard Raspail after an evening at her apartment.

The long years together, Simone wrote in *Force of Circumstance,* didn't lessen the interest they took in each other. "A woman friend has said that each of us listens to the other with great attention. Yet so assiduously have we always criticized, corrected or ratified each other's thoughts that we might almost be said to think in common. We have a common store of memories, knowledge and images behind us; our attempts to grasp the world are undertaken with the same tools, set within the same framework, guided by the same touchstones. Very often one of us begins a sentence and the other finishes it; if someone asks us a question, we have been known to produce identical answers. The stimulus of a word, a sensation, a shadow, sends us both traveling along the same inner path, and we arrive simultaneously at a conclusion—a memory, an association—completely inexplicable to a third person."

She answered those who stigmatized her for insisting women should be independent without ever having been single herself by saying that independence and spinsterhood were not the same thing. She answered charges that she always followed Sartre politically by saying he was ideologically creative whereas she was not: "The real betrayal of my liberty would have been a refusal to recognize this particular superiority of his; I would then have ended up a prisoner of the deliberately challenging attitude and the bad faith which are at once an inevitable result of the battle of the sexes and the complete opposite of intellectual honesty." She said too many women had read *Memoirs of a Dutiful Daughter* because they enjoyed the accuracy of a milieu without being interested in her efforts to escape it. Since *The Prime of Life,* her relationship with her readers had become ambiguous, she wrote, because the Algerian war had brought her loathing of her own middle class to new heights. She admitted she was no longer sure *whom* she was writing for or how she should measure herself. She summed up that the only thing that could happen from now on would be misfortune: "Either I will see Sartre dead or I'll die before him. It is horrible not to be there to console someone for the pain you cause by leaving him. It's appalling that he leaves you and will not speak to you again." The last sentence in the nearly seven hundred-page third volume of her autobiography was so enigmatic she would have to explain it later. All the promises of her youth had been kept, she wrote; yet when she looked back toward the young girl she had been, she felt she had been cheated. "The promises have all been kept. And yet, turning an incredulous gaze toward the young girl ready to believe, I realize with stupor how much I have been gypped."

Sartre and Beaver spent the winter of 1962–63 in Moscow and returned the following summer. With Khrushchev's consent, *Pravda* had published Yevtushenko's poem *Stalin's Heirs* and *Novy Mir* had printed Alexander Solzhenitsyn's *One Day in the Life of Ivan Denisovich,* about Stalin's *gulags,* and the first volume of Ilya Ehrenburg's *Memoirs,* which spoke freely of Western art and culture. Simone loved Moscow under the snow. Simonov and his wife invited them to a Christmas Eve party at a theater where elegantly dressed people danced to recorded jazz.

The ostensible reason for the Moscovite winter was the creation of an East-West writers "community." Under the presidency of the elder poet Giuseppe Ungaretti, the organization was supposed to encourage transideological exchanges, but between the groundwork and the summer assizes in Leningrad, Khrushchev brought the cultural liberation to a screeching halt. On March 8, he defended Stalin and made vehement attacks on formalism and abstractions in writing and the fine arts. Ehrenburg was picked out for the severest criticism and when Khrushchev met the author-journalist privately, he blamed him for having had a bad influence on Sartre—for having incited him to leave the Communist Party. When Ehrenburg observed that Sartre had never belonged to the Party, Khrushchev remained unconvinced. When Sartre and Beaver returned in July, Ehrenburg told them the publication of the remainder of his memoirs and the complete edition of his work had been suspended and that to calm himself he spent a great deal of time working in his garden.

Khrushchev's cold blast reduced the August convention in Leningrad to an exercise in banality. Soviet writers expressed their contempt for Western literature and for a rotten, corrupted West, with Fedin comparing the writer to a pilot whose duty it is to fly his passengers to their right destination, and Alain Robbe-Grillet replying that "the novel is not a means of transportation . . . that by definition a writer doesn't know where he is going." To prevent the convention from fizzling altogether, the Soviet organizers asked Sartre to make a coherent summing up of the proceedings, which he did. The organizers also persuaded Khrushchev to receive a delegation at his country home in Georgia and after two days in Moscow, Sartre, Simone, Ungaretti, Angus Wilson, five other Westerners and a number of Russian authors were flown and bused, on empty stomachs, to a hilltop residence overlooking the Black Sea. Simone had imagined that since they had been invited, Khrushchev would be friendly. Instead he abused them as so many henchmen of capitalism. After his outburst, however, he managed to say, "Still you are against war too, so at least we can eat and drink together." The dinner was splendid, but the master of all Russia remained sullen. Later, Sartre learned that French Communist Party chief Maurice Thorez had seen Khrushchev a few hours before their arrival and warned him he was about to meet a bunch of dangerous reactionaries.

Being given hell by the mercurial Khrushchev apparently had its advantages. Suddenly, Sartre and Beaver felt upgraded to some sort of VIP status that allowed them to travel anywhere they wished. With Lena Zonina, they visited the Crimea, Armenia and Georgia from Yalta to Tbilisi and Yerevan, where they saw a misty Mount Ararat across the Turkish border. The VIP status held the following year when they were invited to Kiev to honor the hundred and fiftieth anniversary of the birth of the Ukraine's national poet, Taras Shevchenko, and they visited the Baltic states, usually very much verboten to foreigners, and stayed in Tallinn where people spoke kindly of emigrated Estonians.

They planned to spend a relaxed fall in Rome and had just settled in at the Albergo Nazionale when Simone received a call from Paris telling her that her seventy-year-old mother had fallen and broken a leg. Friends had transported Madame de Beauvoir to a hospital.

Simone returned to Paris immediately. It was discovered that Françoise de Beauvoir had cancer. Because she had always been afraid of dying of

With Khrushchev and fellow writers in Georgia

cancer, she was not told the truth but led to believe she was suffering from an inflammation of the stomach lining. Her case was diagnosed as hopeless. Poupette joined Simone at their dying mother's bedside. The end was horrible. When Poupette commented to one of the nurses about her mother's sufferings during the final two weeks, the nurse replied, "I assure you, Madame, it was a very easy death."

The nurse's exclamation became the title of Simone's book about her mother's death. *Une Mort très douce* (*A Very Easy Death*) is one of Simone's shortest works.[10] Sartre has called it her best. It is a clinical, at times harrowing, account of an old woman dying of cancer in a modern hospital. The contrast between the messiness of life—the tears, cries, pain, pus, soiled sheets and vomiting—is juxtaposed with the cool efficiency of the terminal ward with its machines attached to the body and its well-groomed almost condescending technicians. *A Very Easy Death* is also a ferocious comment on the French bourgeoisie, contrasting the compassion for the suffering body with an ironic contempt for the values the dying woman continues to express to the end—her preference for this rather than that hospital. The very deceit of never telling the dying woman the nature of her illness itself becomes part of the bourgeois falsehoods she had lived and lived for.

Sartre had to answer Khrushchev and in November used an invitation extended to him and Simone by the Czech Writers Union to say that no East-West dialogue was possible if part of the Western writers' heritage was considered "decadent" by their Eastern confreres. Mentioning three "decadents" singled out at the Leningrad meeting four months earlier—Freud, Kafka and Joyce—as three men who had brought him to Marxism, Sartre said, "We Western leftists cannot accept that some of the basic authors who have formed us, authors we cannot abandon, are considered decadent because that means you condemn our past and make any contribution we might have to any discussion meaningless." His hosts were politely courteous in public and, like their Polish brethren in 1957, passionately cordial in private. Antonin Liehm, an essayist and journalist who had translated a number of books from the French, became a friend. They met with Milan Kundera—and ran one of his cruel, ironic short stories in *TM*—the very young Václav Havel, Eduard Goldstücker, Karel Kosik and others who gave them precious information about "fetishized Marxism." Czechoslovakia was in bad shape economically. To rectify this, the leaders

---

[10] Simone de Beauvoir, *Une Mort très douce*, Paris: Gallimard, 1964; *A Very Easy Death*, New York: G. P. Putnam's 1968.

Françoise de Beauvoir and Simone
GISÈLE FREUND

had worked out a new system, adapting production to the country's needs and its resources. But these reforms were incompatible with extreme centralization of power as they demanded a certain liberalization. The working class, which had lost all political awareness, seemed to side with the old bureaucrats although the reformists intended to provide workers with a certain control over production. The intellectuals were in favor of reform and the old guard Stalinists launched a campaign against Liehm that came to nothing. Kundera underlined the grotesque surrealism of *homo bureaucraticus* that made all men suspect and Kosick claimed the system needed careerists who were mean, blinkered, insensitive and incapable of thinking. Liehm described the ultimate of satellite communism as a scene where hysterical Marxist man falls on his knees and, replacing reason with faith, shouts, "I believe, therefore I am absurd" because he appears to himself as an obstacle to the building of socialism. Truth, they said, was told only because no better lie was available. The country had no idea of its real situation because official lies had destroyed both previous elements of knowledge and all socioeconomic research. It was not even the case of leaders knowing the truth but hiding it from the people. Truth did not exist.

Before leaving Prague, Sartre attended the Czech premiere of *Les Séquestrés d'Altona.*

The big event of 1964 was the Nobel brouhaha. The first hint that Sartre might be the year's winner came in an October 15 dispatch in *L'Aurore* from the morning paper's Stockholm correspondent. Sartre immediately wrote a short statement, which, translated, was read October 22 in Stockholm by a representative of his Swedish publisher. "For personal reasons, I would not want to appear on the list of possible laureates," he wrote, adding that his refusal should not be interpreted to mean that he didn't hold the Swedish Academy in the highest esteem.

Sartre and Beaver were having pork brisket at L'Oriental on Montparnasse when journalists tracked him down to tell him he was the 1964 Nobel Prize winner in literature. Why had the Swedish academicians decided to ignore his refusal? He had no idea, he told the journalists. This time he had to explain himself. In a carefully drafted statement, translated into Swedish to be read in Stockholm and distributed in French by the Agence France-Presse news agency, he said his personal reason was that he had never accepted *any* official honors and that his political reason was that he didn't want to be stamped as belonging to any side of the ideological struggle dividing Europe. "On the cultural front, the only valid battle today is the struggle for peaceful coexistence between the Eastern and

Western cultures," he wrote. "I don't mean we must embrace each other; I know very well that the confrontation necessarily takes on the form of conflict, but it should take place between individuals and cultures without the interjection of institutions. I personally feel very deeply the contradictions between the two cultures; I am the product of those contradictions." [11]

He understood perfectly well, he said, that the prize was not the Western camp's ideological award but that was nevertheless what people saw in it and that events beyond the control of the Swedish academicians had made it into. "It is regrettable that the Nobel Prize has been bestowed on Pasternak before Sholokhov, that the only Soviet works to be honored are those edited in foreign countries and forbidden at home. A gesture could have been made in the other direction to establish a balance. During the Algerian war when we signed the 'Manifesto of the 121,' I would have accepted the prize with gratitude because it would not only have honored me but also the freedom we were fighting for." Finally, Sartre said he was tormented by the 250,000 kroner ($60,000) that accompanied the prize. To accept meant being able to contribute the money to causes of importance—"I for one think of the anti-Apartheid Committee in London"—to refuse meant to deprive such organizations of a needed support.

Sartre didn't want to face the news media until the statement had been read to the Academy in Stockholm and went into hiding at Simone's. At 6 P.M., however, Anne-Marie phoned saying she was besieged by the press at 222 Boulevard Raspail. At midnight Sartre relented and went out to have himself interviewed and photographed. When he got back to Boulevard Raspail the next morning, a television van was parked in front of the building.

The reaction was largely negative. Catholic existentialist philosopher Gabriel Marcel called Sartre a "chronic disparager and systematic blasphemer" [12] and André Breton saw the refusal as a propaganda score for the East bloc. Most painful to Sartre were letters from the poor: "They write harrowing letters, all saying the same thing, 'Give me the money you refuse.'" [13] In Moscow, the gesture was also misunderstood. Sartre's liberal friends in the Writers Union thought he had deserted their cause for the Stalinists' side when he had regretted Boris Pasternak's winning the Nobel Prize before Mikhail Sholokhov. The Soviet liberals were looking for new straws in the wind. A week before the Nobel contretemps

[11] Reprinted in toto in *Le Monde*, October 24, 1964, and in volume in Michel Contat-Michel Rybalka, *Les Ecrits de Sartre, op. cit.*
[12] In *Nouvelles littéraires*, October 29, 1964.
[13] *Nouvel Observateur*, November 18, 1964.

the Soviet Presidium had removed Khrushchev from power and replaced him with Aleksei Kosygin as Premier and Leonid Brezhnev as First Party Secretary.

Two months earlier, President Johnson had answered the alleged attack on a U. S. destroyer in the Gulf of Tonkin by North Vietnamese PT boats by bombing North Vietnam. In March 1965, Sartre made his first protest against the war by refusing to go to the United States to give a series of lectures on Flaubert and philosophy at Cornell University. His refusal was absolute, especially since the U. S. air force was escalating the conflict. When the first U. S. combat troops landed in South Vietnam in April 1965 and seventeen nations called for peace negotiations, he said it was Algeria all over again and that the Vietcong would have to be recognized as valid representatives, just as the French government had been forced to negotiate with the Algerian provisional government. "Teach-in" protests against the war were spreading in America and for a Boston rally Sartre sent a telegram wishing American intellectuals more success than their French counterparts had had in opposing the Algerian conflict. "But even if you don't succeed your demonstration won't have been in vain. Your demonstration comes at a time when irresponsible men are giving the world an odious image of your country." [14]

Playboy and *Vogue* interviewed Sartre at length while in *Harper's* Nelson Algren wrote a disconcerting review of *Force of Circumstance*. The *Playboy* interview rambled from the generation gap to Gaullist politics, from the "nouveau roman" to the recent decline of Jean Genet's writings. Most interesting was Sartre's observation that he had always surrounded himself with women who were pretty because feminine ugliness upset him: "I admit it and I'm ashamed of myself." [15] He preferred the company of women, he said, because he usually found men boring, with their narrow sensitivities and their shop talk, whereas women possessed qualities that stemmed from their situation as both slave and accomplice. The *Vogue* interview was a love hymn to Simone. [16] When asked what he thought of her as a woman, Sartre said, "I think she's beautiful. I've always thought her beautiful, even though she was wearing a hideous little hat when I first met her. I was dead set on making her acquaintance because she was beautiful, because she had, and still has, the kind of face that appeals to me. The wonderful thing about Simone de Beauvoir is that

14 "Up all Night," in *The Nation,* May 31, 1965.
15 "Jean-Paul Sartre, A candid conversation with the charismatic fountainhead of existentialism and rejector of the Nobel Prize," *Playboy,* May 1965.
16 "Sartre Talks of de Beauvoir," *Vogue,* July 1965.

she has a man's intelligence—you can see from the way I'm talking that I'm still a bit feudal—and a woman's sensitivity. That is, I've found in her everything I could possibly want. And we've never really quarreled, except about silly things. For example, in 1939 we quarreled in Naples about whether or not the Neapolitans should be obliged to live in the houses that were built for them. The argument ended with my saying to her, 'You're a fascist!' and with her answering, 'And you, you'll never amount to anything! Never, never, never!' "

Algren's review was a confused lashing-out of a kind rarely seen in American literary magazines, full of snippets of quotes, lines from *Alice in Wonderland,* metaphors of Simone as a parthenogenesis researcher damaging free-spirited sperms and a punch line in italics that read, "Will she ever quit talking?" Without identifying his relationship to the author he was reviewing, Algren quoted from passages about himself and that "certain fidelity" Simone and Sartre had maintained for themselves as a couple. He said procurers had more honesty than philosophers and that Simone appealed to women who had never gambled but lived by proxy. "No chronicler of our lives since Theodore Dreiser has combined so steadfast a passion for human justice with a dullness so asphyxiating as Mme. de Beauvoir." [17]

On January 26, 1965, Sartre had lawyers begin proceedings for the adoption of Arlette Elkaim. At the same time, he returned to the theater, not with his own play but with an adaptation of Euripides' *The Trojan Women.* Directed by Michael Cacoyannis and staged at the Théâtre national populaire, *Les Troyennes* was not so much a tragedy as an oratorio on the antiwar theme. Sartre modernized the play and had Troy symbolize the Third World struggling to free itself from colonialism. A week after the premiere, a court granted Sartre's request to legally adopt Arlette.

Les Temps modernes was quietly returning to the Gallimard fold, from which the tempestuous Malraux had chased it in 1947 after the magazine had compared de Gaulle with Adolf Hitler. The seventeen years with the Julliard publishing house had been happily uneventful but ended in a disagreement with editor-in-chief Christian Bourgeois. The end of the Algerian war had marked a moment of hesitation for the *TM* "family"— Claude Lanzmann, Marcel Péju, Little Bost and Jean Pouillon, Francis Jeanson and, since the very beginning, J. B. Pontalis—who met at Simone's every other Thursday to work out the next issue. Sartre's and Simone's 1957 trip to Warsaw had resulted in a "Polish period" when the magazine

---

[17] "The Question of Simone de Beauvoir," *Harper's,* May 1965.

translated and published numerous texts by far-left Warsaw authors. In 1961, André Gorz, a Swiss journalist who had first met Sartre in Lausanne in 1946, had become a member of the editorial committee, and together with Pouillon, had taken charge of political questions, in effect filling the late Merleau-Ponty's role. Under Gorz, an "Italian period" had started, with the publication of Italian Communist Party debates and discussions of reformist liberalism. Péju had left after his exposé of independent Algeria's socialism had been found too brutal by the others.

With Simone, Sartre spent another summer in the Soviet Union. Alone, he made a sidetrip to Helsinki to attend the World Congress for Peace, National Independence and General Disarmament, which coincided with President Johnson's ordering a major American troop buildup in South Vietnam and an increased draft in the United States. The Chinese Communist Party denounced the Russians' neutrality in Vietnam, calling them collaborators and revisionists. The hostility between Russia and China had Sartre's and Beaver's Russian friends convinced the Chinese were preparing to invade the Soviet Union. Khrushchev's fall seemed to have been beneficial. Solzhenitsyn and Ehrenburg were published and Pasternak's work was appearing again and if Kafka was not yet translated, he was now considered a victim of capitalism instead of a decadent pessimist.

Sartre and Beaver visited Lithuania, where the local writers' union delegates never left them alone, and Pushkin's estate in Pskov. Back in Moscow, Ehrenburg told them the most important form of publishing was now *samizdat*—self-publishing. Writers condemned to silence by censors had their friends help them type up and copy their works and this exceedingly interesting clandestine literature, Ehrenburg said, was developing side by side with official writing. Simone read a *samizdat* short story by Yuli Daniel published in France and, in English, *The Icicle and Other Stories* by Andrei Sinyavsky, another self-publishing author. She had found their stories ironic denunciations of the Stalinist terrorism but in no way anti-Marxist. In October, when Sartre and Beaver were in Rome, Daniel and Sinyavsky were arrested and viciously attacked in *Izvestia* and *Literaturnaya Gazeta*. In February 1966, they were tried and found guilty of having damaged the social and political regime of the U.S.S.R. and sentenced to reeducation in a tough labor camp, Sinyavsky for seven years, Daniel for five. To mark their solidarity with the imprisoned authors, Sartre and Beaver refused to visit the Soviet Union that year and to attend the Tenth Congress of Soviet Writers. The next time they were in Moscow, Sholokhov said Daniel and Sinyavsky should have been punished more se-

verely and Solzhenitsyn refused to see Sartre, apparently because Sartre
was a writer whose work was always published. Russians were never easy
to please.

Were Sartre and Beaver becoming professional protesters? The biggest
protest was just ahead of them.

The Bertrand Russell International War Crimes Tribunal was not so
much the brainchild of the ninety-three-year-old philosopher as of Ralph
Schoenman, a young American who since 1960 had become what his enemies—and they were many—would call Russell's "left-hand man."
Schoenman was a stocky youth of twenty-four who had studied philosophy
at Princeton and continued postgraduate studies at the London School of
Economics, when he had written to Russell about nuclear disarmament
politics and hitchhiked to northern Wales to meet him. Over the following
years, Schoenman had come to exercise a growing influence over Russell's
activities. Variously called a Trotskyite operator, a CIA plant and simply
a young leftwinger with a greatly inflated sense of his own importance,
Schoenman had first become Russell's secretary in Wales, then his spokes-
man in London and secretary of the Bertrand Russell Peace Foundation,
traveling extensively either for the Peace Foundation or as Russell's personal representative.

During the summer of 1965, Schoenman had showed up at the Helsinki
World Congress for Peace and persuaded the organizers to let him read
a "Statement from Bertrand Russell" that members in the audience who
knew Russell called extremely un-Russellian. With the "Statement" finished and the chairman preparing to call the next speaker, Schoenman had
announced he wished to read a statement by the Peace Foundation on the
report by the American delegation. As the report had been read the previous evening, Schoenman had been gaveled out of order, but since he
had the microphone he had continued until the chairman had crawled over
a table and forcibly snatched away the mike. Faced with threats that reports of the incident would be made public, Schoenman had promised "to
be less violent and ill-mannered in the future." His unstoppable enthusiasm had much the same result when he had tried to gain the Foundation
publicity in England. "It was painful on Monday to see Russell slowly
stumbling his way through a prepared text that ignored vital evidence, slid
over the true and suggested the false, and fell back on innuendo instead
of direct accusations," *The Economist* reported on a speech in early 1965.
"Sitting beside him was Mr. Ralph Schoenman, the anti-American American who is now Lord Russell's secretary and who, until he proves the

contrary, will be presumed to produce the stuff the old man takes responsibility for." [18]

When M. S. Arnoni, the editor of the radical American journal *Minority of One,* had proposed a war crimes trial specifically dealing with Vietnam in 1965, Russell had replied that the idea was "attractive" but demanded time and money, and the events in Southeast Asia were moving very fast. By early 1966, however, Schoenman had been sent to North Vietnam to collect evidence and Russell himself was beginning to sound out potential judges for the tribunal. "There is considerable circumstantial evidence that Schoenman was largely responsible for Russell's changed view," Russell biographer Ronald W. Clark would write. "But, as in other spheres, Schoenman reinforced tendencies already present while Russell himself had been influenced during the last months of 1965 by the mounting evidence of atrocities in Vietnam and by the growth of unrest with the war in America itself. He was also—a fact which his enemies were reluctant to concede—a patriot seriously perturbed by the supine attitude of the British government and its reluctance to make any statement which could possibly be construed as critical of American policy." [19]

In July 1966, after $250,000 had been raised by selling Russell's private papers to McMaster University in Hamilton, Ontario, Russell threw his last scruples about "genuinely impartial people" overboard. Any lingering belief in the impartiality of the tribunal was dispelled when Schoenman himself was set to be the secretary-general and he described the tribunal members as "a partial body of committed men."

The first Sartre and Simone heard of the tribunal was when Schoenman knocked at Simone's door in Paris and asked whether Sartre and she would agree to be members. The Russell Peace Foundation would send commissions to Vietnam, he said, and would ask American leftists to supply documents. The point of the whole thing was to arouse public opinion all over the world and particularly in America. Schoenman specifically stated the hearings would be held in Paris and that Sartre and she wouldn't have to attend all of them, but could name their deputies and would be provided with accounts of the proceedings. In fact, they would only be asked to be present for two or three days at the very end. They accepted.

In September and October, Sartre and Beaver visited Japan. All their books had been translated into Japanese—a 1965 paperback edition of *The Second Sex* was a current best seller—and they were received as celebrities, asked to give lectures, wined and dined and shown the country in

[18] Ronald W. Clark, *The Life of Bertrand Russell,* New York: Knopf, 1976.
[19] *Ibid.*

In Tokyo, 1966
A.F.P.

The mid-1960s
GISÈLE FREUND

style. For the first time in his life Sartre was traveling with a camera. He used it, Simone would say, "with the ardor of the Japanese."

Things were changing in literature and during the fall Sartre was sharply challenged by a new "ism" which was largely a reaction against the dialectic and historic process that he incarnated. The occasion was a special Sartre issue which *L'Arc,* a quarterly published in Aix-en-Provence, was bringing out and for which he agreed to speak his mind on "structuralism," which, to the dismay of Marxists, was fast becoming the new rallying point.

Structuralism was the name under which trendy journalists had lumped together somewhat abusively, Roland Barthes' "nouvelle critique," Claude Lévi-Strauss' ethnology, Jacques Lacan's psychoanalytical research into intent and Michel Foucault's linguistic philosophy. The "nouveau roman" authors had changed the novel during the past decade from the sonorous "man's fate" dimension that T. E. Lawrence, Malraux and Bernanos had practiced before the war and Sartre and Camus had continued during the war and postwar years. Alain Robbe-Grillet, Michel Butor and Nathalie Sarraute didn't have the same sense of the tragic as their elders and quite simply gave up judging man and his fate. They refused to make their novels "signify" or explain life. Instead, they invited their readers to join in an organic experience *inside* a mind, a mind which, far from dominating the world, was mere part, or "structure." Their novels were actually a case of applied phenomenology in the Heidegger-Sartre tradition, a "bracketing off" of metaphysical absolutes and meaning, and Sartre had himself hailed Sarraute's "protoplasmic view of our inner universe" in a preface to her novel *Portrait d'un inconnu* (*Portrait of a Man Unknown*).[20] The novel is no longer a story because to tell a story one must dominate one's material and the phenomenological conscience can have no such pretensions. It isn't *above*—authorized to make psychoanalytical judgments—but part of the world's structure.

This modesty of purpose led Barthes and other critics to interiorize critical studies. Barthes also gave up explaining a work of fiction and limited himself to describing its "given," its structures, thus bracketing off principles, values, social context and historical period. At the same time, he tried to ask the ultimate question of intent: Why do writers write? Did Racine write for the same reason as Proust? Sartre had himself moved in

---

[20] Nathalie Sarraute, *Portrait d'un inconnu,* Préface de Jean-Paul Sartre, Paris: Robert Marin, 1948.

this direction in his *Baudelaire* and *Saint Genet,* in which he considered writing as invention, as *project* rather than finished book.

The writer *about* to write fascinated several authors grouped around the magazine *Tel Quel (As Is)*. Philippe Sollers, Jean-Pierre Faye, Jean Ricardou and Jean Thibaudeau felt a novel wouldn't have to be a "re-lived, constructed or imagined adventure," but could be a creative reverie. In *Drame,* Sollers evoked in over three hundred pages the almost cellular, amoebic ideas of a writer thinking about a novel whose subject will never become clear, neither for him nor for his readers, because he remains indecisive in the very act of creating. As Spanish novelist Pio Baroja had foreseen at the turn of the century, "It is impossible to write a novel that has no subject, no architecture and no composition." [21] With the *Tel Quel* group, authors gave up being storytellers and even witnesses to become "present" individuals assailed by sensations that are difficult to define in a universe without apparent form and order. Life is an almost biological experience, which can only be explained by its inner structures. When Jean-Pierre Richard analyzed the landscapes in Chateaubriand's writing, his "neo-critique" took place beyond biographical circumstances. Chateaubriand is a nebula of sensibility—soul or amoeba, who dilates, retracts, moves forward and launches pseudopods and retracts them. To understand a work of fiction we shouldn't start from the outside (biography of the author, sources, influences, literary milieu), but settle *into* it, coincide with it in an intuitive analysis of its emotion and structures, and study it "in the text." The work of fiction becomes dialectically *anterior* to its author. It is not because the young Proust lived a sensual existence as a conspicuous society figure that he painted a mundane milieu. It is because a certain sense of space and time existed within him that he wrote a book on the premise that the whole of our past remains alive, hidden somewhere within us, and may be rediscovered, involuntarily, through sensory perceptions or works of art. It is not because he knew exile and disgrace that Chateaubriand wrote about it, but because his personal and original *aura* included the structure of a "refugee sensibility" that he was exiled. For the *Tel Quel* group and Jean Starobinski, the work of fiction is not the expression of its author or the reflection of the world as seen through the author, it is the initial reality on whose *surface* the writer has lived. It is the work of fiction—not the author—that has structure, organic construction and life.

In his life-long studies of South American Indians, Lévi-Strauss had

[21] R. M. Albérès, *L'Aventure intellectuelle du XXe siècle,* Paris: Albin Michel, 1969.

discovered that the individual's ideas are formed by the myths of the society he lives in, whether primitive or developed, and not the other way around. He discovered that mental structures are not to be found in the individual's thinking but in collective—or mythological—convictions. In linguistics, Foucault came to the same conclusion but went even further. Language is not a "means of expression," but a quasi-biological environment. Man doesn't create a language for himself; from birth he is steeped in a language, a society, a mythology that will condition, mold and assimilate him: "Language is anterior to man." In *Les Mots et les choses,* which caused a sensation when it was published in 1966, Foucault said there is no *continuity* in society or in the human mind.[22] The language that educated Europe spoke in the sixteenth century was an autonomous language that translated that century's world view and pretended to represent reality. In the seventeenth century language wanted to classify and its ideal was a grammar, in the century of Enlightenment language expressed natural history, while the nineteenth-century's undercurrent of language was sociology and scientific psychology. All may have spoken French, but each period "structured" its world view and certain grammatical forms differently and there is no link between different periods of human thought. Foucault claimed that we do not live in an evolving society in which history guarantees continuity, but in a discontinued civilization.

In *La Pensée sauvage (The Savage Mind),* Lévi-Strauss had attacked Sartre's historical underpinning of *La Critique,* saying the French Revolution as we see it today never took place, that historical facts are no more given than any other: "Insofar as history aspires to meaning, it is doomed to select regions, periods, groups of men and individuals in these groups and make them stand out as discontinuous figures, against a continuity barely good enough to be used as a backdrop. A truly total history would cancel itself out." [23]

It was no wonder that Marxists were troubled by structuralism. Marx also believed that man was determined by environment, or structure, but to Marxists the environment *moved* in a dialectic and historic evolution. Lévi-Strauss and Foucault refused all historicism and the new critics studied an author "in the text" without paying any attention to literary history.

Did Sartre want to defend *La Critique,* his Marxist friends or was he

[22] Michel Foucault, *Les Mots et les choses,* Paris: Gallimard, 1966; *The Order of Things,* New York: Pantheon, 1971.
[23] Claude Lévi-Strauss, *La Pensée sauvage,* Paris: Plon, 1962; *The Savage Mind,* London: Nicolson, 1966.

just foolhardy when he agreed to be interviewed for *L'Arc* by *TM* collaborator (and sometime "new critic") Bernard Pingaud? Whatever the motive, he took on the whole gang—Barthes, Foucault, Lévi-Strauss and the *Tel Quel* group—and hit them where they converged—their refusal of history. His argument was simple—"History *produces* structures," he said.[24] Anthropology, for example, was not a static science of frozen human forms but a study of social dynamics, hence of historical deployment. In man's striving for knowledge, man as object, man as inert subject of structural analysis, must get back his humanity, that is, his freedom, his mobility, his sense of history. A phenomenon can only become intelligible when studied in its "totalization," which must include its mobility.

It was not Sartre's finest hour in dialectics. Structuralism was not an ideology, but a method. Despite its arcane terminology, it proposed to start all research with whatever autonomous structures can be discovered, whether the subject is the atom, a language, an Amazonian tribe or a piece of fiction. Structuralism was irreconcilable with Marxism insofar as Marxism studied evolving reality rather than organic reality and the debate was a replay of the pre-Socratic dispute between Parmenides who said nothing can come to be or pass away and Heraclitus' contention that everything flows. On a more immediate level structuralism was also, as R. M. Albérès would underline, the reaction of a new generation "tired of the abuses, in all branches of research, of the historical, dialectic and genetic method, in literature the best example of a reaction against the predominance of literary history that had prevailed during the first half of the century." [25] *Le Nouvel Observateur, L'Express,* Sollers and Foucault had a field day with Sartre's utterances in *L'Arc*—Foucault saying Sartre had obviously never read *Les Mots et les choses*—but the nine-page interview would not be the last word for any of the parties.

Meanwhile, anteriority became Simone's explanation for her feeling "gypped" by life in those closing lines of *Force of Circumstance*. Francis Jeanson's flattering biography, *Simone de Beauvoir ou l'entreprise de vivre,* included a supplementary question-and-answer interview. Here, Jeanson asked her whether she hadn't tried to be dramatic in saying, "I have been gypped." [26] She answered that in a certain way it had been literary dramatics, but, as she had just read in *Tel Quel,* there was no such thing as a truth "anterior to the truth that language expresses." By saying she had

---

[24] "Jean-Paul Sartre répond, entretien avec Bernard Pingaud, *L'Arc*, No. 30, October 1966.
[25] R. M. Albérès, *L'Aventure intellectuelle du XXe siècle, op. cit.*
[26] Francis Jeanson, *Simone de Beauvoir ou l'entreprise de vivre, op. cit.*

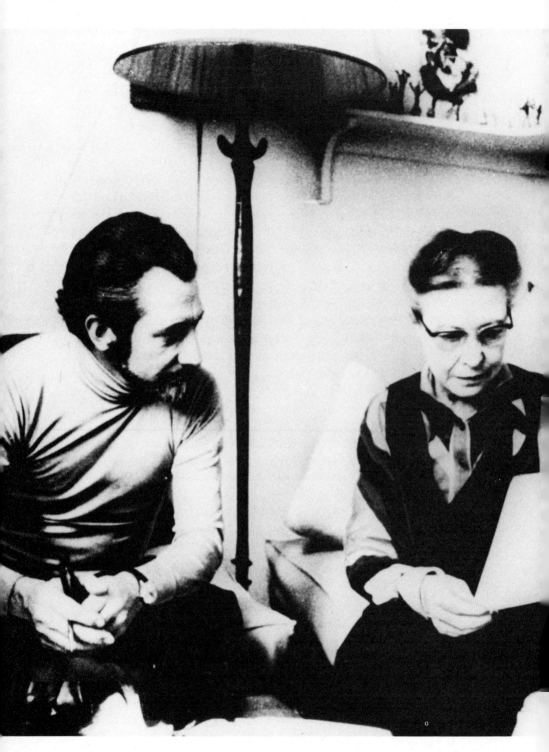

Francis Jeanson and Simone, 1974

been gypped she meant this to translate her *total* vision of life: "I have always thought, like Sartre, that life is a vain search for Being, that we're always looking for the absolute and never reach higher than the relative." Youth in a sense meant promises, and in the "I have been gypped," she meant to measure her adult astonishment in remembering her illusions when she was sixteen.

In November, Russell and Schoenman announced the creation of the Bertrand Russell International War Crimes Tribunal. Troubles began soon enough and before the end of the year Schoenman was complaining to Sartre in Paris that the tribunal's executive committee had met and discussed rules and procedures without letting him know. He was soon to apologize for not having sent documents and other material to the tribunal's chairman, Yugoslav author, World War II partisan and friend of Marshal Tito, Vladimir Dedijer.

What interested Sartre at this point were the *limits* of the tribunal. As he told a *Nouvel Observateur* reporter, the question was not to judge the morality of American foreign policy but to see whether this policy was criminal under narrow and specific "war crimes" definitions. Imperialism had existed throughout history and as such escaped all judicial and moral condemnation. He objected to the term "idealistic," saying it would be idealistically silly to pretend to be a real court, whereas it made sense to be mere citizens trying objectively to judge one country's policies according to judicial precedent such as the Nuremberg Trials. Finally, he justified the fact that the tribunal would only investigate alleged American and South Vietnamese atrocities and not alleged North Vietnamese or Vietcong crimes by saying he refused to equate "the actions of a group of poor peasants, tracked like animals and obliged to institute an iron rule in their ranks, with the actions of an immense army supported by a superindustrialized country of two hundred million people." [27]

In January 1967, Sartre went to London to meet Schoenman and a number of his fellow members, American "black power" radical Stokely Carmichael (who never showed up but sent a deputy), Polish-born British historian (and Trotsky biographer) Isaac Deutscher, former Mexican president Lázaro Cárdenas and British National Union of Mineworkers leader Laurence Daly. Schoenman had difficulties finding a country willing to host the tribunal. Britain ruled itself out by announcing it would not allow into the country any of the North Vietnamese who were willing to give evidence. Russell's plans still remained optimistic, however. "The

[27] *Nouvel Observateur*, November 30–December 6, 1966.

proposal is for a session in New York in July, in Japan in August and in Auschwitz in September," he wrote to Dedijer, who was later to arouse Russell's wrath by declaring, tongue in cheek, that the next session would be held in the Vatican.

While Schoenman looked for another country—and tentatively settled on Switzerland—Sartre and Beaver toured that other potential flashpoint, the Middle East. Was a third solution possible? Was it possible to bridge the gap between Israelis and Arabs through a rapprochement between Israeli and Egyptian leftists? Sartre liked Gamal Nasser's socialistic nationalism and announced he would visit Egypt and Israel and that *TM* would publish a special Israeli-Arab issue. The trip had been set for December but actually took place in February and March 1967. The special *TM* issue went to the printers in late May, one week before the outbreak of the Six-Day War.

Sartre and Beaver visited Cairo first, as guests of the influential *Al-Ahram* newspaper. After excursions to Luxor and the Aswan Dam the Soviets were building, Sartre met politicians and Simone looked into the problem of women, meeting a few feminists—doctors, lawyers and journalists. Toward the end of their stay, Nasser received them at his residence. For three hours they talked, Nasser in a somewhat melancholy voice. To Simone's questions, he said he was a feminist, that he had encouraged one of his daughters to carry her studies to an advanced level. He believed in God, he said, but Islam had thwarted him at every turn. On the question of the Palestinian refugees, he admitted it was a Gordian knot and seemed less than eager to risk a war.

When Sartre and Simone landed in Tel Aviv, he told a news conference he was torn between contradictory friendships. World War II had taught him that no one in Europe could be safe unless Jews were safe and when Jews had fought the British to create Israel he had been passionately on their side. But the Algerians' struggle to free themselves from colonialism had taught him solidarity with FLN combatants and brought about numerous friendships in Arab countries: "Now, when the Arab world and Israel confront each other we therefore feel divided within ourselves and experience the confrontation as a personal tragedy." [28] They were the guests of Histadrut, the labor organization, met with Prime Minister Levi Eshkol and visited kibbutzim where Simone learned that older pioneer women, now in their sixties, had ignored all differences and behaved like men whereas the younger women felt they served Israel just as well carry-

[28] Interview with *Al Hamishmar,* reprinted in *New Outlook,* Tel Aviv, Vol. 9, No. 4, May 1967.

With Lanzmann in front of the sphinx at Giza, Egypt
KEYSTONE

ing out their "women's work" as by competing with the men. After three weeks in the country, Sartre told a news conference that if the new Israeli Man could develop in peace, grasp the contradictions within himself and overcome them, he could be one of the richest men in history. When questioned about his stand on the Israeli-Arab question, he reaffirmed his neutrality and said he recognized "totally" both Israel's right to exist as a nation and the Palestinians' right to return to Israel.

The Bertrand Russell International War Crimes Tribunal had trouble finding a host country. After a hall had been rented in Zurich the Swiss government banned the tribunal from the country. Next came France, where the chosen hotel canceled the reservation. Sartre wrote to de Gaulle asking whether this refusal was based upon a desire to prevent the tribunal from sitting in Paris. Elegantly calling Sartre "mon cher maître," de Gaulle answered Yes. In making de Gaulle's letter public, Sartre said the tribunal would sit, even if it had to be on a ship anchored on the high seas.

Very reluctantly, the Swedish government allowed the tribunal to convene in Stockholm—not out of any awe for the Russell court, but to uphold its own democratic principles. Russell was approaching his ninety-fifth birthday and it was out of the question that he come to Stockholm. Before Sartre and Simone got there with their respective deputies, Claude Lanzmann and Gisèle Halimi, they heard that Schoenman was holding free-swinging press conferences three times a day and it was only when they all foregathered in a big downtown hotel that they learned the composition of the tribunal. Russell was the honorary chairman, Sartre was the executive president and Dedijer was to preside over the hearings, assisted by Laurent Schwartz, a French teacher and veteran of Algerian antiwar protests. There were several no-shows, including Daly, Carmichael and James Baldwin, and new judges included David Dellinger, editor of the U. S. magazine *Liberation, Marat/Sade* author Peter Weiss, a Filipino poet, Turkish, Italian and Japanese lawyers, a Pakistani supreme court justice, a German philosopher and two other Japanese and American pacifists. Besides Simone the only other woman was Melba Hernandez, who had taken part in the Cuban revolution and who, after seeing the miniskirted girls and longhaired youths doing the translating, typing and copying, said she was going to tell Castro that Carnaby Street fashion—strictly forbidden in Cuba—was not incompatible with revolutionary ardor.

After repairing various blunders committed by Schoenman, including his insult of the Swedish prime minister, and overcoming various inner hostilities, the hearings started in an auditorium in the House of the

Arriving in Stockholm
for Russell Tribunal trial
A.F.P.

People under the glare of Swedish TV cameras. The judges were asked to consider two questions: 1) Had the United States committed an act of aggression as defined by international law; and 2) Had there been bombings of purely civilian targets and if so to what extent? In a growing hostility of Swedish press and public, the tribunal heard evidence from Pham Van Bac and other North Vietnamese and Vietcong representatives and in the wee hours of May 10 delivered a guilty verdict on both counts and agreed to meet in a last session in the fall.

The Venice Film Festival was a welcome respite. *Le Mur,* directed by Serge Roullet, was the only film adapted from any of Sartre's works that he really liked, and on September 5 he faced a massive festival press conference to help "sell" the picture. Various critics saw a parallel between Sartre's thirty-year-old short story about Spanish Civil War idealism and current fascination with Chinese Red Guard ideology. Yes, Sartre agreed, idealism both in the best and worst sense.

Festival director Luigi Charini took them to the Lido in a launch and at the landing stage they took a horse-drawn carriage to go and see René Maheu, their Ecole Normale school chum who had introduced them to each other in 1929. Now the director of UNESCO, Maheu was staying at the Hôtel des Bains where Thomas Mann had situated *Death in Venice* and they loved its turn-of-the-century charm. They had not seen Maheu for years. They had drinks on a terrace overlooking a big garden where Maheu told them how Venice and its lagoons were threatened with ecological disaster and how UNESCO was trying to help in the historic preservation.

Two weeks later the Russell tribunal met in Brussels and at the invitation of two Danes agreed to hold the last full session in Copenhagen. The tribunal, which Russell had difficulties keeping afloat financially, was becoming irrelevant where it wanted to make an impact—in the United States. The Spring Mobilization to End the War in Vietnam had sponsored mass marches in New York and San Francisco, which attracted one hundred eighty thousand participants. Carmichael and Martin Luther King, Jr., had brought together major elements of the peace and civil rights movements and King and Benjamin Spock had launched Vietnam Summer. Negotiation Now! had coalesced various moderate antileaders and organizations such as the American Jewish Congress, Americans for Democratic Action and the National Council of Churches. For October, Dellinger was mobilizing a Washington march on the Pentagon to be followed by a Stop the Draft Week.

The tribunal convened, not in Copenhagen, but in a union hall in Roskilde, twenty miles from the Danish capital. Sartre brought along his adopted daughter, Arlette, and Gisèle Halimi was another faithful. When they got to Roskilde, Dedijer told them Schoenman would probably have difficulties entering Denmark. So much the better, they all agreed. Deutscher had died but Carmichael showed up at the end. Three questions were on the agenda: 1) Had American forces used or tried out new weapons forbidden by the laws of war? 2) Were the Vietnamese prisoners subjected to inhuman treatment forbidden by the laws of war? and 3) Had there been acts tending toward the extermination of the population and coming under the legal definition of genocide?

The verdict was a foregone conclusion—the My Lai revelations the following March were to be grim confirmation of atrocities—and only Sartre's sum-up as president of the tribunal was noteworthy. Written in early December 1967 as Hanoi rejected President Johnson's offer to stop all aerial and naval bombings if it would lead to negotiations and if North Vietnam wouldn't take advantage of the lull, *Vietnam: Imperialism and Genocide* condemned the United States because it had no interests in Vietnam and was waging war ten thousand miles from its borders only to set an example. Taking General William C. Westmoreland's claim of October 1967, "We are waging war in Vietnam to show that guerrilla warfare does not pay," Sartre said the war was a precautionary and premeditated genocide addressed to all mankind. "Total war presupposes a certain balance of force, a certain reciprocity," he summed up. "The present example of genocide, the latest result of the unequal development of nations, is total war fought to the bitter end by one side only and without the slightest degree of reciprocity." [29]

When the war ended with Saigon's collapse in 1975 and *Le Monde* asked Sartre what he thought the Russell tribunal had meant, he would answer, Not very much. It had had no impact in the United States and the Soviet Union never took it seriously, he said, but the North Vietnamese put a lot of faith in it and Pham Van Bac got to play a major role in the protracted peace negotiations with Henry Kissinger. "Any free man who is interested in an affair of social importance can, together with other equally free men, make a judgment that may bring others to judge for themselves. The Russell tribunal reaffirmed the old idea that every man is both his neighbor's judge and his keeper." [30]

[29] Published in volume, *Tribunal Russell 2: Le jugement final*, Paris: Gallimard, 1968; translated as *On Genocide*, with summary of the evidence and judgments of the International War Crimes Tribunal by Arlette Elkaim-Sartre, Boston: Beacon Press, 1968.
[30] *Le Monde*, May 10, 1975.

*   *   *

Sartre, Simone and Arlette returned from Roskilde in time to see Camille one last time before she died in a hospital. A recluse since Dullin's death in 1949, Camille in the end had only Sartre and Beaver—Sartre to pay her debts, Simone to visit her in her apartment where she lived as a perpetual drunk in her own filth, scraps of theatrical costumes and food brought up by the concierge and left to rot. When Simone and the concierge finally called the health department to have her taken to the hospital, the ambulance attendants found her in a semicoma on the floor covered with excrement—she even had it in her hair. When Simone visited her at the hospital, she apologized because her hair had been cut. She suffocated a few days later.

For Sartre, the New Year started with a painful attack of arthritis that forced him to cancel plans to attend a cultural congress in Havana. When a Cuban journalist interviewed him via long-distance telephone, Sartre expressed the hope that the congress would elect as its president a Third World representative. In Havana, Sartre's arthritis was rumored to be diplomatic, provoked either by his disapproval of Castro's new policies or by his fear of a confrontation with Arab intellectuals over his pre-Six-Day War neutrality. The rumors were not altogether wrong, even if Sartre's arthritis was very real. Homosexuals were now being persecuted in Cuba, and as soon as the congress ended, Castro stopped supporting Castroism in Latin America and fell in line with Moscow's more cautious policies. And Israel *was* a dilemma for radical leftists. Sartre and Beaver saw the depth of the division when they opened *TM* to Eldridge Cleaver —Simone had admired *Soul on Ice*—and saw him attack Jews. What was painful, as Simone would write in *All Said and Done,* was that the non-communist left was becoming as monolithic as the Party itself: "I understand the claims of Arafat's nationalists; but unlike many of the left I refuse to see Al Fatah as a movement that embodies the hopes of socialism. I am sorry that only a small fraction of the Israeli left attempts to negotiate with the Palestinians."

In March and April, Sartre and Beaver visited Yugoslavia as the guests of Dedijer, eagerly discussing the "Prague spring," which Sartre thought proved it was possible to put an end to the abuses of the regime without doing away with the entire system.

They were back in Paris in early May, Sartre once more picking up Flaubert and Simone working on her book on old age, when student activists escalated their situation at Nanterre and the Sorbonne and within days clashed head-on with steel-helmeted police on Boulevard St. Germain.

Since the end of the Algerian war, Sartre and Beaver had not paid much attention to what was happening in their own country. With the May Events a decade of radical involvement in French affairs was to begin.

CHAPTER

SPRING OF 1977

SIMONE'S SIXTY-NINTH BIRTHDAY was like the others—for friends. Little Bost and Olga were there, Sylvie Le Bon and Lanzmann, too, and the new faithfuls—Pierre Victor, Philippe Gavi, Catherine Clément and Jorge Semprun. And there was a postcard from Zette and Michel Leiris, and a phone call from Poupette. The birthday party was at the studio apartment. Sartre had Victor open the champagne and Olga joked that Beaver's next birthday would be like Sartre's seventieth, with telegrams from all over the world and a monster interview with Michel Contat. The guests stayed late; it was a Saturday. Sylvie and Lanzmann were the last to leave. Sartre stayed. Since his blindness he lived with Beaver.

The next day things were back to normal. With a tape recorder they worked on the continuation of *Les Mots*. In the afternoon, Victor and Gavi took Sartre to lunch at one of the Montparnasse *brasseries* and at 3 o'clock deposited him at 222 Boulevard Raspail, where Beaver joined him at 6 to read him the newspapers. As usual, they returned to her studio at 9 and spent the evening listening to records from Simone's ever-growing collection. As usual, Sartre was in bed by 1 A.M.

It was hard not to be able to write. The tape recorder was a laborious process and turned the biography into a "dialogue book," as they called it—"talked" into the tape recorder, transcribed by a secretarial service, then read back to Sartre by Simone for joint oral editing and actual penciling by Simone.

Like *All Said and Done,* the "dialogue book" dropped chronology in favor of themes. "What I try to explain is how things change, how certain events influenced me," he told this biographer after one such session with Simone. "I don't think a person's life is written in the sands of childhood but that there are important periods when things fall into place. What I see more and more clearly in my own life is that there is a fissure in the middle—World War II—and that I can barely recognize the person I was before the cleft.

"Human lives surprise by their changes, even if somebody's life does form a whole that cannot be cut up into convenient sections. Youth and maturity, the subjective and objective selves, the personal and political identities constantly rub against each other. It is impossible to understand anyone without seeing his or her social dimension. We are all political beings, but I really only understood that at the end of the war."

If it took the hindsight of three score and ten years to realize that he had only discovered *homo politicus* when he was forty, age also made him realize that there was a human need to escape the social dimension. In his seventies, he again marked his distance with Marxism and broke not only with the Soviets but with Castro. He opted for an unstructured "libertarian socialism," in which no man would think for any other man. In the latter half of the 1970s, Sartrian politics sought to overcome constraints and compulsions, to cultivate transparency and to try to bridge the gap between the terribly lonely modern man and the muffled revolt straining at the seams of our allegedly sated and indifferent society. It was no longer possible to accord attenuating circumstances to Marxism or to follow Georges Marchais' Communist Party—let alone President Valéry Giscard d'Estaing's advanced liberalism. Both appeared to him to be the living dead, frozen shadows and left-behinds because they were incapable of crystallizing and channeling new needs. Sartre's politics of generosity was not without its naïveté, but as he gravitated toward a status of "monstre sacré" in his country's conscience, both his enemies and his defenders seemed to have tired, making him dangle, somewhat incongruously, in midair between official admiration and Maoist youths politely holding their fire.

Beaver was with him, revered grandmother of a triumphant sisterhood. She knew how to remain firm in her feminism but also how to keep her head above it. She saw a need for women to remain multiple and even contradictory in the face of feminism as election bait and consumer chic, to remain aloof from ideologies and perhaps to bring about a cease-fire between class struggle and the war of the sexes.

Self-criticism and a sense of having said it all dominated the mid-1970s for both of them, together with the contradictions of being rich and famous while trying to melt into a proletariat that was perhaps more myth than either of them would admit. When Betty Friedan visited France, she was struck by the prim, bohemian elegance of Simone's studio and her suggestion that to avoid compromising temptations young women should forego the very comforts and rewards of elitist careers and fame that Simone's own eminence had earned her. In numerous interviews, Sartre went out of his way to appear unexceptional, to deny ascendancy, to downgrade the role of the intellectual and even to debunk the writer as a neurotic and a freak in whom a period's incongruities are made theater. His urge for personal transparency was accompanied by a passion to share—money and innermost thoughts, and a relentless boring into all pretense. "The truth in writing would be to say, 'I take the pencil. My name is Sartre. This is what I think.' "

Life as perpetual revision had come with the aftershock of the May Events.

They had returned from Prague in December 1968 with their ears ringing with defiance only to see the backlash to the student barricades carry de Gaulle to his biggest-ever election win. But the aging chief of state had transformed the victory into a suspended sentence by insisting on a follow-up referendum, to be held in April 1969.

Sartre and Beaver spent New Year's Day 1969 with Anne-Marie. Sartre's mother was not well. She had high blood pressure, headaches and painful bouts with rheumatism. On January 3, she had a heart attack and was taken to the hospital. When Sartre saw her the next day she was pleased that the pains were gone, but she slipped fast and died of complications from uremia and a second stroke two weeks later. She had often said she didn't want a church service and Sartre and Beaver had her taken directly to the cemetery where family and a few friends were gathered. In July, she would have been eighty-seven.

The universities were seething as newly appointed Education Minister Edgar Faure tried to rein in both students and faculty and loudly announced an upcoming overhaul of the whole system of higher education. Sartre had occasion to protest to Faure when sanctions were taken against a college teacher who had asked his students to do a paper on *Le Mur*. In February, Sartre took part in a meeting protesting the expulsion of thirty-four Sorbonne students. The meeting was held in the old socialist Mutualité Hall and as he got to his seat, he found an anonymous note on it, saying, "Sartre, be brief!"

For the first time he felt challenged to the core by men and women who could be his grandchildren. The student militants who dominated every university were miles to the left of anything he had thought possible. None of them were poor—indeed most of them were the sons and daughters of middle- to upper-class parents—and they had replaced poverty as the prime mover of "revolution" with sovereignty. The notion of *power* in a modern industrial society was more important to them than ownership and they demanded that the individual be defined in other ways than by the objects he produces or the functions he fulfills. This "angry" generation dreamed about masses and spontaneity, criticized the very notion of the *party* as a political, structured organization and, to combat the "serialized individual," demanded a return to "pure Leninism." The real *locus* of revolutionary consciousness was neither in the class, nor in the Party, but in the struggle itself, meaning that the Communist Party was only relevant as long as it was an instrument of struggle. When they said the university should be "open," they meant it should dispense culture instead of grinding out technocrats, that grading should be replaced by collective studies.

Sartre felt the student Maoists were one big contradiction—highly structured and hierarchized yet longing for spontaneity and free forms. But they wanted change, radical change, and Sartre congratulated them, as he said, "without being quite sure what kind of role an old fart like me can play."

The April 27 referendum, which Sartre told a news conference people should boycott, went against de Gaulle, and the next day the nearly eighty-year-old chief of state resigned. For the presidential elections that followed, Sartre supported Alain Krivine without campaigning actively for the minority student Maoist candidate. The elections made Georges Pompidou de Gaulle's successor.

Sartre and Beaver spent the summer in Rome and met with Daniel Cohn-Bendit and several other student leaders already talking with nostalgia about last summer's barricades. "What struck us most of all was that they did in fact have the state of mind of defeated men," Simone would write in *All Said and Done*. "There they were, after the great days of May, empty-handed. They harshly criticized *Les Temps modernes*, accusing it of having become an institution."

Politically, *TM* had supported the May phenomenon and, after the "Polish" and "Italian" periods, now began a Maoist phase, as Sartre and especially Simone threw it open to the sometimes contradictory currents of extreme leftism and the Women's Lib movement. The shift provoked the departure of J. B. Pontalis, who had been with *TM* since the beginning, and of Bernard Pingaud who had joined in 1949.

Malraux said of the May Events, which saw quotations from his books scrawled on college and university walls taunting him with the Faustian pronouncements of his youth, "To know youth is to be part of it; it is not attempts at 'dialogue.' " Malraux, Sartre—and Aragon—were now, despite their differences in character and options, the elder statesmen of French letters. None of them yielded to the reassuring mythology of white-maned Victor Hugo apotheosis, but all three remained the elder "names" above the pack and all three ruthlessly questioned literature itself. In retirement, after a decade as de Gaulle's high-profile Secretary for Cultural Affairs, Malraux plunged into writings on art as man's permanence and continued his *Antimémoires,* mixing fact and fiction because a life is remembered for what is "anti," for what is imagined, amplified and transcended. Aragon remained faithful to his forty years inside the Communist Party but in his explorations of his surrealist youth and of the limits of fictionalized biography in his monumental *Henri Matisse, roman,* he moved into a twilight that was no longer Marxian. In *L'Idiot de la famille,* Sartre also challenged literature and writing. The three heavy volumes of the unfinished Flaubert biography were a political conscience's untiring indictment of literature and, through Flaubert, of the author's caste and his rank in society as guru.

But before delivering *L'Idiot de la famille* to Gallimard, Sartre delivered himself to the student Maoists, knowing full well the radicals were seeking to exploit his name and fame.

The May Events had created a welter of far-out newssheets with such names as *J'accuse, La Cause du peuple, L'Idiot international* and *Revolution!* This "underground" press made the Establishment shudder, but it was noisily hawked on street corners and campuses by enthusiastic "Maos" and avidly read by the under-twenty-five crowd. *La Cause du peuple,* which likened its followers to Resistance partisans, Communist Party members to Nazi collaborators and spoke of the "occupation" of France by the bourgeoisie and the need to liberate the land, became the straw that broke the nervous Pompidou Administration's back. In April 1970, the two young editors of the paper were arrested. With the exception of the German Occupation years, no newspaper editor had gone to jail in France since 1881 and the Palais de Justice was ringed with police vans for the two editors' court appearance. Prosecuting attorneys demanded that the oft-confiscated newssheet be banned permanently—a motion that was re-

Leaving the Palais de Justice with
Gisèle Halimi after testifying on behalf
of the Cause du peuple *editors*
KEYSTONE

fused. The editors were remanded for trial. In June, when the judge sentenced them to one-year prison terms, students clashed with police at several locations until 3 o'clock in the morning. A few days later police surrounded the plant where *La Cause du peuple* was printed to take its owner Simon Blumenthal into "supervisory detention" and to confiscate another press run. The workers surrounded the police vans, making the cops leave without Blumenthal, and seventy-five thousand copies of the paper had already been spirited away.

The next day, the masthead of *La Cause du peuple* carried the name of its new editor—Jean-Paul Sartre—and that evening, passers-by in the Rue Daguerre behind Montparnasse cemetery could see a flock of photographers and TV cameramen surround an elderly couple handing out *La Cause du peuple* to housewives with shopping bags and men returning from work. As Simone was to put it in the closing pages of *All Said and Done,* "We pushed through the crowd, crying, 'Read *La Cause du peuple.* Support the freedom of the press!' and handing out copies; then we went along Avenue Général Leclerc, which was even more crowded. Some people refused the paper with a disapproving look. 'It's banned,' said one man. Others took it without caring one way or another; still others called out for a copy." When a young policeman came up, took a stack of papers from Sartre and grabbed his arm to lead him toward the precinct station, he was blitzed by photographers. Somebody shouted, "You're arresting a Nobel Prize winner!" and the cop let go. Sartre followed him but the cop walked faster and faster, almost running. Together with some twenty supporters they repeated the operation on the Right Bank the following Friday, starting somewhat saucily opposite the *L'Humanité* building. When a police van pulled up, they were told they were not being arrested, only taken in for an identification check. When the paddy wagon stopped in front of the police station, they were all herded inside except Sartre, who was told he was free. He immediately began distributing his remaining papers to the gathering crowd and finally managed to get himself invited inside. The chief was phoning. Plain-clothed higher-ups arrived, took Sartre and Simone aside and told them everybody would be released within half an hour. Sartre made it clear he and Simone would be the last to leave. When they got outside they were surrounded by journalists and TV crews. Sartre told them he was not trying to get himself arrested but to place the government in a state of self-contradiction. Judging from the police confusion, he had succeeded.

It was not that Sartre had chosen the "Maos"—he barely knew them— nor that they chose him. A few months earlier they had ridiculed him. It was the government's clumsiness that brought the two together. And after *La Cause du peuple* came others. By the fall of 1970 Sartre had assumed responsibility for two other papers, *Tout!* and *La Parole au peuple,* and helped the provincial newssheet *Secours rouge,* backed by a splinter group of the same name.

Pierre Victor was the bushy-haired twenty-nine-year-old radical who had come to Sartre and asked him to take over the editorship of *La Cause du peuple.* Victor was an Althusserian Leninist-Marxist, a Spontex Maoist and a neo-*Tel Quel* believer. Sartre was fascinated. Althusser was a Sorbonne professor (and a *pieds-noir* of Alsatian origin, born in 1918) who had articulated a major theoretical system by the most sweeping retroactive assimilation of pre-Marx philosophers—Spinoza especially but also Montesquieu—into a kind of "western Marxism," the most ambitious attempt at giving Karl Marx forefathers and thereby developing radically new theoretical directions to contemporary Marxism. Sartre didn't agree with Althusser's theory that all ideology was a necessary illusion to bind society together but agreed there were curious similarities in his and Althusser's parallel pessimism when it came to the structures of socialism and the idea of a true dictatorship of the proletariat.

Sartre liked the young Maoists' rejection of bureaucratization of socialist revolutions. He knew that purist Maos, who believed in spontaneous political action, had adopted the trade name Spontex for themselves because it made scouring sponges rhyme with "spontaneism," but he wasn't *au courant* on what the *Tel Quel* group had been up to since the May Events. Victor explained. "Textual writers" rejected committed literature as a trap and as bourgeois flimflam. If an author wanted to contribute to the triumph of social revolution, he should start by applying structuralism to his own writing, that is, he should try to integrate his Marxism into his writing instead of his politics. Somewhat like American radical feminists proposing to take sexism out of English with "chairperson" if not "herstory," Sollers, Thibeaudeau, Julia Kristeva and others tried to invent a preconscious language stripped of lazy metaphors and references, a language moving forward in a kind of perpetual motion of cutoff phrases and a verbal jubilation often without punctuation marks but replete with neologisms and repetitions. As critics, they used Lacan's research into subterranean ideology "in the text." That these Althusserian Leninist-Marxists were applying Barthes' critical theories, Lacan's psychoanalysis and the semantics of Foucault and Noam Chomsky was of course interesting, considering it was only four years since Sartre had taken the structuralists to task for ignoring historical evolution. But then again, Spontex Maoists looked past Moscow toward Peking and, sometimes, Havana.

Victor was a cool intellectual who had read most of Sartre's philosophy and rejected a good part of it. Sartre found Victor's thinking solid and enjoyed the confrontation with this radical theorist who said it all came down to "the masses." If intellectuals felt unwanted it was because the masses didn't need them; not because theory was in the praxis but because theory only became clear when tried out in the real world. All human beings were equal—radically equal, Victor intoned with the seriousness of a born leader that made Sartre make fun of him until he realized that his ascendence over the Gauche prolétarienne, the party behind *La Cause du peuple,* was perhaps pernicious. Victor, on the other hand, showed Sartre he was his own contradiction—a radical, yes, but also an institution, the Voltaire the government wouldn't arrest.

Revisionists—as Victor and his Spontex Maoist followers called card-carrying communists—claimed morality was a bourgeois hang-up, something that militants should dispense with and instead concentrate on practical rules leading to concrete results. Not true at all, said the Maos. Spontaneous explosions of popular violence were profoundly moral. Even if such violence had economic and political motives, it could only be understood on a moral basis as a revolt against man exploiting man. When the bourgeois claimed his conduct was human—work, family, fatherland —he was only hiding the profound immorality of alienating the masses. Which was the reason, Victor explained, why the intellectual as "knowledge technician" was doomed to disappear. The intellectual may have discovered exploitation and oppression, but only in the abstract and as a contradiction of bourgeois morality, as a "No!" to the bourgeoisie's eternal "Obey!"

Sartre could not follow his young disputant into his idolatry of the proletariat. The Maos found worker "occupation" of factories and the holding of executives hostage for hours and sometimes days—a practice that got dubbed "séquestration"—examples of a dictatorship *of* the proletariat rather than the party dictatorship *for* the people. What had to be preserved at all cost was this spontaneous violence because it alone could lead to true self-government. Political parties were no longer making the changes, individuals were, unpredictable individuals.

But, said Sartre, the Maos were also a party and a party would always try, to the degree that it wanted to see itself as "in the service" of concerted action, to control such action. If Althusserian neo-Leninist-Marxists wanted real social reform and, at the same time to remain revolutionary, the political element of Marxism would have to self-destruct because a society marching toward self-government would eventually abolish, along with the state, *political* action.

In 1973, the Gauche prolétarienne self-destructed as its own contradiction—as party dedicated to a proletarian self-rule that could only be self-generated. "Little by little Pierre came around to my point of view, particularly regarding freedom and the refusal of *all* hierarchy, of the very idea of leadership," Sartre would say in 1976. But Victor's influence on Sartre was also important. The intellectual as fleshed-out contradiction was Victor's idea—although foreshadowed in Sartre's notion of writing as neurosis. Victor forced Sartre to examine his own position in society as well-paid "knowledge technican." On his own, Sartre realized that he couldn't progress very far. He could not, as some intellectuals had done, look for a job in a Renault factory because that was just as monstrous and showed a self-loathing that the liberated individual was supposed to have left behind. "It is true that intelligence stinks, but no more than stupidity," he had said in 1948. Now, he said that if the intellectual should self-destruct so should the working class. True revolution meant going beyond class. If the state was the last Bastille to storm before the millennium of social universalism, then "the dictatorship of the proletariat" was the next-to-last obstacle.

Simone didn't exactly have blind faith in Mao's China and said she wouldn't be surprised if one day she would hear about Chinese *gulags*. She found many of the Spontex Maos' assertions naïve and was ambivalent about their using Sartre's fame while vehemently denouncing all intellectual "star system" pecking orders. But she liked their focus on the young, the women and that bottom "other France," which progress always seemed to neglect. During the Gaullist 1960s the robust economy had almost tripled, yet the prosperity had mainly benefited the slowly expanding middle class and the country's pampered farmers while totally bypassing the aged and the wage earners. Two thirds of the country's twenty million workers struggled along on annual incomes nearly five times less than upper-level executives—the highest spread between employer and employee income in Europe. Millions still lived without the conveniences common to other industrial economies. One out of three French homes was officially considered to be "overpopulated," a quarter of them had no hot water and over half lacked baths. Taxes were regressive and the French worker had come to expect little from a capitalist, conservative society and to put all his faith in changing government. The traditional left defined itself as that electoral alternative, whereas the Maos sought small-scale solutions to immediate problems.

In the fall of 1970, members of the Mouvement de Libération des Femmes (MLF) asked Simone to speak on behalf of a new abortion bill coming before the National Assembly. The MLF found the bill hopelessly inadequate and several of its members felt the way to dramatize the issue was for a number of women, both well-known and anonymous, to admit that they had had abortions. Together with Françoise Sagan, Simone Signoret, Catherine Deneuve, Jeanne Moreau and hundreds of unknowns, Simone signed what became The Manifesto of the 343—women who admitted having had illegal abortions and now invited the Pompidou Administration to prosecute them (something that after some hemming and hawing it decided not to do). Simone took part in the "occupation" of a school for unwed mothers run according to quasi-medieval rules and in the fall of 1971 took part in the Paris version of the worldwide Woman's Day manifestations and marches.

The point was no longer to emancipate but to "decolonize" women. Simone had liked Betty Friedan's *The Feminine Mystique* in 1963. She had followed the flood of American feminist literature, from Kate Millett's *Sexual Politics* to Robin Morgan's collection of studies, *Sisterhood Is Powerful,* and corresponded with some American militants; an American paperback edition of *The Second Sex* sold three quarters of a million copies in 1969 alone. She was gratified that these feminists quoted *The Second Sex* as an authority and all followed her twenty-year-old lead in saying that women were manufactured by civilizations, not biologically determined. Repeatedly, she said that if she were to write *Le Deuxième sexe* in the 1970s, she would emphasize the materialistic foundations for the oppression of women. In an advanced society woman's status as housewife-consumer was economically very profitable, but emancipation had not come to women in socialist countries either. Abstract socialists would say capitalism oppressed women; radical feminists now answered that *all* societies were male supremacist, and she was the first to admit that the dying Fanon's predictions about Algerian—and by extension, African, women escaping male oppression the moment the colonial powers were defeated were nothing more than fabulations. "Algeria's foreign policy is held out as 'progressive' and it is indeed anticolonialist and antiimperialist," she wrote in *All Said and Done,* "but the country's home policy is both nationalist and reactionary."

If she didn't rewrite *The Second Sex* or pour her consciousness-raising into a new feminist book, she wrote a long, absorbing essay on that truly neglected minority—the aged. *La Vieillesse* (*The Coming of Age*) is a fierce indictment of society's indifference and cruelty toward old people, a seven-hundred-page inquiry into old age as social phenomenon and private anguish.[1] More prodigious recapitulation than original thesis, *La Vieillesse* draws on scientific and artistic evidence, on ethnology, psychology, medicine and sociology in establishing the causes and effects of aging —the steady degradation of old age and the harrowing neglect reserved for the aged throughout history. *La Vieillesse* is divided into old age as seen from the outside—old age and biology, old age through history and today—and from the inside—the individual's discovery and assuming age in time, and everyday life and, as lived by a number of exceptional beings. Here is Victor Hugo who prepared himself to become a patriarch and enjoyed a grand old age; here is Tolstoy's pathetic jealousy of his wife until his death at eighty-one, Michelangelo's obsession with death, Verdi accepting age with difficulty despite magnificent health, Chateaubriand's atrocious aging and Lou Andreas Salomé, the remarkable woman whom Nietzsche and Rilke had loved, who at fifty became Freud's friend, and Freud himself, cancer-ridden and writing totally fresh works in his late seventies and dying at eighty-three after having undergone thirty-three cancer operations during the last sixteen years of his life. Her final judgment is severe: "Society only cares about the individual insofar as he is profitable. The young know this. Their anxiety as they enter the labor market matches the anguish of the old when they are thrown out of it. Between these two ages, routine masks the problems . . . When we have understood what the state of old age is, we cannot satisfy ourselves with calling for a more generous 'old-age policy,' higher benefits, decent housing and organized leisure. It is the whole system that is at issue and our claim can only be radical—change life itself."

Sartre's craziest, most poetic and most important critical enterprise reached the bookstores in installments in 1971 and 1972. *L'Idiot de la famille* was a critical event, a three-volume attempt at "totalizing" the experiences by which Flaubert made himself the author of *Madame Bovary*.[2]

Flaubert had interested Sartre since childhood. He had read *Madame Bovary* again at teachers' college, *L'Education sentimentale* during the

[1] Simone de Beauvoir, *La Vieillesse,* Paris: Gallimard, 1970; *The Coming of Age,* New York: G. P. Putnam's, 1972.
[2] Jean-Paul Sartre, *L'Idiot de la famille,* Paris: Gallimard; tome I and II 1971, tome III 1972.

1930s and, during the war, the four massive volumes of Flaubert's correspondence, finding the author unsympathetic but deciding one day to
write his biography. The idea had resurfaced in 1954 when Communist
Party guru Roger Garaudy had proposed a contest in which each would
explain a commonly known figure according to Marxist and existentialist
modes of perception. In a short time, Sartre had filled twelve school notebooks with a Marxist and psychoanalytical outline of Flaubert, but nothing
had been published. After *The Words,* Sartre had again taken up Flaubert
and spent the next seven years writing four successive versions of the
biography before totally rewriting it in its final form in 1970 and, with
its publication, promising a fourth volume.

The Idiot of the Family is a monstrous—some critics would say a mon-
umentally perverse—portrait of Flaubert. It is an all-encompassing attempt
at "totalizing" Flaubert "in the text." Sartre uses psychoanalytical research
that psychoanalysts reject, "applied" Marxian dialectics that Marxists have
denounced and a method of reading Flaubert that is particularly attentive,
if it isn't actually structuralist, to show how Flaubert—and through him
everyone else—reflects the contradictions of his milieu and class, and
how, with the right tools and methods, the "total" Flaubert can be laid
bare.

Sartre pays special attention to the scribblings of Flaubert's youth
(which literary criticism usually finds unrewarding) and compares letters
from different periods of Flaubert's life. This allows Sartre to discover
that Flaubert was sexually passive—something that letters of his maturity
confirm—and to see the young, unhappy Flaubert as someone for whom
neurosis became a *solution.* Sartre finds that Flaubert delivers himself in
his letters as if he were on a psychiatrist's couch whereas George Sand,
one of his more important correspondents, constantly tries to hide herself
behind words. In scrutinizing *Madame Bovary* structurally, Sartre discovers
both defeat and victory. Flaubert was a man who missed important turns
in his childhood and adolescence, later outgrew his neuroses to some extent and put his defeat into *Madame Bovary,* which he wrote slowly and
painfully, laboring for more than five years. But *Madame Bovary* is a
masterpiece and Sartre's next step is to show that the great novel demanded
a different author from the unhappy Flaubert who projected himself in his
heroine, Emma Bovary, as he admitted in a famous remark. If the defeated
Flaubert is to be found in the text—there are numerous passive verbs de-
noting inner paralysis despite Flaubert's determination to find in style
alone the beauty that does not exist in banal reality—the author's triumph
must also be in the printed page. Sartre analyzes the defeats in the first

volumes and promises his readers to discover Flaubert's triumphs in a fourth volume. Sartre uses Lacan's latest psychoanalytical notions (the self as imaginary construction assumed by the individual after the fact), the latest discoveries in semiotics and analytical criticism—after Sartre, Gérard Ginette and others begin to break up the *Decameron* structurally, as well as Proust's subjectivism and horror fiction—to show that anyone is completely knowable. *The Idiot of the Family* is ultimately an attempt at showing that there is no "mystery" in the development of a life, that all structures of the self can be discovered and its inner dynamics made clear.

Critics generally held off judging *L'Idiot de la famille,* pending the promised concluding volume. Many, however, noted Sartre's own transparency, his total freedom from desire to prove anything. "It is a text that can go far because it is itself mobile, perpetually on the prowl to produce bubbling, effervescent effects," *Le Nouvel Observateur*'s Michel Sicard wrote. "The mocking tone, the passion, the hatred are not the residue of old polemics, coded disputes or phony intelligence, it is total violence. The analysis bores in, corrodes, undermines; what is left must die. This is guerrilla warfare, cruelty. The text has its own unbearable tension, in many places the charges are massive and blood is spilled as the self-analysis of the narrator and of history, the fact that fascism and capital can also be within us."[3]

Sartre started the fourth volume in October 1971, but didn't get very far before the Maos and what Jean Genet called his "genius for being a pain in the ass" of the bourgeoisie swallowed him again. The government had stopped harassing the "revolutionary press" after too much Keystone Kops ridicule had been heaped on police, and foreign news crews had filmed Jean-Luc Godard, Delphine Seyrig and other members of the radical chic crowd emerging from the Panthéon precinct station, and the French national network had featured Simone, Sartre and Blumenthal handing out papers on Boulevard St. Michel with a paddy wagon discreetly following them. In June, however, Sartre's nominal but very legally binding editorship of counterculture newspapers finally brought him charges of slander for articles printed in *La Cause du peuple* and *Tout!* As he told TV audiences, his directorship of the various newssheets was not the action of a liberal defending the freedom of the press but an act that committed him to people he had faith in, even if he didn't entirely share their ideas.

In private, he was less enthusiastic. He felt none of the papers had found the right approach and tone, and, more seriously, that they lied more often than the bourgeois press, that their "triumphalist" reporting

[3] "Décrire l'Oncle Gustave," *Le Nouvel Observateur,* May 1975.

of successful work actions without ever mentioning failures, was a dis-service to the supposedly proletarian readers. The truth should be revolu-tionary, but revolutionaries, as he told one short-lived newssheet, "don't want to know the truth; they have been brainwashed and live in their own dream world." Together with "old timer" novelist Maurice Clavel, who with *La Perte et le fracas* wrote the first May Events novel, Sartre founded Libération, a counterculture news agency.

Although Simone wrote on delinquent teenage girls in *La Cause du peuple* and took part in several protests, she also managed to say No to a lot of things and to stay at her work table to finish *All Said and Done*. Sartre's activist's calendar for 1971 and 1972 included actively supporting a prison hunger strike, marching for racial tolerance in the Arab-domi-nated Goutte d'or section of Montmartre, intervening in a prisoners' revolt, leading a takeover of a Renault car plant—from which he was bodily ex-pelled—investigating the murder of a Renault Maoist and attending the youth's funeral, noisily breaking with Castro over the jailing of the Cuban poet Padilla, forewording a book on the French Maos, flying to Brussels to speak on "Justice and the Government" to the young bar association of Belgium, attending his defamation trials and, together with Simone, sitting still for three weeks of filming for a documentary directed by their old friend Alexandre Astruc.

All Said and Done picked up where *Force of Circumstance* left off, but the last volume of Simone's now 2,200-page autobiography dealt not so much with chronology as with themes—the notion of change, her work, Rome in the summer, political travels (one of the few comic touches in the book is the description of a man in bathing trunks puffing along the beach in Crimea with Lenin's portrait tattooed on one side of his chest and Stalin's on the other), womanhood, the May Events and her and Sartre's radicalization. She called meeting Sartre "the most important event in my life" and wrote unsentimentally—if sometimes long-windedly—about the last ten years. Critics found the book lacked intimacy—V. S. Pritchett say-ing she had hardened too much into seeing people in the light of concepts [4] —but also that it was the voice of a wise and admirable woman. She was radical in her feminism, but rejected the idea that all sex was rape and the hatred of men and "masculine patterns" because it implied an equally specific feminine nature: "For women it is not a question of asserting themselves as women, but of becoming full-scale human beings."

* * *

[4] In *New York Review of Books,* August 8, 1974.

Sartre was not happy with *La Cause du peuple* and in the fall of 1972 plunged into an endeavor that was totally to submerge him—turning the Libération news agency into a daily newspaper. What he wanted to help create was a newspaper that would practice participatory democracy, a "people's daily," in which, if the readers wouldn't actually write their own news, they would furnish it. The idea had come during Spontex Maoist protests in Lens, in Lille and in Lyons, where workers, and, in one particularly moving case, nurses from a retirement hospital, had come up and said, "Would you say this? We've tried to have the local newspaper say this!" Whenever a social event would take place, the actors in the event—the strikers, protesters, young people—would be the source of the news, which "liberation committees" of volunteers would then sift and check out. The paper would not be a party organ like *L'Humanité,* whose editors and journalists no longer had a gut feeling for the weariness, anger and needs of the people in whose name they spoke. The newspaper would have to invent a journalism capable of expressing the immediacy of workers protesting inferior work safety or delinquent teenage girls in state institutions demanding why priests were allowed to visit them but not family-planning volunteers. If the people had to talk to the people subtleties would be lost, but the popular sense of justice would be restored. This would be a justice that the bourgeoisie couldn't accept because it lacked finesse, but it would be a justice without sophistry, loopholes and too clever bias.

Sartre poured 200,000 francs ($40,000) of seed money into the venture and by January 1973 could tell a radio audience that donations of five thousand francs (one thousand dollars) were coming in every day, most of it in the equivalent of twenty-dollar bills. When his talk-show host wondered if it wasn't regrettable to see Sartre abandon literature and philosophy for advocacy journalism, he answered that he was abandoning philosophy only for six months. After that he hoped *Libération* would be sufficiently robust for him to tiptoe into the wings. When asked whether *Libération* would succeed, he said he didn't know, that he and his friends were only launching an idea and that its survival was up to the people at large.[5]

The "revolutionary press" made him neglect *Les Temps modernes,* although he tried to attend the fortnightly get-togethers and to give his opinion like Simone, Bost, Lanzmann, Pouillon and Gorz. They were all in agreement that *TM* should not pronounce itself on every political issue that popped up, but try to present digested, thought-out views. With the

[5] Interview with Jacques Chancel, broadcast over ORTF February 7, 1973.

With Michelle Vian, "Spontex Maos"
and journalists at the Renault factory
gate at Boulogne-Billancourt
KEYSTONE

Abandoning philosophy for only six months;
Sartre during campaign to launch Libération
KEYSTONE

exception of Pouillon and Gorz, none of them actually wrote anything in the magazine any longer, but Simone read all contributions sent in and began a column on sexism, written by revolutionary feminists, while Pouillon and Gorz took turns actually putting issues together. The circulation was eleven thousand—the same as in 1945 practically—and if *TM* was no longer the revered official bulletin of existentialism, it was still there, with a track record that few "little magazines" could match—over three hundred issues of "articles de combat," of comments and analysis covering almost thirty years of hopes, failures and accomplishments on the left. "If I am less involved and less interested now, it's because *TM* has its own existence," Sartre would say in 1976.

He worked on and off on Flaubert—defending himself for doing so to Victor and other Maos by saying that even if no worker would read *L'Idiot de la famille,* for him to abandon something he had worked on for fifteen years would be very unliberated. "There's a certain ambiguity, I realize. On the one hand to go and find a nineteenth-century character and concentrate on what he did on June 18, 1838, one might call that escapism—and maybe I do try to escape a bit—but if, on the other hand, I look at it from the viewpoint of the method I use, I have a feeling that I'm contemporary," he told Michel Contat and Michel Rybalka, two new "Sartrologues" who published a 788-page inventory of all Sartre's writings.[6] Contat, who was also collaborating with Astruc on the documentary, was a thirty-five-year-old French literature teacher and jazz musician from Lausanne and Rybalka a forty-year-old UCLA doctor of philosophy who had written an essay on Boris Vian. They were the last interviewers that Sartre actually saw. In June, he was blind.

In March, overexertion had provoked a mild heart attack which had forced him considerably to reduce his activities just as *Libération* was being launched. He was there on May 22 when the first issue appeared, but hypertension had persisted and three weeks later he suffered an acute hemorrhage behind the left eye. It was the only good eye since he had practically lost the use of his right eye at the age of three. When he left the hospital and Simone took him convalescing in southern France, he could see light and color but no longer distinguish objects or faces. When he held a page to his face, he could see black lines but not the words. When he picked up a pen, he could not see what he wrote. The pharmacological treatment of the hypertension gave him moments of delirium. In Avignon, he had Simone lead him through the streets toward a bench where he said a young girl was going to meet him. The rendezvous was nonexistent.

[6] Michel Contat-Michel Rybalka, *Les Ecrits de Sartre, op. cit.*

Simone was far from well herself. She suffered excruciating arthritic pain and began taking the powerful drug cortisone, which caused a fattening of the facial tissues but effectively killed the pain.

Eye specialists all gave the same prognosis on Sartre's eye—the condition was irreversible. Sartre should feel crushed—as a writer he was no more, as he told Contat—but somehow he didn't feel sad. To write was to rewrite—as many as six times in some of his fiction, and even when Simone read something to him, he could only make the simplest oral corrections. Style was a way of saying several things in one sentence, he told Contat. Literature wasn't scientific paper writing; it was words disposed in such a way as to reverberate with meaning. Friends suggested a tape recorder, but playback time was dictated by the machine's mechanism, not by the speed of mind and eye. Juxtaposition of sentences was awkward and the control of the flow of thought was lost. But he did try one out—"loyally," he said.

From the Riviera, they went to Rome, but he could no longer venture out-of-doors alone and felt ineffectual when newspapers were read to him or when he was left alone to listen to the radio.

And he couldn't see *Pourquoi Israel?* which Lanzmann finished in June. The three-hour-plus movie was "written, conceived and directed" by Lanzmann and featured Simone among its producers. It used interviews intercut with other footage for a provocative and sometimes ironic look at Israel in 1973. Without recourse to newsreel or stock footage, Lanzmann looked at the Israeli Black Panthers, mostly Jews from North Africa who felt discriminated against by the Ashkenazi establishment. He showed a police chief who had known the concentration camps react to being called a Nazi by young demonstrators and a newcomer from Russia emotionally visiting the Wailing Wall, later only to seek to emigrate to the United States.

The October War saw Sartre and Beaver back opposing sides for the first time. Israel's victory robbed Jews of the traditional image as victims, and the far left, from Maoists to Trotskyites, supported the Palestinian cause. In interviews with *Libération* and Tel Aviv's *Al Hamishmar,* Sartre called for direct talks between the Palestinian Liberation Organization and Israel and refused to associate himself with an Appeal for Israel that Simone signed. She deplored Israel's refusal even to admit to a Palestinian plight, but said she couldn't support the Palestinian alternative—the destruction of Israel.

Their political differences carried over into the 1974 presidential elections brought about by Pompidou's sudden death. In what was the most exciting election campaign in decades, Simone supported the United left candidate François Mitterand against former economy and finance minister Valéry Giscard d'Estaing, whereas Sartre, together with the Maoists, was for "revolutionary abstention." When Mitterand was asked to comment on Sartre's refusal to vote for him, the socialist leader politely answered that the institutions Sartre refused to acknowledge "are nevertheless worthy of respect." Giscard d'Estaing's election, with a razor-thin majority over Mitterand, moved France from Gaullism into a pragmatism, where the problems of the times were, first and foremost, technical and economic.

Libération had its troubles. The new government was much too cool to send paddy wagons trailing "Voltaire" up Boulevard St. Michel and the defamation trial had ended quietly with Sartre condemned to pay a symbolic one-franc fine. The newspaper's problem was finding its stride, tone and relevancy. After a wobbly start that had forced Sartre to pour still more money into the venture, "Lib," as its very young readers called it, and its dedicated, under-thirty staff headed by Philippe Gavi, became a politicized tabloid. The choice of news was eccentric and items were treated for their baroque, unjust, absurd or contradictory values, leaving four pages toward the back of the sixteen-page daily to a readers' forum that by 1976 looked more like the personal ads section of New York's *Village Voice* than participatory democracy journalism. The items, printed without comment, were visibly written by disoriented people trying to call each other from behind walls of solitude and incomprehension—a convict writing from within "the French *gulag*" but actually saying all he wanted when he got out was a girl friend, day-care centers and newly founded gay clubs advertising themselves, collectives seeking crash pads and "the people of Maronne-la-Maine organizing against the abusive powers of warrant-serving marshals." Sartre got involved in one running story —the rape of a militant of Vietnamese origin by an African militant. The case had divided the readership, some writing in to say macho aggressiveness had no place in revolutionary ranks; others to caution that to strike out against a black was playing into the hands of right-wing scare tactics to expel African and Algerian aliens. "A man who protests against the way society treats him and who at the same time oppresses a woman is certainly not a true revolutionary," Sartre wrote in, suggesting that the Comité de Soutien, which had expelled the African worker, try to talk him into mending his ways.[7]

Together with Victor and Gavi, Sartre "talked" a book into existence,

[7] *Libération*, November 15, 1973.

On a raison de se révolter (You are Right to Rebel),[8] but in May 1974, one year to the day after publication of *Libération* had started, new blood-pressure complications forced him to give up the directorship of the paper —but not his financial support—and his sponsorship of other combative newssheets still publishing. A month later, as he and Beaver went to Rome for the summer, he abandoned *L'Idiot de la famille.* He felt that the fourth volume was both the most difficult and the least interesting, that the essential of what he had to say was done and that someone else could write the conclusion from the three volumes he had already written.

Arlette was there, too, to soothe and to distract. Before Sartre's blindness, father and adopted daughter had tinkered with music on certain evenings, he playing his upright piano in the studio on Boulevard Raspail, she bringing her teachers' college violin. Now, Arlette was there for several hours every other day, to read and to talk, and, friends would say, he surely needed both Simone and Arlette.

Giving up Flaubert was painful. He tried to be philosophical about it, telling friends and interviewers that all human toil was, ultimately, unfinished. But something was gone. He had swallowed Corydran to write parts of Flaubert also, as if he had obeyed what in *The Words* he had called "commandments sewn under the skin," the compulsion to write or to die. *On a raison de se révolter* showed him the limits of printed conversations, devoid of the density of written ideas. Interviews were frustrating because the to and fro of questions and answers begged new questions. In Rome in 1974, he decided he was no longer bounded by commandments sewn under the skin and that, perforce, he had said what he had to say. "It's not exactly true; if I put myself in the stead of a man who has years ahead of him and plenty of good health, I haven't said everything, far from it," he would tell this biographer two years later. "If I still have ten years, however, that's already a lot."

But folded-arms idleness was not in the Sartrian vein, and, with a tape recorder between them, he and Simone began a series of "autobiographical conversations" that would constitute the continuation of *The Words.* And when they returned to Paris, the reorganized state radio and television corporation offered Sartre an opportunity to review the twentieth century in a television series for the new Antenne 2 second network. NO ONE HERE BUT US LIBERALS, *Time* had headlined its report of Giscard d'Estaing's election and promises of change [9] and the new president's

[8] Philippe Gavi, Jean-Paul Sartre, Pierre Victor, *On a raison de se révolter,* Paris: Gallimard (collection La France Sauvage), 1974.
[9] *Time,* June 10, 1974.

choice of Marcel Jullian to head the A 2 network was a piece of inspired liberalism. Jullian was the editor-in-chief of the Plon publishing house and as TV "czar" immediately began looking for flashy ideas. When Maurice Clavel suggested delivering France's intellectuals to a TV audience's judgment, Jullian said, "Fabulous. Let's begin with Sartre." In 1971, when Malraux had turned seventy, the occasion had been marked with a series of nine hours of rambling reminiscences by this unique witness and protagonist of fabulous decades. Clavel almost became Sartre's agent in the preliminary negotiations. Sartre would agree, he told Jullian, if he had total freedom. Sure, answered Jullian, Sartre could conceive his series as he pleased and name his own collaborators. Sartre reviewing the century was a bright feather in the cap of the new A 2 chief and the upcoming series was roundly advertised on network time.

It sounded too good to be true, but Sartre "hired on" Simone, Gavi and Victor and immediately began outlining what was tentatively called "The History of the Century as seen through the Subjectivity of an Intellectual born in 1905." They decided each episode's events would have a feminist point-counterpoint. On January 6, 1975, Sartre submitted a synopsis of ten one-hour segments and reiterated that he demanded total freedom, meaning "no obstructions by judicial, bureaucratic or financial authorities." The TV "essay" didn't seem to fit existing programming, but the preliminary go-ahead came without delay and Sartre's team swelled to eighty as research, writing and preproduction work went into high gear. The cost was figured at ten million francs ($2.2 million), a hefty but not necessarily outrageous sum for a prestige series that could probably be sold in scores of markets. Jullian authorized a first eighty thousand francs advance payment.

The trouble began in August when Sartre and crew disbanded for a month's vacation after six months' work. Sartre and Beaver repaired to Rome, where Jullian wrote him saying it would be necessary to make a pilot that would allow program directors to get an idea of where the project was going before the network could give the full production go-ahead. "In other words, I have to pass an exam," Sartre retorted at a news conference a month later. "The public is the only judge. To slip a jury of 'superior' judges between work and public means to determine the work in advance. It's a detail but here we go again, censorship." On the eve of the September 25 news conference, Jullian had countered with a scaled-down four-million-franc proposal, which Sartre said might have been viable if offered six months earlier when a different script could still have been written. When Sartre went public with his news conference Jullian answered, saying it was hard to talk about censorship when the "piece of work doesn't exist yet." He was appalled and at *Le Nouvel Observateur*'s Jean Daniel's suggestion tried one more patch-up. But Sartre was hurt and—regretfully, it seemed to Jullian—repeated it was too late, that he no longer trusted the network and that he would never be seen on television again.

The press largely backed Sartre, *Le Monde* saying "our liberalism has perhaps moved forward but it remains an outdistanced liberalism" [10] and *Le Nouvel Observateur* that at seventy Sartre could be proud to be considered a fearsome subversive. "So at the last moment the government backed off, dizzy before that liberal and progressive jump into the corrosive unknown. At the idea of a new Socrates preparing to corrupt our youth for months to come . . . our anxious leaders have thrown up financial obstacles." [11]

An appalling news item popped up at the end of September—some of Sartre's young Maoist friends tried to collect, retroactively, the $60,000 Nobel Prize money. After a flurry of Associated Press and Agence France-Presse reports, Stig Ramel, the director of the Nobel Foundation, confirmed in Stockholm that a letter had been received laying claim to the 250,000 kroner that had been awarded to Sartre in 1964. The letter originated from "circles close to Mr. Sartre," Ramel said, adding that he did not know if it had been authorized by the author but that, in any case, the Nobel rule stipulated that any claim should be made no later than a year after the prize-awarding ceremony. In Paris, Sartre formally denied having said he wished to receive the money.[12]

Sartre *was* broke. His last reserves had been swallowed up by *Libération*, and together with Contat he recorded a seventieth-birthday conversation that was copyrighted, serialized in straight question-and-answer form in *Le Nouvel Observateur* and sold to major magazines abroad.[13] He revealed he had paid $36,000 in taxes in fiscal 1974, but that, for the first time, he wondered how to make ends meet.

The long interview was not only a sentimental birthday trip down memory lane. Contat asked penetrating questions and yielded such replies as Sartre admitting that to his regret, he had never learned anything about himself in the scores of books written about him, Sartre calling the division of public and private man an illusion, and his believing that

[10] *Le Monde,* September 28, 1975.
[11] *Le Nouvel Observateur,* September 29, 1975.
[12] *Le Monde* and *International Herald Tribune,* September 28, 1975.
[13] *Le Nouvel Observateur,* June 23, 30, July 7, 1975; in volume, Jean-Paul Sartre, *Situations X,* Paris: Gallimard, 1976.

despite a darkening horizon, humanity was marching forward, even if a socialist revolution would never happen. When asked whether he would say he had been "gypped," he said No: "I haven't been disappointed by anything. I've seen people, good and bad—the bad are only bad in relation to certain goals—I've written things, I've lived, there isn't anything to be sorry about." The taped conversation ended with a burst of laughter as Sartre realized the disillusionment of his saying that his life had also made him understand that it hadn't amounted to much. "You must keep in the laughter," Sartre told Contat. "You must put, 'An accompaniment of laughter.'"

Simone was being sucked into the quarrels of feminism. From America came books packed with rage, pain, irony and affluent angst and a personal visit from Betty Friedan, trying to share "with someone wiser, older" her own groping fears that the women's movement was coming to a dead end. They talked for a long time and came down on different sides of "the system," Simone saying such gains as better jobs, token positions and apparent sexual integration were counterproductive, that the role of feminists was to "sap this regime but not play their game," while Friedan wondered how women could achieve the millennium if they denied for themselves the skills and expertise even to have a voice in changing the system. The author of *The Feminine Mystique* came away disappointed, feeling Simone distant and cold, uttering fashionable clichés and repudiating elitism and elevating the anonymous "working class" woman in the abstract.[14]

In reality, Simone was more "pretext than prow," as she liked to say. She had been overtaken by a younger generation of Frenchwomen who, in fact, saw a certain patronizing optimism in parts of *Le Deuxième sexe*. *L'Arc* celebrated the quarter-century anniversay of *Le Deuxième sexe* with a Simone de Beauvoir special issue. "She has found a way of remaining present without making herself a controlling factor, even a disguised, underhanded authority," wrote the editors in their introduction. For the special issue, Simone interviewed Sartre on women, saying there were traces of "phallocracy" in his books and making him admit he was not totally innocent when it came to exploiting women. But she said he had always considered her his equal, something that made him wonder if, curiously, this hadn't fortified his machismo when it came to other women. She said that if he had accepted *The Second Sex,* the book hadn't changed

[14] "Sex, Society and the Female Dilemma, A Dialogue between Simone de Beauvoir and Betty Friedan, *Saturday Review,* June 14, 1975.

Simone, 1974
GISÈLE FREUND

him a bit—or her, she added as an afterthought: "We had the same attitudes then," she said, "we believed socialist revolution would necessarily
bring about the emancipation of women. We've sure had to change our
tune." [15] More interestingly, they deepened the sap-the-regime vs. taking-
over-from-within debate by addressing the question of whether a working
woman should rebel against her working husband, whether the husband
was the only refuge from capitalist oppression or just one more oppressor.
Simone said it was a very real issue for feminists and Sartre felt the working woman should try to find a compromise between the bigger and lesser
evils—the battle of the sexes being the bigger of the two—but that, yes, a
working woman should rebel against an oppressive husband because it was
the only way to move forward. On the crucial issue of a specific woman's
nature, which Simone and radical feminists denied ("feminitude" is social
conditioning, not biology), Sartre wondered whether certain feminine
qualities wouldn't be lost in triumphant feminism, whether indeed it
wouldn't be better to transfer those positive qualities to men rather than
suppress them in women. This brought Simone to admit that women
possessed perhaps a deeper, inner knowledge of the self and Sartre to
say that a male civilization was "comical," that woman's oppression had
made her less comical and made her escape certain masculine faults and,
in the end, made her almost freer than man because fewer principles were
dictated to her.

If Sartre's political beliefs had not yet dissolved into hearty laughter
at man's comical society, he was, in blindness, achieving a longed-for
transparency in which everything could be said, where nothing needed to
be hidden and the isolated individual could come forward to join with
others.

Politics made him travel. With Cohn-Bendit he went to Stuttgart to
talk to Andreas Baader—with Ulrike Meinhof, the leader of the extreme
leftist Red Army. While denouncing the Baader-Meinhof gang's terrorism,
Sartre also deplored the conditions of Baader's detention, something that
earned him brickbats in the German press. With Simone and Victor,
Sartre went to Lisbon to hail the Portuguese revolution and to express his
hopes for a country living in a state of mild anarchy after forty-one years
of right-wing dictatorship. With the end of the Vietnam War, Maoists
told him the Enemy No. 1 was no longer the United States but the
Soviet Union.

Sartre's health improved during the summer of his seventieth year and

15 *L'Arc,* No. 61, 1975.

he talked about doing an essay on "Power and Freedom" and met with Astruc to discuss the documentary started in 1973 and never finished. In January 1976, Gallimard published *Situations X,* the tenth collection of his shorter texts, this time forewords to books on the Burgos trial of Basque separatists and on Maos in France, his speech to the young bar association of Belgium, a pamphlet against elections—the last piece he wrote in *TM* before going blind—and the marathon q-and-a interview with Contat, now titled "Conversations with Myself." Books on Sartre kept coming. Francis Jeanson and Colette Audry were the latest biographers; [16] John Gerassi, the son of Stépha and Fernando, was writing a political biography and Contat was named executor and overseer of posthumous publication of as yet-unpublished texts, including the unfinished "Morale" of 1949, two chapters of *La Critique* and the beginning of the fourth volume of *L'Idiot de la famille.* If Sartre scholarship in America seemed arrested in *La Critique* circa 1960, American feminism kept Simone in view. University presses published a study of the complexity of Simone's attitudes toward women by Jean Leighton.[17] In the fall of 1976, Simone joined Eugene Ionesco and Raymond Aron in asking UNESCO to reverse its two-year-old decision barring Israel from taking part in its work.

They were in Rome when they learned that Martin Heidegger had died at the age of eighty-six and had said, "I won't really be read for another three hundred years." Sartre had met Heidegger once, in 1952, on his way back to Paris from a peace conference in Vienna, and liked Heidegger's assessment of his future readers. When this biographer asked Sartre whether he thought he would be read in three hundred years, he said he couldn't care less, that certain ideas germinated more slowly than others and that he didn't so much have the impression he was misunderstood as perhaps recognized for the wrong reasons. He was sure future generations would change in the way individuals talk to each other, that once inequality and privilege have been eliminated, the true revolution would surely be in the way we perceive each other and express ourselves with increased translucence. To make the self obvious to the other. "We can only see the somber recesses in ourselves if we try to become transparent to others."

16 Francis Jeanson, *Sartre dans sa vie,* Paris: Seuil, 1975; Colette Audry, *Sartre,* Paris: Seghers, 1976.
17 Elaine Marks, *Simone de Beauvoir, Encounters with Death,* New Brunswick, New Jersey: Rutgers University Press, 1973; Jean Leighton, *Simone de Beauvoir on Women,* Rutherford, New Jersey: Fairleigh Dickinson University Press, 1975.

Jocular transparency was the hallmark of *Sartre par lui-même,* the Astruc-Contat documentary finally released in October 1976, four years after it was filmed. The three-hour film, which Sartre swore would never be shown on television, featured a superhonest and captivating Sartre, going over his life and its itinerary with a mixture of astonished scruples and exacting insistence, with Simone furnishing affectionate corrections and the *TM* faithfuls, Gorz, Pouillon and Bost, forming a Greek chorus of amiable questioners. The chain-smoking Sartre is seen sitting in his studio at 222 Boulevard Raspail, telling in his famous metallic rasp of his childhood and school years, of his discovery of contingence and his own physical ugliness—the two seem linked in the seventy-year-old Sartre's mind—of his friendship with Nizan, his meeting Beaver, the nauseous years in Le Havre, the 1940 POW camp and the postwar existentialist fame and fights with the communists. Newsreel clips show him attending rehearsals of his plays, visiting Cuba—with Che Guevara lighting his cigar—and, after 1968, hawking revolution in the street and, with Beaver, being escorted into a police van.

Sartre and Beaver were not in Paris for the premiere of *Sartre par lui-même.* They were in Israel where he accepted an honorary doctorate from the Hebrew University in Jerusalem. "My acceptance of this title," he said, "has political significance. It expresses the friendship I feel for Israel since its birth and my desire to see it prosper in peace and security."

Next year it would be forty years since *La Nausée* had come out and the year after it would be fifty years since they had met. Fifty years since that Monday after the Easter recess when René Maheu had introduced them to each other. Looking back, Sartre thought it had been a good life. "I cannot see what I can blame life for. Life has given me what I wanted and at the same time made me realize that it isn't much." And Beaver, "My days now are to a great extent the continuation of former days, but that is with my whole-hearted agreement. Since I was twenty-one I have never been lonely."

CHAPTER

EXIT WITH LAUGHTER

As Jean-Paul Sartre and Simone de Beauvoir prepare to enter history, they are a revered first couple giving way without disappearing, enemies of stagnant serenity, unbelievers in an afterlife but warm supporters in the value of happiness and truth-telling. In a France where the Trotskyites keep trotting and the great debates of our time are often missed on the pretext that French culture is different and original, Sartre and Beauvoir are both beyond polemics and surprisingly present, a twin conscience that younger intellectuals keep debating, but also a fused pair of ancestors about whom everything has been said.

The assessments of them vary—now it is Sartre who is seen as the leader and Beauvoir as the piggy-backing also-ran; now it is she who is perceived as the richer mind. Sartre has been accused of believing too many things; Beauvoir of being, essentially, a school marm. Half of Sartre wants to be home writing that *magnum opus* he should have written; the other half of him regrets not being out there on the barricades making a bigger dent on current events. She has realized that character traits—her own youthful puritanism included—end up losing their edge, that it is possible to consider old age and death as scandalous without believing in God, that to write, that is, to invent and create, is more of an undertaking than to live. She has realized that feminism can be a trap and that with Sartre a certain kind of humanist writer is coming to an end. She has expressed the unity

Simone today
GISÈLE FREUND

Sartre today
KEYSTONE

of existentialist thought better than he, but his theater is not mere evening classes in phenomenology.

Sartre is an author of unfinished works. The promised "Morale" complementing *Being and Nothingness* was never written. *La Critique de la raison dialectique* never received its promised conclusion, nor did *The Roads to Freedom*, *The Words* or *L'Idiot de la famille*. The reason is also a question of context, of a cultural crisis.

The image of the resourceful and activist intellectual that Sartre, Beauvoir, Camus and their friends forged for themselves during the first flush of peace in 1945 was neither unreasonable nor particularly innovative. It belonged to a long tradition of literature as the privileged *locus* for thinking out man's fate and giving meaning to life. Despite the piquant flavor of St.-Germain-des-Prés bohemia, their ambition was that of Emile Zola and Charles Péguy magnified by a heightened confidence in their power.

While Sartre in particular never stopped launching his defiant "J'accuse," he and his peers were robbed of their power and turned into mandarins, respected but disarmed. In 1945, a self-righteous France could execute Robert Brasillach for the passionate pro-Nazi articles he had written during the Occupation. Fifteen years later, when the Algerian war threatened to tear a divided country apart, Sartre couldn't get himself arrested (as a half-impotent government limited itself to lashing out at teachers and civil servant signers of the Manifesto of the 121). Another decade and it is no longer as novelist and playwright that he flees a derisive Nobel Prize and public honors, but as militant. What is literature when culture is no longer considered a life-giving force but a class privilege (when not a particularly devious form of alienation)? The Sartre of 1947 believed—together with a long line of writers—that a book could, by itself, change its reader. The Sartre of 1970 believed no one should think on behalf of anyone else and, by implication, that no one had anything to tell anyone else. Beauvoir had traced the outer limits of this evolution in *The Mandarins* when she commented that her hero was "opposed to the old humanism he had believed in, a new, more realistic, more pessimistic humanism in which he gave a large share to violence and very little to ideas of justice, liberty and truth. Triumphantly, he showed that this was the only adequate morality, but to adopt it personally he would have to throw so many things overboard that he couldn't do it."

Sartre is the freelance, the fellow traveler who lived through an era when Marxism could not tolerate the smallest independent pronouncements on major political issues except in the most oracular form and the advanced industrial world went through its most dynamic and triumphant expansion.

Sartre was tempted to join the Party but never crossed the Rubicon, remaining instead alongside, articulating political ideas that the Party itself refused to admit.

If politics gradually robbed literature of its powers—one wonders where Camus would have stood after the May Events had he lived—the prodigious advances in structuralism also deprived belles-lettres of authority. Once Barthes, Foucault and Cie. had picked literature apart—and Sartre himself had "totalized" Flaubert—a certain kind of writer was no more. Philosophers, psychologists, sociologists, linguists and, with them, writers no longer deal in absolutes but propose a *method* that is valid insofar as it is verifiably coherent and convincing, a method that is superbly phenomenological and brackets off questions of divine existence, the dialectic meaning of historical will or the beautiful and tragic dimension of man. Like science, literature has become relative. Fundamental questions have become optional as literature has fissioned into picaresque fiction destined for what is politely called the general public and an intense if marginal and often pedantic critical avant-garde. If Sartre has left part of his enormous work unfinished, he is, in the words of Jacques Audiberti, "the night watchman on hand at all fronts of our intelligence." And as such, Sartre dominates his generation and has no successor.

Beauvoir is the author of diminished ambitions. *She Came to Stay,* her first published novel, breaks the behavioral analysis that its subject seems to impose in order to dramatically present the dilemma of the self and the Other. Through its opposite feminine characters, Beauvoir etches a portrait of a clear-eyed, forthright and energetic womanhood that is new. As a chronicle of the hopes and disillusions of a generation, *The Mandarins* is more than a *roman à clef.* It marks the end of existentialism and, with its refusal of an esthetic viewpoint, the end of the existentialist novel. With her essays she gave herself the task of describing and demythifying feminine existence and, later, old age. By their ambition and success, *The Second Sex* and *The Coming of Age* are felicitous applications of the existentialist method, but as memorialist and biographer she lacks the vigor of conception and composition that heightened her first novels. Her sense of her own limits—and those of others—is acute. She has said about Camus that "it is hard to depend on others when you have believed yourself to be sovereign, an illusion that bourgeois intellectuals share and none of us has been cured of without pain." She has found lancing phrases to puncture her and Sartre's youthful idealism. "We refused to touch the wheels of History, but we wanted to believe that it turned in the right direction. To have thought overwise would have brought too many things into question." Or, "To look for the reasons for not walking on someone's face, is already to walk on his face." She has said that to open up is to become less moralizing and more understanding, but that total lucidity is also an illusion, that the bottom line is perhaps a certain kind of courage to live, a courage that is both intellectual and practical.

Sartre and Beauvoir are exegesis made passion. Supreme Evil is to fumble mutely in the dark; it is not to be able to cry out. Poulou and Simone were the gifted children of a class they learned to hate because of the way it deprived others of what young intellectuals would naturally consider everyone's birthright—a voice. What filled the young Sartre and Beaver with that deep, lifelong and absolute loathing of the bourgeoisie was the way it deprived others of the means of expressing themselves. Privileged people can, even when they have suffered, explain their suffering, Beauvoir has written. What revolted her most in the Algerian atrocities was that behind the tortures were men and women whose chance birth more or less condemned them to die without having been able to tell themselves—in telling others—what happened to them. It is because she felt this insult so deeply that she tried to cry out for others.

Political passion, however, seems to ebb. Sartre and Beauvoir are keenly aware that the late 1970s are a time for disenchantment and fading causes, even for the extreme left. Settling Mao Tse-tung's succession "at the top," far from the Chinese people, should have provoked embarrassment, if not indignation, in Western radical circles. The Chinese Revolution was the last refuge for radical ideology, and the Chairman's succession should not have been reduced to a vulgar palace power struggle. And in Western Europe, Beauvoir has come to believe, Marxism can only save itself by pushing its self-doubt toward total self-reappraisal. Europe, she feels, may again have to discover its own lights because only uncomfortable doubts can propel political imagination.

To the aging Sartre the Evil standing in the way of translucence, the Evil locking each of us into our alienation and secrets is whatever obstructs one human being from communing with another. We may deliver our bodies to each other's gaze and, in the sexual act, to contact, but we have not yet learned to give each other our minds, although ideas, too, are variations of the flesh. If social concord is to exist one day we must learn to exist entirely for each other. If demands are empty, Beauvoir has said, they result in discontent To demand happiness means already to possess a capacity for happiness.

Contradictions persist, as in any living thought. Isn't our assuming responsibility for what circumstances have made of us precisely what stands in the way of our clasping hands across class? In his search for universals, Sartre has produced a lot of simplifying abstractions, but, as he tells his most recent visitors, one day, after his death and after his listener's death, when our economic, cultural and emotional differences have been sorted out, there may indeed be new antagonisms that none of us can dream of. But these new differences will not necessarily prevent the existence of a society, perforce global and more just than our own, where each individual will be able to give himself fully to someone else who will give himself in equal measure.

In the meantime, to write is to express what is hidden, convoluted, obscure and masked in the human psyche. The most interesting books, Sartre predicts, are not the ones that try to conceal, but the ones that give us a glimpse of our recesses and, better still, bear witness to what we are to each other.

WORKS

BY

SARTRE

AND

BEAUVOIR

WITH THE EXCEPTION of one of Sartre's early philosophical works, all of his and all of Beauvoir's books have been published in the original by Gallimard. (Editions in English are all published in New York unless otherwise noted.)

SARTRE

NOVELS

La Nausée, 1938	*Nausea,* translated by Lloyd Alexander, Norfolk, Conn.: New Directions, 1949
Les Chemins de la liberté 1 *L'Age de raison,* 1945 2 *Le Sursis,* 1945 3 *La Mort dans l'âme,* 1949	*The Roads to Freedom,* tr. E. Sutton 1 *The Age of Reason* 2 *The Reprieve* 3 *Troubled Sleep* Knopf, 1950 and 1951

SHORT STORIES

Le Mur, 1939 (Le Mur—La Chambre—Erostrate—Intimité—L'Enfance d'un chef)	*Intimacy and Other Stories,* tr. Lloyd Alexander, London: Peter Nevill, 1953

THEATER

Les Mains sales, 1948
Le Diable et le Bon Dieu, 1951

Théâtre I, 1947, Les Mouches
  Huis Clos
  Mort sans sépulture
  La Putain respectueuse
Kean, adapted from Alexandre Dumas,
  1954
Nekrassov, 1956
Les Séquestrés d'Altona, 1960

Red Gloves or Crime Passionnel
Lucifer and the Lord or The Devil
  and the Good Lord
The Flies
No Exit or In Camera
The Victors
The Respectful Prostitute

The Condemned of Altona or Loser
  Wins
Three Plays, Dirty Hands, The Respect-
  ful Prostitute, The Victors, tr. Lionel
  Abel, Knopf, 1949
No Exit and Three Other Plays, No
  Exit, The Flies, Dirty Hands, The
  Respectful Prostitute, tr. Lionel
  Abel, Vintage, 1955

LITERATURE

Situations I, 1947; II, 1948; III, 1949;
  IV, 1964; V, 1964; VI, 1964; VII,
  1965; VIII, 1972; IX, 1972; X,
  1976
Saint Genet, Comédien et martyr, 1952

Baudelaire, 1947
Les Mots, 1963

Qu'est-ce que la littérature?, 1964

L'Idiot de la famille, I, II, 1971, III,
  1973 (Gustave Flaubert)
Un Théâtre de situations, 1973

Saint Genet, Actor and Martyr, tr.
  Bernard Frechtman, Braziller, 1963

The Words, tr. Bernard Frechtman,
  Braziller, 1964
What Is Literature?, tr. Bernard
  Frechtman, Philosophical Library,
  1949

PHILOSOPHY

La Transcendance de l'ego, esquisse d'une description phénoménologique, Paris: Librairie Vrin, 1965

L'Imaginaire, psychologie phénoménologique de l'imagination, 1940
L'Etre et le néant, 1943

Critique de la raison dialectique, 1960

Questions de méthode, 1967

The Transcendence of the Ego: An Existentialist Theory of Consciousness, tr. Forrest Williams and Robert Kirkpatrick, New York: Noonday, 1957

Being and Nothingness, tr. Hazel E. Barnes, Simon & Schuster, 1956
Search for a Method, tr. of first chapter *Critique de la raison dialectique,* by Hazel E. Barnes, New York: Knopf, 1963

POLITICAL ESSAYS

Réflexions sur la question juive, 1946
Entretiens sur la politique, 1946
  (with David Rousset and Gérard Rosenthal)
L'Affaire Henri Martin, 1953
On a raison de se révolter, 1974
  (with Philippe Gavi and Pierre Victor)

Anti-Semite and Jew, Schocken, 1948

BEAUVOIR

NOVELS

L'Invitée, 1943

Le Sang des autres, 1945

Tous les hommes sont mortels, 1947

Les Mandarins, 1954

Les belles images, 1966

She Came to Stay, tr. L. Drummond, Cleveland and New York: World Publishing, 1954
The Blood of Others, tr. Roger Senhouse and Yvonne Moyse, Knopf, 1948
All Men Are Mortal, tr. Leonard M. Friedman, Cleveland and New York: World Publishing, 1955
The Mandarins, tr. Leonard M. Friedman, Cleveland and New York: World Publishing, 1956
Les Belles Images, tr. Patrick O'Brian, G. P. Putnam's, 1968

SHORT STORIES

La Femme rompue (Monologue—
L'Age de discrétion), 1967

The Woman Destroyed (The Age of
Discretion—The Monologue—The
Woman Destroyed), tr. Patrick
O'Brian; G. P. Putnam's, 1969

"RÉCIT"

Une Mort très douce, 1967

A Very Easy Death, tr. Patrick O'Brian,
G. P. Putnam's, 1966

THEATER

Les Bouches inutiles, 1945

ESSAYS AND LITERATURE

Le Deuxième sexe, 1949

The Second Sex, tr. H. M. Parshley,
Knopf, 1953

L'Amérique au jour le jour, 1954

America Day by Day, tr. Patrick
Dudley, Grove Press, 1953

Pyrrhus et Cinéas, 1944
Pour une morale de l'ambiguité, 1947

The Ethics of Ambiguity, tr. Bernard
Frechtman, Philosophical Library,
1948

Privilèges, 1960
La Longue marche, essai sur la Chine,
1958

The Long March, tr. Austryn Wain-
house, Cleveland and New York:
World Publishing, 1958

La Vieillesse, 1970

The Coming of Age, tr. Patrick
O'Brian, G. P. Putnam's, 1972

AUTOBIOGRAPHY

Mémoires d'une jeune fille rangée, 1958	*Memoirs of a Dutiful Daughter,* tr. James Kirkup, Cleveland and New York: World Publishing, 1959
La Force de l'âge, 1960	*The Prime of Life,* tr. Peter Green, Cleveland and New York: World Publishing, 1962
La Force des choses, 1963	*Force of Circumstance,* tr. Richard Howard, G. P. Putnam's, 1964
Tout compte fait, 1972	*All Said and Done,* tr. Patrick O'Brian, G. P. Putnam's, 1974

POLITICS

Djamila Boupacha (with Gisèle Halimi), 1963

BIBLIOGRAPHY

Albérès, R. M., *L'Aventure intellectuelle du XXè siècle,* Paris: Albin Michel, 1969.

Alleg, Henri, *La Question,* Lausanne: La Cité, 1958.

Anderson, Perry, *Considerations on Western Marxism,* London: New Left Books, 1976.

Aron, Raymond, *L'Opium des intellectuels,* Paris: Calmann-Levy, 1955.

Audry, Colette, *Sartre,* Paris: Seghers, 1976.

Bersani, Jacques; Autrand, Michel; Lecarme, Jacques; Vercier, Bruno, *La Littérature en France depuis 1945;* Paris: Bordas, 1970.

Brée, Germaine, *Camus and Sartre,* New York: Delta, 1972.

Camus, Albert, *The Rebel,* tr. Anthony Bower, New York: Random House, 1960.

Chapsal, Madeleine, *Les Ecrivains en personne,* Paris: Juilliard, 1960.

Clark, Ronald W., *The Life of Bertrand Russell,* New York: Knopf, 1976.

Contat, Michel; Rybalka, Michel, *Les Ecrits de Sartre,* Paris: Gallimard, 1970; *The Writings of Sartre,* tr. Richard McCleary, Evanston: Northwestern University Press, 1974.

Desan, Wilfred, *The Tragic Finale,* Cambridge: Harvard University Press, 1954.

———, *The Marxism of Jean-Paul Sartre,* New York: Doubleday, 1965.

Donohue, H. E. F., *Conversations with Nelson Algren,* New York: Hill & Wang, 1963.

Fanon, Frantz, *Les Damnés de la terre,* Paris: Maspero, 1961; *The Damned,* tr. Constance Farrington, Paris: Présence africaine, 1963.

Funk & Wagnalls Guide to Modern World Literature, Martin Seymour-Smith, ed.; New York: Funk & Wagnalls, 1970.

Jeanson, Francis, *Le Problème morale et la pensée de Sartre,* Paris: Myrte, 1947.

———, *Simone de Beauvoir ou l'entreprise de vivre,* Paris: Seuil, 1966.

Leighton, Jean, *Simone de Beauvoir on Women,* Rutherford, N. J.: Fairleigh Dickinson University Press, 1975.

Leiris, Michel, *L'Age d'homme,* Paris: Gallimard, 1939; *Manhood,* tr. R. Howard, New York: Grossman, 1964.

Lévi-Strauss, Claude, *La Pensée sauvage,* Paris: Plon, 1962; *The Savage Mind,* tr. George Weidenfeld, London: Nicolson, 1966.

Madsen, Axel, *Malraux,* New York: Morrow, 1976.

Marks, Elaine, *Simone de Beauvoir, Encounter with Death,* New Brunswick, N. J.: Rutgers University Press, 1973.

Masters, Brian, *Sartre, a Study,* New York: Rowman & Littlefield, 1974.

Merleau-Ponty, Maurice, *Humanisme et terreur,* Paris: Gallimard, 1947; *Humanism and Terror,* tr. John O'Neill, Boston: Beacon Press, 1969.

———, *Les Aventures de la dialectique,* Paris: Gallimard, 1953.

Mournier, Emmanuel, *Malraux, Camus, Sartre, Bernanos,* Paris: Seuil, 1953.

Russell, Bertrand, *Wisdom of the West,* London: Rathbone, 1959.

Sarraute, Nathalie, *Portrait d'un inconnu,* Paris: Robert Marin, 1948.

Tynan, Kenneth, *Tynan Right and Left,* New York: Atheneum, 1967.

Werner, Eric, *De la violence au totalitarisme: essai sur la pensée de Camus et de Sartre,* Paris: Calmann-Levy, 1972.

INDEX